Unfinished
Transformation

Unfinished
Transformation

Domestic Politics and International
Relations since the COVID-19 Pandemic

Wonhyuk Lim

BROOKINGS INSTITUTION PRESS
Washington, DC

Published by Brookings Institution Press®
1775 Massachusetts Avenue, NW
Washington, DC 20036
www.brookings.edu/bipress

Co-published by Rowman & Littlefield
Bloomsbury Publishing Inc, 1385 Broadway, New York, NY 10018, USA
Bloomsbury Publishing Plc, 50 Bedford Square, London, WC1B 3DP, UK
Bloomsbury Publishing Ireland, 29 Earlsfort Terrace, Dublin 2, D02 AY28, Ireland
https://www.bloomsbury.com

Typeset in Minion Pro
Composition by Circle Graphics
Printed and bound in the United States of America

The Brookings Institution is a nonprofit organization devoted to research, education, and publication on important issues of domestic and foreign policy. Its principal purpose is to bring the highest-quality independent research and analysis to bear on current and emerging policy problems. Brookings' publications represent the sole views of their author(s).

Library of Congress Control Number: 2024950635

ISBN: 978-0-8157-4019-3 (cloth : alk. paper)
ISBN: 978-0-8157-3989-0 (pbk. : alk. paper)
ISBN: 978-0-8157-3990-6 (ePub)
ISBN: 978-0-8157-4115-2 (ePDF)

For product safety related questions contact productsafety@bloomsbury.com.

⊖™ The paper used in this publication meets the minimum requirements of American National Standard for Information Sciences—Permanence of Paper for Printed Library Materials, ANSI/NISO Z39.48-1992

Contents

Preface and Acknowledgments

The origin of this book goes back to January 2020, when I started teaching at the Johns Hopkins School of Advanced International Studies in Washington as a visiting professor from the KDI School of Public Policy and Management. Just a month before, I had arrived from South Korea, leased a townhouse, and taken a family vacation at Disney World, enjoying some downtime and thinking about what I wanted to do for the next two years. I learned that a mysterious infectious disease had broken out in Wuhan, China, and that health officials in Korea were on high alert. Back in 2003–4, Korea had luckily managed to avoid the Severe Acute Respiratory Syndrome (SARS) epidemic; but in 2015, Korea had a near panic with Middle East Respiratory Syndrome (MERS). Health officials were awfully unprepared for the disease at the time, with inadequate testing and contact-tracing, low stockpiles of personal protective equipment, and no separation of infected patients from other patients in emergency rooms at major hospitals. As the disease spread through hospitals, Korea, in Northeast Asia, wound up with the second-highest number of confirmed deaths from MERS, after Saudi Arabia. Although the Korean government implemented major institutional reforms and increased critical stockpiles to improve crisis response and management in the wake of the MERS epidemic, health officials were nervous about the spread of the new infectious disease, COVID-19, as they contact-traced the rapidly increasing number of confirmed patients.

The contrast in the United States was rather stark. Although the first confirmed case of COVID-19 in the United States occurred about at the same time as in Korea, there seemed to be very little public concern. Life went on as before, and a simple protective measure such as wearing a mask was not encouraged in January and February. Even as COVID-19 quickly spread from China to other parts of the world through international air travel and domestic transmission in this era of globalization, the US government behaved as if COVID-19 was not very transmissive and could be easily contained. Instead of securing test kits and critical supplies in the first two months of 2020, government officials, including President Donald Trump, spent most of their time criticizing China for the outbreak and reassuring the public that there was no reason to panic.

When COVID-19 finally exploded in America in March, people were caught so unprepared that there was a near panic. They were basically on their own for a crisis they had no idea about; in their lifetime, they had never experienced a crisis like this, they did not know when it would end, and they could not trust their government to look after them. When I went grocery shopping, pasta and pasta sauce shelves were empty, as people stocked up on food supplies. For some unfathomable reason, toilet paper was gone, too, and people fighting for toilet paper was an indelible image from the early days of the pandemic. Unlike in most other countries that tried to preserve employment by providing wage subsidies, there was massive unemployment in the United States, as restaurants, hotels, and other businesses shut down their operation and laid off workers. To make up for inadequate unemployment insurance and prevent social turmoil, the US government provided massive consumption subsidies in the form of stimulus checks. Even so, there was social turbulence, as the pandemic highlighted the great inequality in America, with racial undertones. In May, a man named George Floyd died after a police officer had him on the ground and pressed his knee against his neck for 8 minutes and 46 seconds. The viral video clip from the scene seemed to ask: How could a human being do this to another human being in a society so rich as America?

At about this time, Korea's National Research Council for Economics, Humanities, and Social Sciences asked me to lead a research project on the "Post-COVID World." It seemed rather premature to talk about the post-COVID world less than five months into the outbreak of the COVID pandemic. I knew that the so-called Spanish Flu pandemic, the closest historical parallel I could think of, had played out over the course of three years. At the same time, I felt it was important to think about how the COVID shock would interact with preexisting conditions and other factors, including crisis response measures, to shape the world after the pandemic. It seemed to me that preexisting conditions were defined by a slowdown in globalization, rising inequality and a populist reaction in advanced industrial countries, and intensifying strategic competition between the United States and China. In the first months of the pandemic, the COVID shock seemed to exacerbate these conditions as it disrupted global trade, highlighted economic and social disparities, and aggravated United States–China relations. If these trends were allowed to continue, the world would be faced with increasing risks of international war and social conflict.

At the same time, the COVID shock led many countries to think outside their usual boxes and take extraordinary measures. In addition to providing immediate relief, they used the crisis as an opportunity to improve the system for public health and social protection. The United States engaged in industrial policy without calling it that, by launching Operation Warp Speed to develop COVID-19 vaccines in record time. Although countries understandably focused on securing their own supplies of therapeutics and vaccines at first, they quickly set up arrangements to distribute critical medical supplies around the world. Instead of drawing inward and isolating themselves from the rest of the world, they began to build more resilient supply chains through international cooperation. I thought the post-COVID world would need to reflect these tantalizing possibilities along with dangerous preexisting trends.

In concluding this project, I would like to thank the National Research Council for its generous funding and support. I would also like to thank the KDI School and the Johns Hopkins Johns Hopkins School of Advanced International Studies (SAIS) for encouraging me to continue this research in the middle of the pandemic. Professor Kent Calder, in particular, helped me to feel at home at SAIS under difficult circumstances, and recommended some of his colleagues as chapter authors for this project. Bill Finan and Yelba Quinn at the Brookings Institution Press patiently guided me though the publication process, and Alfred Imhoff provided excellent copyediting of the manuscript. Last but not least, I would like to thank my family, who navigated the pandemic with me.

Introduction
UNFINISHED TRANSFORMATION
OF THE WORLD IN DISARRAY

WONHYUK LIM, *KDI SCHOOL OF PUBLIC POLICY AND MANAGEMENT*

The coronavirus disease of 2019—COVID-19—was the biggest global health shock since the so-called Spanish Flu influenza pandemic of 1918–20. According to the World Health Organization, the COVID-19 pandemic led to more than 7 million confirmed deaths around the world over a four-year period, starting with the first reported mass outbreak in Wuhan, China, at the end of 2019.[1] This death toll amounts to about 0.08 percent of the global population. Although this is much lower than the worldwide fatality rate of 2 percent for the influenza pandemic of 1918–20, the COVID-19 pandemic was a huge shock as people around the world feared for their everyday safety and experienced social distancing and lockdowns for the first time in their lives.[2]

In the early phase of the pandemic, there were primarily three views on how it would affect the world: as a fundamental game changer, as an accelerator of preexisting trends, or as a disruptive but transient shock. Some believed that the pandemic would fundamentally transform the world. For example, Thomas Friedman felt that the pandemic would mark a new historical divide: the world before COVID-19 and the world after it.[3] He believed that we would get through the crisis because of the depth of talent and selfless commitment in "Big Government: the scientists, the medical professionals, the disaster professionals, the environmental experts." Citing scholarly work, he noted that disaster-prone nations have learned that tight rules and order save lives, unlike countries like the United States that had been spared major disasters like famines and disease outbreaks. He concluded that tighter rules and more generous rescue packages would make America a stronger and kinder society after corona. In other words, he felt that COVID-19 could serve as a catalyst for a fundamental transformation by changing people's ideas about the role of the government and their own role as citizens. Others believed that the pandemic would accelerate preexisting trends. Noting that "not every crisis is a turning point," Richard Haass expressed his belief that the pandemic would "accelerate history rather than reshape it," reinforcing such trends as democratic backsliding and United States–China strategic competition, to produce "a world in even greater disarray."[4] A third possibility was that the pandemic would be a transient event despite its huge toll in human lives and livelihoods, much like the influenza pandemic of 1918–20.

Of course, this pandemic on its own would not determine the future of the world. It would also depend on how people and their governments responded to the pandemic and whether this response was institutionalized and sustained beyond the pandemic. Missing from each of the three perspectives was the idea of interaction between the pandemic and human agency in the long term. For the "game changer" view, even if tighter rules and more generous rescue packages are successfully introduced, they may not be sustained if this response is framed as a one-time event, to be phased out after the pandemic is over. For the "accelerator" view, even if the pandemic reinforces preexisting trends and leads to "a world in even greater disarray," this world would be deeply unstable, fraught with the risks of international war and social conflict. Russia's invasion of Ukraine in 2022 is a reminder of what would likely happen if dangerous trends are allowed to accelerate. People and their governments would have to reverse, or at least decelerate, such dangerous trends, if they are to avoid a catastrophe. Last but not least, viewing COVID-19 as a transient shock may be shortsighted, given its large impact on people's perceptions. The pandemic exposed serious gaps in public health and social protection as well as international cooperation, but it also highlighted tantalizing possibilities if people and their governments can come together to address major challenges, ranging from poverty reduction to vaccine development. If sustained, these tantalizing possibilities would constitute a fundamental transformation.

Although COVID-19 infections have yet to disappear, enough time seems to have passed to assess the impact of the pandemic. This book provides a comprehensive and interdisciplinary perspective on preexisting trends before COVID-19 and envisions the post-COVID future. After this introductory chapter, the book looks at emerging changes in international relations, largely driven by United States–China competition (chapters 1 and 2) and other countries' efforts to secure their strategic autonomy (chapters 3 through 6). The book then looks at remaining challenges, such as economic inequality (chapter 7), political polarization (chapter 8), and global cooperation in the face of rising United States–China tensions, vis-à-vis public health (chapter 9), development cooperation (chapter 10), and climate change (chapter 11).

The end of the Cold War, the acceleration of globalization, and the Rise of the Rest ("Great Convergence") posed serious challenges to the existing international order based on World War II settlements and Cold War modifications. The bipolar world order led by the United States and the Soviet Union briefly gave way to a unipolar moment after the disintegration of the Soviet bloc in the 1990s, but it soon had to contend with new developments, such as the expansion of the European Union and the rise of developing and emerging countries such as Brazil, China, and India. The global financial crisis of 2008–9 provided an opportunity to reform global governance arrangements, as evidenced by the emergence of the Group of Twenty at the leadership level, but this adjustment, reflecting a sea change in international economic and political realities, was by no means a smooth process. Domestically, in many advanced industrial countries, there was a nativist and populist backlash against "the global elite" as increasing socioeconomic disparities and interaction with the outside world produced economic anxiety and status anxiety. Politicians who promised to take back control and bring jobs home appealed to a large number of voters, using us-versus-them rhetoric to divert attention from socioeconomic problems (chapters 7 and 8). The combination of international power shift and nativist and populist backlash made global cooperation a precarious proposition, even though the proliferation of global value chains, infectious diseases, and climate change made global cooperation more imperative than ever before. Instead, as the world experienced a slowdown in globalization in the wake of the global financial crisis, the United States–China strategic competition and the absence of global leadership came to define the international order in the 2010s (chapters 1 and 2). Many countries in Asia and Europe began to express concern and skepticism about both the United States and China, but they did not have the necessary leverage to promote global cooperation (chapters 4 through 6). In short, a slowdown in globalization, rising inequality and populist reaction in advanced industrial countries, and intensifying United States–China strategic competition constituted preexisting trends before the outbreak of the COVID-19 pandemic at the end of 2019.

The slowdown in globalization in the wake of the global financial crisis represents the latest phase in the history of globalization. Since the second quarter of the nineteenth century, trends in international trade and financial

Figure I-1. Trade and Financial Globalization

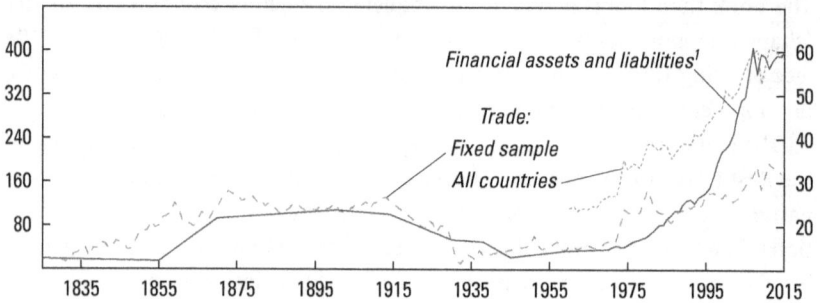

[1]Before 1970, calculated as external financial assets multiplied by 2.
Source: Bank for International Settlements, 2017.
Note: Trade openness is measured as a percentage of exports plus imports to global gross domestic product (GDP). Financial openness is measured as the percentage of external financial assets plus liabilities to global GDP. The fixed sample includes 18 countries, including major advanced and emerging economies.

flows relative to global GDP show two waves of globalization, each of which consists of three phases: rise, expansion, and crisis (figure I-1).[5]

In the first wave of globalization, the rising phase (1830–70) was driven by the combination of the First Industrial Revolution and imperialism. The First Industrial Revolution provided Britain and other industrializing countries in Europe with significant technological and military advantages over non-European states to open up their markets, if not conquer them outright. Within Europe, the Concert of Vienna helped to facilitate peace and prosperity after the Napoleonic Wars, as the major powers of the day (namely, Austria, Britain, France, Prussia, and Russia) regularly consulted with each other to manage risks. The confluence of these factors led to a dramatic increase in trade and financial flows relative to global gross domestic product (GDP).

In the expansion phase (1871–1913), trade and financial flows increased in volume and geographic scope, but their ratios to global GDP were relatively stable. Although international trade rapidly expanded in this period, it mostly involved simple commodities and manufactured products that did not cross national borders multiple times in their production process.[6] In this phase, the Second Industrial Revolution, centered on electricity and chemistry, further widened the gap between Western and non-Western states. However, international rivalry within Europe made the situation increasingly precarious, with the breakdown of the Concert of Vienna and the rise of unified Germany after the Franco-Prussian War. Subsequently, the formation of competing alliance systems in Europe in the early twentieth century foreshadowed the demise of the first wave of globalization.

In the crisis phase (1914–44), trade and financial flows suffered a steep fall relative to global GDP. World War I and its contentious postwar settlement led to a decline in trade and financial globalization, and this trend accelerated in the wake of the Great Depression, as protectionist measures were increasingly adopted around the world. High unemployment and economic hardship set the stage for significant reform in countries with relatively strong democratic traditions, such as the New Deal in the United States, but similar economic background factors led to the rise of totalitarianism in other countries with weak democratic traditions, most notably in Germany, Italy, and Japan. By the middle of the 1930s, the world was divided into competing blocs, which culminated in World War II.

In the second wave of globalization, the rising phase (1945–78) was characterized by a strong recovery in international trade and financial flows under the ideology of "embedded liberalism," or liberalism embedded in social democracy and nondiscriminatory multilateralism.[7] The ascendancy of social democracy (or the welfare state) in advanced economies led to broad-based growth.[8] The Bretton Woods institutions—the International Monetary Fund, the World Bank, and the General Agreement on Tariffs and Trade—established after World War II, together with the United Nations, promoted nondiscriminatory multilateralism and progressive liberalization. The Third Industrial Revolution, centered on information technology, helped to set the stage for a sustained economic expansion. However, this resurgence of globalization was really "half-globalization," as it mainly took place in the capitalist bloc led by the United States against the communist bloc led by the Soviet Union, in the context of the Cold War. Although economic interaction between the two blocs was limited and ideological competition was intense, the logic of mutually assured destruction helped to preserve peace between the two nuclear-armed superpowers.

The expansion phase (1979–2008) of the second wave of globalization saw the increasing influence of neoliberalism, as social democracy was weakened in many Western countries in the wake of the oil shocks and stagflation in the 1970s. At the same time, a number of socialist countries, beset by economic stagnation, embarked on reform and opening up, starting with China in 1978, Vietnam in 1986, the Central and Eastern European countries in the late 1980s, and the Soviet Union itself in the early 1990s. The end of the Cold War came without a major conflict and led to a dramatic increase in economic integration. The establishment of the World Trade Organization in 1995, and China's accession to it in 2001, ushered in a period of "hyperglobalization," as multinational corporations built extensive regional and global value chains.[9]

The rise of emerging economies such as Brazil, China, and India highlighted the latter part of this phase.

Finally, the current phase (2009–present) represents a potential crisis or reversal in globalization—a slowdown in globalization combined with worsening inequality and intensifying geopolitical competition. The combination of skill-biased technological change, expanding trade, and declining social protection has undermined workers' position in many advanced economies since the 1980s (chapter 7). The Fourth Industrial Revolution, centered on smart robots, and the response to climate change seems to provide opportunities for leap-frogging, at least to those countries that made successful catch-up efforts in industrialization. During this phase, China, under its dual circulation strategy, has pushed for the vertical integration of production and has become central to global value chains, accounting for the largest share of exports of intermediate goods globally. Unlike the crisis phase of the first wave of globalization, however, the current phase—at least so far—has not been stricken by a world war or a Great Depression, and has avoided the dangerous dynamic of belligerently competing blocs. The logic of mutually assured destruction continues to prevent a major war among nuclear-armed powers. Having benefited from the second wave of globalization, especially since the end of the Cold War, most developing and emerging economies would like to avoid another Cold War and maintain their strategic autonomy. In contrast, advanced economies have had to cope with difficult domestic politics of globalization in recent years, as evidenced by Brexit in Britain and the election of Donald Trump in the United States (chapter 8).

Table I-1 summarizes the different phases of the two waves of globalization, including the leading ideology, major elements, and "finishing shocks," which triggered major changes in the trajectory of globalization. In the first wave, the dynamic of competing blocs and the outbreak of world wars led to the decline of globalization. In the second wave, the logic of mutually assured destruction has helped prevent another world war, and the challenges to globalization have been more economic rather than military, related to domestic discontent and international rivalry for economic power.

The intensifying United States–China strategic competition should be understood in this historical context, which is characterized by the logic of mutually assured destruction, the absence of competing alliance systems, the reality of extensive international economic interaction, and the desire of third parties to enhance their strategic autonomy. In his book—*Destined for War: Can America and China Escape Thucydides's Trap?*—Graham Allison looks at historical cases of power transition and explored possibilities for war and

Table I-1. Two Waves of Globalization

Phase	Ideology	Major elements	Finishing shocks
Rise I, 1830–70	Imperialistic liberalism	First Industrial Revolution, Concert of Vienna, imperialist aggression	Franco-Prussian War
Expansion I, 1871–1913	Liberalism vs. Socialism	Second Industrial Revolution, breakdown of the Concert, competing alliance systems	World War I
Crisis I, 1914–44	Liberalism vs. Totalitarianism	World War I and contentious postwar settlement, Great Depression, competing blocs	World War II
Rise II 1945–78	Embedded liberalism	Third Industrial Revolution, social democracy, multilateralism, Cold War, mutually assured destruction, decolonization	Oil shocks and stagflation
Expansion II, 1979–2008	Neoliberalism	Weakening welfare state, socialist transition and end of Cold War, financialization, rise of emerging economies	Global financial crisis
Crisis II, 2009– present	Rise of nationalist populism	Fourth Industrial Revolution and climate response, worsening inequality and populist reaction, US–China strategic competition	Major risks to future trajectory: domestic discontent and geopolitical tensions

Source: Wonhyuk Lim, "Globalization and the Asian Century," in *New Global Dynamics: Managing Economic Change in a Transforming World*, ed. Zia Qureshi and Daehee Jeong (Brookings and KDI, 2024).

peace between an established power and an emerging power (table I-2).[10] However, for nuclear weapons powers following the logic of mutually assured destruction, historical war outcomes based on conventional weapons have limited applicability, as nuclear weapons would destroy both sides. Even among outcomes of peaceful coexistence, some are more relevant than others in the current context. For example, Portugal and Spain could agree to a sphere-of-influence arrangement by drawing a line in the middle of the Atlantic back in 1494, as the two powers could assert their naval superiority over other European countries at the time and try to subjugate weak countries in the Americas and Africa. In today's world, however, it would be much more difficult for the United States and China to agree to a sphere-of-influence arrangement by drawing a line in the middle of the Pacific. Other countries would push back and call for an open and inclusive approach rather than letting the United States and China establish their respective exclusive sphere of influence, as they would like to engage with both the United States and China as well as among

Table I-2. Possibilities for War and Peaceful Coexistence, Based on Historical Cases

Outcome	Type	Cases
War	Preemption by established power	Spanish Armada's attack on England, 1588
	Preemption by emerging power	Japan's surprise attack on Pearl Harbor, 1941
	Collision	France and Britain: Seven Years' War, 1756–63 Britain and the Netherlands: Fourth War, 1780–84 Franco-Prussian War, 1870–71 World War I and World War II
Peaceful coexistence	Sphere of influence	Portugal and Spain: Treaty of Tordesillas, 1494
	Concert	Concert of Vienna after Napoleonic Wars European integration after World War II
	Accommodation	Britain's acceptance of America's rise, early 1900s
	Deterrence based on mutually assured destruction	US–Soviet Cold War, 1947–91

Source: Author's formulation, based on historical cases given by Graham Allison, *Destined for War: Can America and China Escape Thucydides's Trap?* (New York: Houghton Mifflin, 2017).

themselves. Moreover, the United States is unlikely to give up on the forward deployment of its military and economic influence in Asia, and China likewise is unlikely to give up on its economic and political relationship with countries in the Americas. In addition, the accommodation outcome is unrealistic unless the United States wholeheartedly accepts China's rise and decides to get on the bandwagon, instead of competing for supremacy. As a result, the relevant outcomes in the current context are largely reduced to concert and deterrence, or some combination of the two.

In fact, the United States' approaches to China have reflected these realities (table I-3). Although the United States had discussed the possibility of using nuclear weapons against China during the Korean War (1950–53), this became an unrealistically risky proposition once China itself successfully developed nuclear weapons in 1964. After Richard Nixon went to China in 1972 to normalize relations between the two countries, the US policy toward China for the next four decades was characterized by strategic engagement, combining military deterrence and economic engagement.[11] Under this approach, the United States, while acknowledging the One China policy, used its forward-deployed military presence in Asia to deter China from unilaterally changing the status quo with regard to Taiwan and the rest of the region. At the same time, the United States promoted economic engagement with China, utilizing complementarities between the two economies to derive mutual benefits. However,

Table I-3. American Approaches to China since the Normalization of Relations

Approach	Objective	Note
Strategic engagement	Economic engagement and military deterrence	The United States' nostalgia about its golden age working against bilateral cooperation, as China becomes increasingly competitive
America First	Pursuit of self-interest on case-by-case basis	The United States is reluctant to incur financial and political costs to strengthen the liberal international order
New Cold War	Decoupling, containment, implosion	Weak ideological competition, a strong track record of cooperation, an absence of alliance blocs, and the increased autonomy of third parties
Strategic competition	Competition without catastrophe, in coordination with allies	An issue-by-issue approach vulnerable to spillovers, the United States' interest in pursuing cooperation in key areas, given China's market size (e.g., finance and manufacturing)

Source: Author's formulation.

the United States had begun to question the wisdom of strategic engagement by the end of the 2000s. China, by this time, had emerged as a peer competitor to the United States. In contrast, despite massive personnel and material commitments, the United States had experienced setbacks in Iraq and Afghanistan and suffered heavy economic losses during the global financial crisis. As a result, strategic engagement with China had become an unpopular approach in the United States (chapters 1 and 2).

Instead, three different approaches to China emerged. First, Trump's America First approach is fundamentally transactional and pursues self-interest on a case-by-case basis. Under this approach, the United States is reluctant to incur financial and political costs to strengthen the liberal international order, unlike right after World War II—as demonstrated by the Marshall Plan, through which the United States provided an equivalent of 2.5 percent of the GDP of Western Europe. As Trump made clear as early as 1987, when he ran a full-page ad in major US newspapers, his main concern was to bring jobs back home and avoid getting "ripped off" by other countries, including American allies. After he was elected US president in 2016, Trump tried to drive a hard bargain with China and American allies alike, using tariffs and other measures. Second, as exemplified by Mike Pompeo's speech at the Nixon Library in 2020, the new Cold War approach toward China basically tries to replicate the United States–Soviet Cold War, through decoupling, containment, "bloodletting" through proxy wars, and implosion, where various campaigns are waged to incite a popular uprising. Third, strategic competition aims at competition without catastrophe, in coordination with allies.[12] Since the global financial crisis, the US approach toward China has shifted from strategic engagement to America First, and then to strategic competition, while keeping the new Cold War as a possible option.

The COVID-19 shock broke out at the end of 2019 against the background of these preexisting trends: namely, a slowdown in globalization, rising inequality and populist reaction in advanced industrial countries, and intensifying United States–China strategic competition. In economic terms, even though a pandemic and a war both result in a great number of human deaths, a pandemic is different from a war in that it has a far less destructive impact on capital stock (except for the kind of capital that becomes less usable due to changes in human behavior in the postpandemic world). So, a pandemic is a labor supply shock without a capital supply shock, and, as such, tends to have a negative effect on the marginal rate of return on capital. Its effect on wages seems to depend on the magnitude of the labor supply shock.[13] If the magnitude of the shock is as large as the one due to the Black Death (with deaths amounting to more than 30 percent of the population), it is likely to have a positive effect on wages and strengthen the bargaining power of workers. However, if it is about the magnitude of the shock due to the 1918–20 Influenza Pandemic (with deaths amounting to 2 percent of global population), previously underemployed workers may be able to step in and fill the gap. In terms of the fatality rate, the COVID-19 shock was much smaller, with confirmed deaths amounting to 0.08 percent of the global population over a four-year period. International restrictions on mobility during the pandemic had a significant effect on the labor markets of those countries that rely heavily on immigration; but overall, the COVID-19 pandemic had a relatively small and transient effect on labor.

Despite its comparatively small quantitative impact, the pandemic exposed serious problems in public health and social protection and also in international cooperation. Historically, a disease outbreak like the Black Death could act as "a great leveler," affecting both the rich and the poor. In contrast, COVID-19 highlighted socioeconomic disparities in coping with the pandemic. The most privileged people left crowded cities and worked remotely from their second home in the countryside. Many workers were laid off in the person-to-person service sector as the fear of infection led to a precipitous decline in demand for dining, leisure, and hospitality services. Those deemed "essential workers" had to face the threat of infection on the frontlines so that others could access the goods and services they needed in order to isolate safely at home.[14] The adoption of the term "essential workers" ironically highlighted the fact that these workers who kept the world functioning were treated as "disposable."[15] As the pandemic exposed gaps in health care and the social safety net, many people felt that they had been abandoned by their government and society and left to cope with the crisis on their own. To be fair, this sense of abandonment was addressed to a different degree in different countries. After offering immediate relief to mitigate the economic impact of the pandemic, some countries used the crisis as an opportunity to shore up public health and social protection; other countries did not go beyond providing stimulus checks and emergency loans.[16]

The pandemic also demonstrated the importance of risk management. Just-in-time delivery over global value chains proved inadequate in this time of demand surge and supply disruption, which highlighted the value of having strategic stockpiles and a domestic manufacturing base to produce critical supplies, as well as diversified international cooperation. Last but not least, COVID-19 delivered a number of "emperor has no clothes" moments for everyone to see. China, which was supposed to have reformed its public health system after the 2003 SARS epidemic, still mishandled the COVID-19 crisis in its early stage. Many Western countries squandered precious time in January and February 2020 by condemning China's political system, and they were caught off guard in March, when COVID-19 exploded. Populist politicians in Italy, the United Kingdom, Brazil, and the United States showed that anti-intellectualism was no match for a contagious virus that knows no politics. Although the United States, China, and other countries still have formidable economic and military power, the loss of credibility they suffered was unmistakable.

At the same time, the response to the pandemic also highlighted tantalizing possibilities. Fiscal measures such as stimulus checks proved effective in mitigating the economic shock.[17] In the United States, the magnitude of the rescue package was well in excess of the GDP gap, and, combined with supply chain disruptions, it later fueled inflation, but at least it showed that an activist government can provide relief to people. Institutional reform to strengthen social protection had a positive effect on poverty reduction. Operation Warp Speed led to the successful development of COVID-19 vaccines in record time. Prior public support for research and development on m-RNA technology and advanced market commitments for vaccines proved critical for this breakthrough, with important implications for innovation and industrial policy. The pandemic also accelerated the digital transformation, as businesses and households alike adopted information technology to facilitate work from home and replace in-person services and meetings.[18] Although countries initially focused on securing their own supplies of masks, personal protective equipment, therapeutics, and vaccines, they set up arrangements to sell or distribute these critical medical supplies around the world. Also, although this proved to be transient, the pandemic showed what the world would look like if it could achieve a sharp reduction in pollutants, including greenhouse gases.

Overall, each of the three early views on how COVID-19 would affect the world had its merits and limitations. The pandemic initially seemed to serve as a catalyst for fundamental transformation. For example, in the United States, the pandemic prompted long-overdue action to strengthen social protection in addition to providing immediate relief. The Child Poverty Reduction Act, legislated in 2020, was one of the most effective antipoverty measures in decades. However, it was terminated a year later.[19] Concern about "welfarism" resurfaced once the crisis subsided. Basically, when massive unemployment in the immediate wake of the pandemic, combined with weak social protection, seemed to raise the specter of social turmoil in 2020, the United States threw lots of money at the problem in the form of stimulus checks, and it adopted some social protection measures—only to phase them out once the perceived threat faded away. Many workers were once again relegated to precarious existence, under the implicit assumption that such a precarious existence would discipline them. However, unless these workers feel secure enough about their livelihoods, they are unlikely to support policy measures to address global challenges on trade, health, and climate. The COVID-19 pandemic also accelerated preexisting trends, by further slowing down globalization, highlighting socioeconomic disparities, and intensifying United States–China strategic competition. It is evident that these accelerating trends cannot lead to stable outcomes, because they exacerbate the risks of crisis and conflict if they continue. As the pandemic response demonstrated with tantalizing possibilities, people and their governments need to work together to reverse these dangerous trends. Domestically, instead of blaming "the global elite" and "outsiders," investing in people should receive priority, given the challenges of automation and globalization. Unless workers and the middle class feel secure enough, governments will find it difficult to push for international initiatives. Internationally, a new order should reflect changing economic and political realities, with guardrails to prevent conflict and mechanisms to promote global cooperation. Countries should exercise their strategic autonomy to work toward a common security and economic framework founded on the principle of openness and inclusivity. Although the COVID-19 pandemic exposed serious problems and offered tantalizing possibilities both domestically and internationally, these transformational changes remain unfinished.

Notes

1. See https://data.who.int/dashboards/covid19/deaths?n=c. Officially, the World Health Organization's public health emergency of international concern, in conjunction with COVID-19, was in effect from January 30, 2020, to May 5, 2023.

2. Robert J. Barro, Jose F. Ursúa, and Joanna Weng, *The Coronavirus and the Great Influenza Pandemic. Lessons from the "Spanish Flu" for the Coronavirus's Potential Effects on Mortality and Economic Activity*, NBER Working Paper 26866 (Cambridge, MA: National Bureau of Economic Research, 2020).

3. Thomas L. Friedman, "Our New Historical Divide: BC and AC—the World Before Corona and the World After," *New York Times*, March 17, 2020.

4. Richard Haass, "The Pandemic Will Accelerate History Rather Than Reshape It: Not Every Crisis Is a Turning Point, *Foreign Affairs*, April 7, 2020, https://www.foreignaffairs.com/articles/united-states/2020-04-07/pandemic-will-accelerate-history-rather-reshape-it.

5. This section on the history of globalization draws from Wonhyuk Lim, "Globalization and the Asian Century," in *New Global Dynamics: Managing Economic Change in a Transforming World*, ed. Zia Qureshi and Daehee Jeong (Brookings and KDI, 2024).

6. Richard Baldwin, *The Great Convergence: Information Technology and the New Globalization* (Belknap Press of Harvard University Press, 2016).

7. John Gerard Ruggie, "International Regimes, Transactions, and Change: Embedded Liberalism in the Postwar Economic Order," *International Organization* 36, no. 2 (1982): 379–415.

8. Paul Krugman, *Conscience of a Liberal* (New York: W. W. Norton, 2007).

9. Arvind Subramanian and Martin Kessler, *The Hyperglobalization of Trade and Its Future*, Working Paper 13-6 (Washington: Peterson Institute for International Economics, 2013); Dani Rodrik, "Globalization's Wrong Turn," *Foreign Affairs* 98, no. 4 (2019): 26–33.

10. Graham Allison, *Destined for War: Can America and China Escape Thucydides's Trap?* (New York: Houghton Mifflin, 2017).

11. Fareed Zakaria, "The New China Scare: Why America Shouldn't Panic About Its Latest Challenger," *Foreign Affairs*, December 6, 2019.

12. Kurt Campbell and Jake Sullivan, "Competition without Catastrophe: How America Can Both Challenge And Coexist with China," *Foreign Affairs*, September–October. 2019,

13. Guido Alfani and Tommy E. Murphy, "Plague and Lethal Epidemics in the Pre-Industrial World," *Journal of Economic History* 77, no. 1 (2017): 314–43.

14.   Nancy Fraser, "American Interregnum," *Sidecar: New Left Review,* April 2021, https://newleftreview.org/sidecar/posts/american-interregnum.

15.   Eric Klinenberg, "We Were Wrong About What Happened to America in 2020," *New York Times,* January 31, 2024.

16.   World Bank, *Inequality and Shared Prosperity: Correcting Course* (Washington: World Bank, 2022).

17.   P. Deb, D. Fuceri, J. D. Ostry, N. Tawk, and N. Yang, *The Effects of Fiscal Measures during COVID-19,* IMF Working Paper 2021-262 (Washington: International Monetary Fund, 2021).

18.   Yuval Noah Harari, "Lessons from a Year of COVID," *Financial Times,* February 26, 2021.

19.   Klinenberg, "We Were Wrong."

One

The COVID Shock, American Domestic Transformation, and Transpacific Relations

KENT E. CALDER, *REISCHAUER CENTER FOR EAST ASIAN STUDIES, JOHNS HOPKINS UNIVERSITY, SCHOOL OF ADVANCED INTERNATIONAL STUDIES*

With over 12 million Americans infected by the coronavirus, and more than 250,000 fatalities, as the turbulent 2020 US presidential election season finally drew to a close, the COVID-19 pandemic became the most tragic American civilian health emergency in over a century.[1] Only the Spanish Flu pandemic of 1918–19 can compare. And more Americans died from the coronavirus infections of 2020, in the first eight months of the pandemic, than in all the foreign conflicts in American history, save only World War II.

China, Iran, and several European nations were also hit hard by the coronavirus pandemic in its early stages. Most of them, however, were able to suppress the pandemic quite rapidly, at limited cost in human lives and lost economic output. The United States, however, consistently had more difficulty, despite the high technical quality of its health care system, with both infections and fatalities rapidly rising to the highest levels on Earth, and lingering there stubbornly throughout 2020. The length and intensity of America's confrontation with COVID-19 were thus distinctive.

The economic, social, and political dimensions of the COVID Shock for the United States were all substantial, by virtue of the scale and intensity of disruption. The implications are only beginning to unfold, but they already show prospects of also being substantial and disruptive. During the second quarter of 2020, US gross domestic product (GDP) dropped by over 9 percent—the greatest fall since systematic quarterly record keeping began in 1947. Indeed, since that time, US quarterly GDP had never previously exceeded even a 3 percent non-annualized GDP decline.[2]

Figure 1-1. Unemployment Dimensions of the United States' 2020 COVID-19 Shock

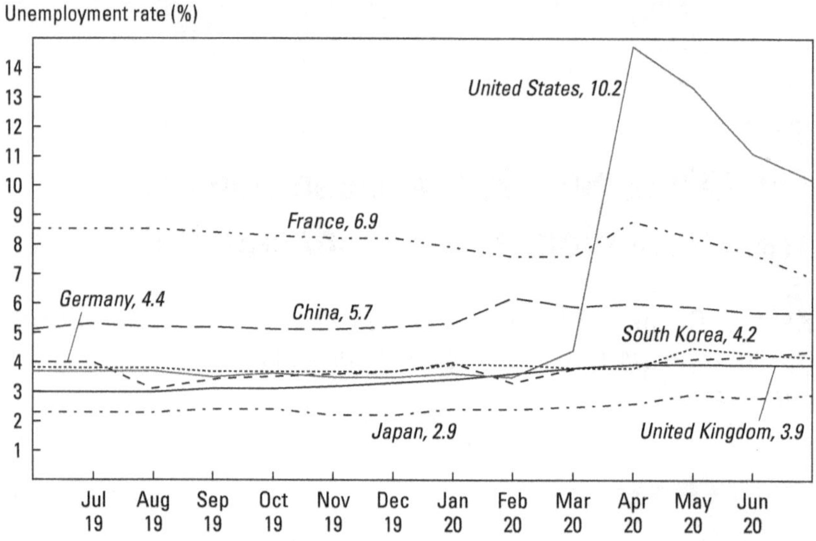

Unemployment rate (%)

Sources: Data for countries that belong to the Organization for Economic Cooperation and Development are taken from its "Data: Unemployment Rate," https://data.oecd.org/unemp/unemployment-rate.htm. Data for China are from the National Bureau of Statistics of China, https://tradingeconomics.com/china/unemployment-rate.

The early employment implications of COVID-19 were also highly disruptive. By mid-2020, more than 50 million people were out of work in the United States, as businesses shut down permanently and restrictions continued across much of the country. Unemployment surged to over 10 percent of the American workforce—significantly higher than in most major Asian and European nations affected by the virus, as noted in figure 1-1. Indeed, the United States was the only Group of Seven member nation to have unemployment *triple* as a result of the COVID Shock.

At the heart of the massively deflationary economic impact of the pandemic in its earliest phases was the way it struck some of the key economic centers of the United States with such ferocious intensity. The virus forced extensive lockdowns that brought economic activity across much of the country to a virtual standstill in its initial stages. After some early dislocations on the West Coast, especially in the Seattle area, the pandemic struck metropolitan New York, where the virus had infiltrated from Europe and quietly bred undetected for weeks before emerging with full force in mid-March. By the end of April, over 25,000 residents of New York and New Jersey alone were dead, and close to 430,000 were infected.[3] In subsequent weeks, the virus also spread virulently to the South and Southwest, with California and later Florida, as well as Texas, surpassing New York's case rate.[4] Its rampage later spread throughout the Midwest and across the Great Plains to the Rocky Mountains.

Consumer spending makes up more than two-thirds of aggregate demand in the United States, and it fell sharply in the early stages of the pandemic crisis—13.6 percent in the month of April 2020 alone.[5] A massive $2 trillion stimulus package under the CARES Act—the largest in the world, in quantitative terms—blunted the macroeconomic impact to some degree, after its passage on March 27.[6] The US federal budget deficit expanded to almost 16 percent of GDP—one of the highest levels in the world.[7]

At the individual level, weekly supplementary unemployment payments of $600 provided under the CARES Act initially helped to bolster household income.[8] Those payments, however, expired on July 31, and Congress was slow to agree on a substitute. Republicans and Democrats differed sharply on the trade-offs between health security and economic growth, leading to a protracted stalemate.

Trillions of dollars were borrowed to counter the crisis, by individuals, corporations, and where feasible by local governments as well. The massive public and private borrowing led to a rapid expansion of the US money supply (known as M2). The Federal Reserve injected massive sums into the banking system, as well as directly into private firms, engaging in an unprecedented expansion of its balance sheet.[9] Yet despite this massive injection of money into the system, inflation dropped to almost zero, suggesting the massive deflationary pressures operating on the economy.

Monetary expansion and surprising resilience in the stock market did provide some bright spots in the economic picture, however.[10] After a sharp drop in late March, the stock market began to surge, with the Standard & Poor's 500 index rising over 25 percent during the second quarter alone. Federal stimulus packages, in particular, stimulated optimism in the markets, with the Federal Reserve at one point buying $41 billion in financial assets daily.

Under pressure from the palpable dangers of direct interpersonal contact that were generated by the virus, digitalization, remote communication, and e-commerce grew explosively. These disruptive changes made Big Tech the largest corporate beneficiary of the pandemic, even as most of the real economy itself was slumping.[11] Amazon's earnings, for example, doubled year on year, compared with 2019.[12] Apple experienced double-digit earnings growth as well.[13] Together, the four largest tech firms—Apple, Amazon, Facebook, and Alphabet (Google)—reported revenue of $206 billion and net income of $29 billion for the three months ending in late June.[14]

Although Big Tech responded dynamically to the COVID Shock, and profited enormously in the process, America's politics were far less responsive. Decentralized, fragmented government made a rapid, coherent administrative response difficult, and the White House provided little leadership, apart from supporting the quest for a vaccine. Deepening inequities in civil society, and rising frustration at the impact of the virus, kindled an assertive nationalism that in turn complicated transpacific relations, as we shall see.

The Pre-COVID Era: Benchmark for Understanding the Future?

Transformation in the American political economy clearly began long before the COVID-19 pandemic, and is ongoing. We know enough already to appreciate that some powerful new forces were unleashed by the initial COVID Shock, many of them synergistic with one another, that showed promise of transforming the country in fundamental ways. Many of those transformation agents, however, have their origins deep in the pre-COVID era. To fully understand the impact of the 2020 COVID Shock in the United States itself—particularly why it diverged from patterns in other major nations—it is important first to understand how the US political economy was structurally configured before this pandemic began.

State structure, as institutionalist social scientists have come increasingly to understand, is a good place to begin.[15] The American political system, for the purposes of health care policy formation, and response to issues of global health care policy, has five basic structural features of critical comparative relevance: (1) its pluralist federal structure; (2) its vigorous, independent, opinionated, and increasingly polarized civil society; (3) its large, affluent, multinationally oriented private business sector; (4) its unwieldy, often opinionated Congress; and (5) its potentially powerful presidency. All these elements predated the COVID Shock, but together they powerfully conditioned the distinctive American domestic response to it. These structural traits of US politics and political governance will likely also condition America's post-COVID foreign policy response to the transpacific relationship.

The United States—like Australia, Canada, and Germany, but unlike South Korea or France—has a decentralized, federal political system. Even though federal powers have increased substantially over the history of the American republic in many areas, extensive responsibilities are still reserved, either by custom or statute, to state and local governments, or to the people themselves. This state and local autonomy is often jealously guarded, and federal intervention is resisted, especially in the country's more conservative South and

Midwest—areas that have long expressed open skepticism of centralized political-economic power.

Fatefully, one of the political-economic sectors where central responsibilities are traditionally underdeveloped in the United States, compared with most industrial democracies, is health care. The United States has no universal health insurance, and nearly 28 million Americans (almost 9 percent of the country's population in 2018) still lacked what in much of the world is considered a basic right.[16] Another 43 percent are underinsured.[17] The United States has no powerful central health ministry; instead, important regulatory responsibilities are distributed to a broad range of specialized agencies, or to the states. The Food and Drug Administration, for example, authorizes new pharmaceuticals, and the Centers for Disease Control and Prevention (CDC) monitors the progress of pandemics and recommends countermeasures. Pandemic countermeasures, such as mandating the wearing of masks or the details of economic lockdowns, are traditionally the province of the states.

Even though the US health care policy structure is relatively decentralized, in past crises it has generally produced coherent policy, based on rigorous federal guidelines issued by the CDC, to which politicians at all levels have deferred. Since 2006 the Biomedical Advanced Research and Development Agency (BARDA) has also had the capacity to support the rapid development of therapeutics. In the 2020 COVID crisis, however, neither the CDC nor BARDA was able to play a centralizing and stabilizing role, because they were inhibited by the White House, which failed to either lead or defer to the public health professionals. White House inaction thus seriously intensified the negative consequences of the underlying structural vacuum when the COVID Shock exploded on the world.

The fragmented and decentralized configuration of public power in the United States facilitates democratic debate—a tendency further accentuated by the vigor of civil society in the country. In contrast to coordinated market economies—be they technocratic-developmentalist, democratic corporatist, or authoritarian—the United States has an iconoclastic, market-oriented civil society, closely interrelated with an opinionated and disputatious mass media.[18] This civil society is well configured to uncover and criticize inequity, but not well equipped to provide operational solutions.

Over the past three decades, America's civil society has grown increasingly polarized, and the political economy itself has grown progressively more unequal. Cultural conflicts, reinforced by deepening polarization in political party preferences, have grown more and more pervasive, as conceptions of identity have become more sharply defined and passionately held.[19] Indeed, it is difficult for Americans at times to agree even on matters of elemental health care importance, as the recent controversy over mask wearing during a global pandemic clearly showed.

A third structural factor configuring America's response to the health care crisis is the configuration of the country's private health care sector, which has helped in the rapid development and marketing of vaccines, even where broader policy responses have been incoherent. The United States has some of the largest multinational pharmaceutical enterprises in the world, rivaled only by Germany, as well as enterprising start-ups. Firms such as Pfizer, Johnson & Johnson, Eli Lilly, and Merck stand in the forefront of global research and development, with massive budgets and global marketing networks, while startups like Moderna attract equity and government research funds. US vaccine innovators are also well protected at home by strong US intellectual property laws, and generally favorable regulatory treatment, reinforced by strong lobbies on Capitol Hill. Cooperating with the government under Operation Warp Speed, they developed credible vaccines in record time, before the end of 2020.[20]

Although America's health care sector made extraordinary progress, in cooperation with government, in developing a vaccine, it was far less successful in the realm of testing, which requires qualitatively different kinds of government operations and coordination. Delays in implementing testing within the United States have occurred for a variety of reasons, including unavailable reagents in supply chains; spikes in case load demand due to economic reopenings; and decentralization of testing, leading to widespread inconsistencies by area in the availability of tests and testing supplies. Common to all these difficulties has been a lack of overarching national supervision.

Unlike vaccine production, where the US government was able to funnel huge resources efficiently into specific vaccine development firms, testing operated under a very different institutional dynamic. The pharmaceutical firms supported their own vaccine candidates internally under conditions of intense external competition that accelerated development through the organized and highly dynamic Operation Warp Speed process. Testing was far less organized. The availability and distribution of tests varied dramatically across state and local lines, with much less federal oversight or support than prevailed in the vaccine area. Vaccine development and testing also had very different target groups, with respect to scale and size. Testing needed to reach out to the entire US population, while vaccine clinical trials were able to focus on much smaller groups.[21]

Vaccine distribution, as a challenge for public policy, presents emerging difficulties in the United States similar to the experience with testing. Distribution is inevitably a somewhat decentralized process, involving multiple local organizations. Slowness and inconsistencies in implementation are thus a significant danger.

The US Congress, seen in comparative perspective, has unique strengths and weaknesses which contribute in the aggregate to America's often halting policy responses to the COVID Shock. As one of three branches of government, Congress is by no means dominant, or even unified, and often cannot sway the White House. Congress does, however have the power to autonomously propose legislation, and can act decisively when unified, as with the CARES Act in the spring of 2020.

A final structural feature of American politics—capable of countervailing all the other features in a crisis—is the institutional power of the American presidency. In stages since the Civil War, and especially since the Great Depression and the advent of the Cold War, the president has steadily accumulated more and more capacity to reconfigure national policy in a crisis.[22] This presidential power, to be sure, is more circumscribed in health care than in many other areas, such as national security, but nevertheless has latent potential if the incumbent desires to use it. The Constitution, after all, puts Congress at an institutional disadvantage, and it provides the president with an institutional edge, because presidents are charged constitutionally with the execution of the laws. Decisions made by Congress are carried out by the president, while presidents execute their own decisions.[23]

Apart from preexisting structure, an important historical consideration predisposed America's response to the COVID Shock as it suddenly erupted at the beginning of 2020. In contrast to the major nations of East Asia and Africa, in particular, the United States has had little recent direct experience with pandemics. The major global pandemics of the past two decades—such as SARS, MERS, H1N9 swine flu, and Ebola—did not touch its shores with any serious virulence.

To be sure, the United States does experience an annual flu season, with as many as 40,000 annual fatalities.[24] This is considered a matter of course, however, and not a matter that mandates much special policy preparation. America's last traumatic experience with a pandemic was the Spanish Flu crisis of 1918–19. That tragic scourge, which killed 675,000 Americans, left a deep scar on the lives and psyches of those affected, to be sure.[25] It was, however, rapidly forgotten by the general public, and by many politicians. Despite insistent warnings over the past decade of impending dangers, repeated by respected figures such as the philanthropist and former Microsoft chairman Bill Gates, Trump administration policymakers were so oblivious to the potential peril of pandemics that in 2018 they disbanded the National Security Council's Directorate for Global Health Security and Biodefense. Only a fraction of the team members were reassigned to roles dealing with pandemic response.[26]

The Disjointed American Response

Few Americans expected the COVID Shock when it suddenly exploded in the early spring of 2020. And few even dreamed of the anguished, agonizing, fragmented, and protracted national response that was to ensue. By the end of November 2020, over 12 million Americans were infected, and over 250,000 were dead—the highest figures, in both categories, for any nation in the world, for a country spending more on medical care, per capita, than any other.[27] With only 4 percent of the world's population, the United States was suffering over 20 percent of the infections and nearly 19 percent of fatalities worldwide.[28]

As might be expected, given the structural and historical considerations outlined above, the American policy response to COVID 19 was halting and spasmodic.[29] With little experience of pandemics in its own living memory, unlike many Asian nations, the United States was extremely slow to become conscious of the COVID Shock at the policy level. When policymakers did begin considering countermeasures, one of the few decisive early actions taken was closing American borders to foreign travel, beginning with China, from which the virus originated. In May 2020, Operation Warp Speed was created to coordinate vaccine development, but only after the pandemic had begun to rapidly accelerate in the United States, and existing interagency structures had proven unable to cope with it.[30]

Attempts to set up a coherent testing program also failed, and contract tracing was employed only half-heartedly, if at all. Even after research confirmed the aerosol transmission of COVID 19, and the disturbing reality of asymptomatic spread, many Americans were loath to embrace masking, even in the face of strong medical insistence. And the federal government failed to impose nationwide standards.

The protracted, generally disorganized American response to the COVID Shock over the course of 2020 was devastating at the macro level, in many ways. Some sectors, to be sure, were stimulated, such as the digital economy. Yet the conventional smokestack economy in the industrial Midwest was badly hit, and ravaged late in 2020 by both structural change and a resurgent virus. Many service sectors were also badly hit, including the airlines, mass transit, and the hospitality industry. By the end of the summer of 2020, for example, domestic air travel in the United States was down 44 percent from prepandemic levels, while international flights from the United States were down 75 percent.[31] With ridership losses ranging from 70 to 90 percent in major cities since March, bus and rail providers project gaping budget holes that meant lasting consequences for riders and operators.

Income inequality had been deepening across the United States for more than thirty years before the COVID Shock hit, intensified by the impact of globalization, declining labor cohesiveness, and differential returns to capital and wage labor.[32] In 1975 the top quintile of US wage earners received 43.6 percent of aggregate income; by 2015, that share had become 51.1 percent.[33] The top 1 percent of Americans alone was receiving 20 percent of total income, and that share was steadily rising.[34] Inequities in the distribution of net assets were even more substantial, with the richest 1 percent of Americans owning more than half the value of equities in the whole country.[35]

The COVID Shock has made matters worse, particularly along the racial divide that has plagued America throughout its history. Disproportionately Black counties account for over half of total infections and nearly 60 percent of deaths due to COVID during 2020, although African Americans make up only 13.4 percent of the population as a whole.[36] Disproportionately exposed to the airborne virus, due to their concentration in blue-collar service occupations, African Americans also suffered from poorer, more crowded housing conditions; poorer medical care; and in many cases, poorer diets—conditions that in turn rendered them more vulnerable to COVID.[37] Other low-income communities of color are also often confronted with similar similar health care challenges. Nearly a quarter of Blacks and Hispanics (24 percent) are employed in service industries, compared with 16 percent of whites, putting the former at increased risk for job losses, loss of income, or COVID exposure if they maintain their jobs. Groups of color also may have more limited ability to absorb income declines due to more limited incomes. Over a quarter of Blacks, Hispanics, American Indians, and Alaska natives are low-wage workers, compared with less than 17 percent of whites.[38]

The COVID Shock thus intensified a long-standing yet combustible situation just waiting for a catalytic spark. The brutal, senseless police killing of George Floyd, a Black resident of Minneapolis, accused only of passing a counterfeit $20 bill, provided that spark in late May 2020, leading to a wave of demonstrations nationwide.[39] Further similar incidents led to more demonstrations, and larger outpourings of violence across the country. A counterprotest backlash emerged, in cities ranging from Portland, Oregon, to Kenosha, Wisconsin, and the socioeconomic frustrations provoked by the COVID Shock itself became even more deeply entwined with frustrations about America's unequal and increasingly polarized society as a whole.

The COVID Shock and Changing Domestic Political Imperatives

Populism on both the left and the right, provoked by individual injustices and frustrations, resurged against a broader backdrop of deepening economic inequality. This inequality, mixed with the traumas surrounding COVID, produced an increasingly combustible sociopolitical mix across the United States, in a presidential election year. There were clearly temptations to engage in short-run posturing, demagoguery, and opportunism. Yet beyond these short-run tendencies, what longer-term political consequences of the 2020 COVID Shock will persist into the future?

One long-term consequence of the COVID Shock is likely to be the intensification and acceleration of the polarization in the American political economy that has been advancing over the past four decades, and that is unusually pronounced from a comparative perspective.[40] Simply put, the haves and the have-nots of American society are growing ever farther apart. In the wake of the COVID Shock, an accelerated digitalization of the US economy, and a buoyant stock market, have generated windfall returns for those with financial assets and an ability to remain at a distance from the virus. Meanwhile, those in manual occupations, subject to more cramped housing conditions, and being forced to commute on crowded public transportation, are also confronting much more severe economic circumstances, with less of a financial cushion. One group rationally prefers stability, yet does little to make resources available to the have-nots, relying heavily on "law and order" measures, while the other is increasingly obsessed with the need for change.

The COVID Shock has thus naturally bred political turbulence. If the same structural conditions continue to persist, the likelihood is for such turbulence, and the demagoguery that exploits it, to also persist, and to breed. One likely outgrowth is intensified, if inchoate, nationalism, which could well advance into matters of international trade, investment, and finance, without producing plausible solutions to public health and economic-inequality challenges.

Another likely political-economic consequence of the COVID Shock, with prospects enhanced by Biden's November 2020 electoral victory, is the rebirth of state activism in microeconomic policy. Americans have been impressed often, amid the COVID crisis, with the lack of medical supplies and equipment at home, and the difficulties of securing them readily from abroad. This existential imperative has stimulated insistent and widespread calls—from the media, members of Congress, and government officials—for "reshoring"—producing an increasing share of essential medical supplies and equipment at home.[41] This medically induced impulse, spurred by the pandemic, has led to a broader revival of interest in industrial policy, which has been largely dormant in the United States for over two decades.

The Post-COVID Transpacific Relationship

As suggested in the foregoing pages, the COVID Shock has had several important implications for the American domestic political economy. It has sharply accelerated digitalization and, with it, has stimulated revolutionary new forms of remote communication. This disruptive technological shift has sharply intensified income inequality, by enriching information and communications technology entrepreneurs, while at the same time decimating smokestack industries and exacerbating widespread unemployment in traditional sectors of the economy. The collapse of aggregate demand in the early stages of the pandemic greatly magnified the impact of the digital revolution, and spurred massive government fiscal outlays that caused a sharp deterioration in government finances.[42] America's fitful, delayed response to the pandemic further depressed growth and compounded fiscal difficulties.

America has thus begun emerging from the pandemic a changed nation—much more "wired" technologically than before, but also more indebted, with higher structural unemployment. It has become a nation more deeply rent by sociopolitical divisions, especially with regard to race and socioeconomic standing. These divisions impart a deepening populist and nationalistic cast to its politics and foreign policy, as it faces out across the Pacific.

Biden's November 2020 election as president of the United States moderated this equation, although it is unlikely to fundamentally transform it. Biden speaks of working toward national reconciliation, and more support for multilateralism. Persistent socioeconomic inequities, the structural problems a divided America has in dealing with them, and the efforts of Donald Trump's narrowly defeated populist movement to exploit discontent have made it difficult for US policymakers to return to the cosmopolitanism and free trade orientation of earlier years. Developments across the Pacific, however, make some constructive reformulation of US trade policy imperative, as we shall see.

Transpacific relations, of course, are a product of developments on both sides of the world's broadest ocean, mediated through embedded institutions and sociopolitical networks that have a powerful stabilizing impact of their own. In the cases of South Korea and Japan, alliance ties naturally have a stabilizing impact, while in the case of China, massive American direct foreign investment and financial interdependence also have a residual stabilizing impact. Within China itself, however, political-economic transformations induced by the COVID crisis itself—notably increased legitimacy for the current government due to its seemingly victorious battle against the virus at Wuhan, and the revived nationalism stimulated by the ensuing return to rapid Chinese economic growth—cannot be ignored.

Despite their underlying stability bias, transpacific relations in the post-COVID world are confronting an unavoidably redefined political-economic reality, born of East Asia's earlier exit than the United States from the pandemic, along with the Trump administration's persistent neglect of multilateral trading relationships. Many East Asian nations maintained significantly better economic records than the United States in the early aftermath of the COVID Shock, especially during the spring and summer of 2020. China, for example, maintained 3.1 percent real growth for 2020:Q2, year on year, and 5.5 percent for 2020:Q3,[43] compared with –9 percent and –3 percent for the United States.[44]

The major nations of Asia have also begun to go their own way without the United States on trade policy to an unprecedented degree, as the United States continued to struggle with COVID. In January 2018, eleven of them signed the Comprehensive and Progressive Agreement for Trans-Pacific Partnership. In November 2020, fifteen Asia-Pacific nations, accounting for 30 percent of the world's GDP, including US allies Japan and South Korea, signed the Regional Comprehensive Economic Partnership (RCEP) without the United States.[45] The RCEP, in particular, is notable as the first free trade arrangement (FTA) to bring China, Japan, and South Korea together under a single FTA, thus streamlining rules of origin, facilitating intra-Asian value chains, and deepening prospects for follow-on China–Japan–Korea and also Free Trade Area of the Asia-Pacific agreements. Positive growth prospects in China, South Korea, Japan, and Vietnam, as a result of successfully confronting the virus, were no doubt important catalysts.

The greatest impact of the COVID Shock on transpacific relations will most likely be on United States–China ties. United States–China relations are, to be sure, significantly deeper in socioeconomic terms than casual observers might suspect: bilateral goods trade of nearly $660 billion was America's largest overseas trading relationship, while US investment in China totaled over $107 billion.[46] Chinese direct investment in the United States, while not nearly as large, more than tripled during the years 2014–19, to $37.7 billion in the latter year.[47] China also held over $1 trillion in US Treasury securities,[48] while nearly 370,000 young Chinese studied in the United States during the 2018–19 academic year.[49]

Despite this high level of interdependence—much higher than ever experienced between the Soviet Union and the United States during the Cold War—important new political-economic pressures had begun pulling the United States and China more deeply into conflict. Most importantly, key new digital technologies began emerging, such as artificial intelligence and 5G, where advances had both civilian and military applications. One nation's advance thus became an existential threat to the other.

Rising frictions over technology, intensified by how the COVID Shock accelerated digitalization, have been compounded by deepening geopolitical mistrust. The United States and its allies have been sobered by Chinese assertiveness in new locations, ranging from Hong Kong and the South China Sea to Southern and Central Europe. This has been compounded by normative differences, intensified by a deepening perception that China, rather than evolving politically toward Western-style pluralism, has instead deepened its own authoritarian cast. A nuanced shift in the political-economic leverage of Washington and Beijing, flowing from China's more rapid exit from the COVID crisis, and its conclusion of the RCEP agreement excluding the United States, counterbalanced by a regional backlash against Chinese assertiveness, were also sources of tension. These have been aggravated by rising nationalism on both sides of the Pacific.

There are, of course, partisan and regional differences in US China policy, which were especially pronounced in presidential election years like 2020. Even so, the central tendency of US China policy as the 2020s began was already more critical of China than at any time since Tiananmen in 1989. On top of that, after the COVID Shock, Americans also began to blame China for allowing the coronavirus to escape overseas, and to inflict the world, including especially the United States itself, in such a disastrous fashion.

Populist pressures, and rising nationalism, intensified by the COVID Shock, have no doubt deepened American suspicions about China as a rising peer competitor. They do not, however, seem to have affected US perceptions of South Korea and Japan in a parallel fashion. As recent international opinion polls indicate, American attitudes toward Korea and Japan appear to have been both remained positive and remarkably stable.[50] Sensitive gestures during the pandemic seem to have reinforced this sentiment.[51]

Positive American attitudes toward its two Northeast Asian allies, however, rest on a precarious foundation. Economic ties with both nations, while deep, are highly unbalanced, with trade favoring the two Asian partners by substantial margins. Military ties are also often seen on both sides of the Pacific as unpleasantly asymmetrical. And cultural communication, despite massive economic interdependence, remains remarkably limited. US relations with both Japan and South Korea are vulnerable to rising populist and nationalist sentiments, stimulated on both sides of the Pacific by the COVID crisis.

Although Northeast Asia has traditionally been the core of the transpacific equation for the United States, Southeast and South Asia have become more important over the past several decades. Immigration to the United States from India, Vietnam, and the Philippines has increased substantially, with the South and Southeast Asian American population combined exceeding 14 million, or 4.3 percent of the entire US population, in 2018.[52] With nearly 5 million members, Indian Americans had become the second-largest group of Asian Americans in the United States, after Chinese Americans.[53]

The South and Southeast Asian American diaspora has also become politically active, and increasingly influential. Indeed, two US presidential candidates for 2024—Vice President Kamala Harris and former UN ambassador Nikki Haley—are of Indian American origin. And strategically, the geographical ambit of American political-military concerns has broadened markedly in recent years, from "Asia-Pacific" to "Indo-Pacific."[54]

The extreme magnitude and duration of the American COVID crisis, relative to those across the Pacific, is also likely to affect transpacific relations in ways that the world is just beginning to perceive. Although figures at the margin may be disputed, China escaped the COVID crisis with less than 90,000 fatalities, and did so after only three months of concerted struggle with the virus. Japan suffered only about 2,000 fatalities,[55] and South Korea even fewer, with less than 600.[56] Although Japan and Korea struggled over a somewhat longer period, they never had to engage in economic lockdowns nearly as severe as in the United States.

Policy Options for the Future

America's disastrous early response and protracted struggle with the coronavirus cost it dearly, not only in human terms but also economically. And the costs it suffered were far greater than those across the Pacific. As a consequence, America's fiscal burden is becoming far greater, intensifying "burden-sharing" pressures on Asian allies, in such areas as military host nation support, while also putting downward pressure on the dollar.

Another strong new impulse in the United States, flowing from the COVID Shock, is toward "reshoring," especially of medical goods, including pharmaceuticals and medical equipment. US senators and representatives have introduced myriad legislative measures mandating reduced reliance on China, which has recently supplied fully 25 percent of the global mask market, and about half of total personal protective equipment imports into the United States.[57] As early as March 19, 2020, Senator Marco Rubio (R-FL) introduced legislation requiring the secretary of defense to report to Congress on the Defense Department's reliance on imports of critical pharmaceutical products, and to establish postmarket reporting requirements for pharmaceuticals.[58] At almost the same time, Senator Tom Cotton (R-AR) introduced several bills intended to protect the US medical supply chain from China.[59] These bills were intended, among other purposes, to ban the use of federal funds for the purchase of, or reimbursement for, drugs manufactured in China.

In May, Senator Gary Peters (D-MI) introduced a reshoring bill to establish a new center within the Department of Health and Human Services to invest in domestic medical manufacturing. Two months later, in July 2020, senators Marco Rubio and Elizabeth Warren (D-MA) jointly introduced the "United States Pharmaceutical Supply Chain Review Act," directing the Federal Trade Commission and the Treasury to conduct a study of US reliance on foreign pharma supplies. Also in July 2020, Senator Josh Hawley (R-MO) introduced legislation directing the Federal Emergency Management Agency to report on personal protective equipment supply chain resiliency.

Apart from this flurry of legislation, the US government has also begun taking administrative action to facilitate reshoring, through the US International Development Finance Corporation. Concrete actions, however, remained relatively small and incremental during the course of 2020, despite the massive destruction and dislocation caused by the pandemic.[60] On June 22, the Development Finance Corporation and the Pentagon agreed to collaborate in dispensing $100 million in funds appropriated under the CARES Act to support supply chain reshoring. By late summer, the 337-person Development Finance Corporation had a 15-person team devoted to reshoring.

Attitudes toward reliance on allied foreign nations, however, are considerably more ambiguous and potentially malleable. Procurements of coronavirus test kits from South Korea were greeted with considerable appreciation in Maryland early in the crisis, just as technical advice on drive-in testing, pioneered in Korea, was appreciated in New York. The experience of the COVID crisis shows that health care cooperation, leading to near-shoring reliance on Northeast Asian allies, rather than on China, may well be a more realistic solution to the health care supply issue—and to nationalistic burden-sharing tensions than reshoring itself.

Multinational firms are another key dimension of the transpacific relationship that can potentially help to stabilize US relations with traditional Cold War US allies. Multinationals such as Samsung and Hyundai—or Mitsubishi, Mitsui, and Itochu—have deep stakes in stable trade relations across the Pacific, and the versatile ability to both generate and to finance trade flows of all kinds. They could be helpful partners of government in creating stable medical supply relationships, both in dealing with current challenges and in preparing for the next pandemic.

A final option for stabilizing transpacific relations in the post-COVID era, one that is especially relevant to America's two free market North Pacific allies, is an intensified domestic policy dialogue. Throughout the post–World War II period, American policy interaction with its Pacific allies overwhelmingly dealt with issues of mutual national security concern, but the concept of national security itself was defined very narrowly, to include almost exclusively political-military questions. But now, in the shadow of the pandemic that cost more American lives than all the foreign wars in American history save World War II, there is a strong argument for defining national security more broadly, and drawing on the positive experiences of US allies, especially South Korea, in dealing successfully with COVID-19, to launch a series of health security and pandemic contingency planning dialogues across the Pacific. Hopefully, the Biden administration, whose key figures stressed human security during the 2020 presidential campaign, is adopting such an approach. Other parallel policy dialogues could deal with medical supply and reshoring issues; and others with broader industrial policy concerns, which have gained increasing credence in the United States since the COVID-19 pandemic.

Notes

1. The author wishes to thank Wonhyuk Lim and Luke Chen for their comments, as well as Vivian Chen, Luke Chen, and Monica Weller for research support.

2. Nick Routley, "Charts: The Economic Impact in the US So Far," *Visual Capitalist*, July 31, 2020, https://www.visualcapitalist.com/economic-impact-of-covid-h1-2020/.

3. "April 30 Report Update," Johns Hopkins CSSE, *Daily Reports*, April 30, 2020, https://github.com/CSSEGISandData/COVID-19/blob/master/csse_covid_19_data/csse_covid_19_daily_reports_us/4-30-2020.csv.

4. Sarah Sidner and Jason Kravarik, "After Bending the Curve, California Has Overtaken New York for the Most COVID-19 Cases," CNN, July 22, 2020.

5. Sarah Chaney and Gwynn Guilford, "Consumer Spending Fell a Record 13.6% in April," *Wall Street Journal*, May 29, 2020.

6. The $2 trillion US package was largest in absolute terms, with Japan second at $1.1 trillion. The United States was second, however, relative to GDP, with 13 percent, compared with Japan's 21.1 percent. See Niall McCarthy, "How Global Coronavirus Stimulus Packages Compare," *Forbes*, May 11, 2020, https://www.forbes.com; as well as Yuko Takeo and Takashi Hirokawa, "Japan Doubles Down to Deliver World's 'Biggest' Stimulus Package," Bloomberg, May 27, 2020, https://www.bloomberg.com/news/articles/2020-05-27/japan-to-unveil-another-1=trillion-in-stimulus-document-shows.

7. Britain was the only major nation with a larger deficit relative to GDP in 2020:Q2, at 18.1 percent. By comparison, France was at 11.5 percent, Germany at 7.2 percent, and Japan at 5.3 percent. Takeo and Hirokawa, "Japan Doubles Down."

8. These payments come on top of about $320 a week average unemployment insurance payments.

9. The law creates disclosure requirements, an inspector general post, and a congressionally mandated board to monitor a $425 billion bailout fund to be administered by the Federal Reserve. It also bars companies that receive government infusions from doing stock buybacks for as long as they are benefitting from federal aid, in addition to a year afterward. See Emily Cochrane and Sheryl Gay Stolberg, "$2 Trillion Coronavirus Stimulus Bill Is Signed into Law," *New York Times*, March 27, 2020, https://www.nytimes.com/2020/03/27/is/politics/coronavirus-house-voting.html.

10. Catherine Thorbecke, "Why the Stock Market Is Divorced from the Pain of a Pandemic Economy," ABC News, August 15, 2020, https://abvnews.go.com/Business/stock-market-divorced-pain-pandemic-economy/story?id=72325808.

11. Ian King, "Big Tech Earnings Surge during Pandemic While Economy Slumps," *Edge Markets*. July 31, 2020, https://www.theedgemarkets.com/article/big-tech-earnings-surge-during-pandemic-while-economy-slumps.

12. Amazon posted $5.2 billion in profits in the second quarter, doubling its bottom line from the same quarter a year ago, despite spending more than $4 billion on COVID-19 initiatives. See *GeekWire*, July 30, 2020, https://www.geekwire.com.

13. Mark Gurman, "Apple Smashes Revenue, iPhone Estimates in Record 3Q," *Edge Markets*, July 31, 2020, https://www.thedgemarkets.com.

14. See *Edge Markets*, https://www.theedgemarkets.com.

15. Among the early advocates of "bringing the state back in," see Theda Skocpol, *States and Social Revolutions* (Cambridge University Press, 1979); and Stephen Skowronek, *Building a New American State: The Expansion of National Administrative Capacities, 1877–1920* (Cambridge University Press, 1982).

16. In 2018, 8.5 percent of the American people, or 27.5 million, did not have health insurance at any point during the year. The uninsured rate and number of uninsured increased for 7.9 percent, or 25.6 million people, in 2017, according to the US Census Bureau. See Edward R. Berchick, Jessica C. Barnett, and Rachel D. Upton, "Health Insurance Coverage in the United States: 2018, US Census Bureau. Report P60-267 (RV), November 8, 2019, https://www.census.gov/library/publications/2019/deom/p60-267.html.

17. Sara R. Collins, Munira Z. Gunja, and Gabriella N. Abdoulafia, "US Health Insurance Coverage in 2020: A Looming Crisis in Affordability," Commonwealth

Fund, August, 2020, https://www.commonwealthfund.org/sites/default/files/2020-08/Collins_looming_crisis_affordability_biennial_2020_sb.pdf.

18. See Peter A. Hall and David Soskice, eds., *Varieties of Capitalism: The Institutional Foundations of Comparative Advantage* (Oxford University Press, 2001).

19. On conceptions of identity in contemporary American society, see Francis Fukuyama, *Identity: The Demand for Dignity and the Politics of Resentment* (New York: Farrar, Straus & Giroux, 2018).

20. Operation Warp Speed was to deliver 300 million doses of a safe, effective vaccine for COVID-19 by January, 2021, according to the US Department of Health and Human Services. See the HHS website, https://www.hhs.gov/about/news/2020/06/16/fact-sheet-explaining-operation-warp-speed.html.

21. See David Lim and Alice Miranda Ollstein, "Why the US Still Hasn't Solved Its Testing Crisis," *Politico*, July 5, 2020.

22. Article II of the Constitution leaves wide swaths of open space, in which presidents can flexibly interpret their powers. Often, the president's power is prescribed only by the norms created over the course of two centuries of practice, rather than by explicit provisions of Article II. See Noah Feldman, Jack Goldsmith, Michael Klarman, Mark Tushnet, Daphna Renan, and Neil Eggleston, "Presidential Power Surges," *Harvard Law Bulletin*, July 17, 2019, https://today.law.harvard.edu/feature/presidential-power-surges/.

23. Alexander Hamilton, *Federalist No. 70,* in *The Federalist Papers*, edited by Charles R. Kesler (New York: Penguin, 2003), 421–29.

24. Joe Palca, "US Flu Season Beginning to East, Modelers Say," NPR, March 9, 2020, https://www.npr.org/sections/health-short/2020/03/09/813641072/u-s-flu-season-beginning-to-ease-modelers-say.

25. On the details, see Nancy Bristow, *American Pandemic: The Lost Worlds of the 1918 Influenza Epidemic* (Oxford University Press, 2012).

26. See Deb Riechmann, "Trump Disbanded NSC Pandemic Unit That Experts Had Praised," Associated Press, March 14, 2020; and Kaiser Family Foundation, "Trump Administration Faces COVID-19 Pandemic without NSC Global Health Security Team: Pandemic Preparedness Faltered Across Four Administrations, Experts Say," April 7, 2020, https://www.kff.org/news-summary-trump-admionistration-faces-covid-19-pandemic-preparedness-faltered-across-four-administrations-experts-say/.

27. JHU Coronavirus Resource Center, "COVID-19 Data in Motion: Tuesday, September 1, 2020," https://coronavirus.jhu.edu.

28. On November 22, 2020, 20.8 percent of total global confirmed COVID-19 cases were in the United States, and 18.5 percent of the fatalities. See JHU Coronavirus Resource Center, "COVID-19 Data in Motion: Tuesday, September 11, 2020," https://coronavirus.jhu.edu.

29. On the details, see Ed Yong, "America Is Trapped in a Pandemic Spiral," *Atlantic*, September 10, 2020, https://www.theatlantic.com/health/archive/2020/09/pandemic-intuition-nightmare-spiral-winter/616204/.

30. On the evolution of pandemic decision-making inside the Trump administration, see Stephanie Baker and Cynthia Koons, "Inside Operation Warp Speed's

$18 Billion Sprint for a Vaccine," *Bloomberg Business Week,* October 29, 2020, https://www.bloomberg.com.

31. Niraj Choksh and Ben Casselman, "Airline Job Cuts Could Pressure Congress and Trump on Stimulus," *New York Times,* August 25, 2020, https://www.nytimes.com/2020/08/25/business/american-airline-furlough-19000.html.

32. See Thomas Piketty, *Capital in the Twenty-First Century,* translation by Arthur Goldhammer (Harvard University Press, 2014).

33. US Census Bureau, "Historical Income Tables: Households," August 29, 2019, https://www.census.gov/data/tables/time-series/demo/income-poverty/historical-income-households.html.

34. Katherine Schaeffer, "Six Facts About Economic Inequality in the US," Pew Research Center, February 7, 2020, https://www.pewresearch.org/fact-tank/2020/02/07/6-facts-about-economic-inequality-in-the-u-s/.

35. Robin Wigglesworth, "How America's 1% Came to Dominate Equity Ownership," *Financial Times,* February 10, 2020, https://www.ft.com/content/2501e154-4789-11ea-aeb3-955839e06441.

36. US Census Bureau, "Quick Facts United States," July 1, 2019, https://www.census.gov/quickfacts/fact/table/US/PST045219.

37. Dayna Bowen Matthew, Edward Rodrigue, and Richard V. Reeves, "Time for Justice: Tackling Race Inequalities in Health and housing," Brookings, October 19, 2016, https://www.brookings.edu/research/time-for-justice-tackling-race-inequalities-in-health-and-housing/.

38. Samantha Artiga, Rachel Garfield, and Kendal Orgera, "Communities of Color at Higher Risk for Health and Economic Challenges Due to COVID-19," Kaiser Family Foundation, April 7, 2020, https://www.kff.org/coronavirus-covid-19/issue-brief/communities-of-color-at-higher-risk-for-health-and-economic-challenges-due-to-covid-19/.

39. Matt Furber, Audra D. S. Burch, and Frances Robles, "What Happened in the Chaotic Moments Before George Floyd Died," *New York Times*, June 10, 2020.

40. May Wong, "America Leads Other Countries in Deepening Polarization," Stanford Institute for Economic Policy Research, January 20, 2020, https://siepr.stanford.edu/news/america-leads-other-countries-deepening-polarization.

41. Andrea Shalal, Alexandra Alper, and Patricia Zengerle, "US Mulls Paying Companies, Tax Breaks to Pull Supply Chains from China," Reuters, May 17, 2020, https://www.reuters.com/article/us-usa-china-supply-chairns/u-s-mulls-paying-companies-tax-breaks-to-pull-supply-chains-from-china-idUSKBN22U0FH.

42. E.g., public debt/nominal GDP in the United States rose from 197.7 percent of GDP in 2020:Q1 to 135.6 percent of GDP in the next quarter—the highest ratio in over fifty years. See US Department of the Treasury, "Fiscal Service, Fiscal Debt: Total Public Debt," FRED, Federal Reserve Bank of Saint Louis, https://fred.stlouisfed.org.

43. Organization for Economic Cooperation and Development, "Current Price GDP in China," http://www.oecd.org.

44. OECD, "Current Price GDP in the United States," http://www.oecd.org.

45. Kentaro Iwamoto, "Asia Forms World's Largest Trading Bloc RCEP After Years of Talks," *Nikkei Asia Review,* November 15, 2020, https://aska.nikkei.com.

46. Office of the US Trade Representative, "The People's Republic of China," https://ustr.gov/countries-regions/china-mongolia-taiwan/peoples-republic-china.

47. US Department of Commerce, Bureau of Economic Analysis, "Balance of Payments and Direct Investment Position Data: Foreign Direct Investment in the US, Foreign Direct Investment Position in the United States on a Historical-Cost Basis," https://apps.bea.gov/iTable/iTable.cfm?ReqOD=2&step=1/.

48. As of July 2020, China held $1.07 trillion in US Treasuries, second only to Japan, which held $1.29 trillion. See the Treasury website, at https://ticdata.treasury.gov/Publish/mfh.txt.

49. This number also more than tripled over the previous decade, from around 100,000 during 2008–9. See Institute of International Education, "Number of International Students in the United States Hits All-Time High," November 19, 2019, https://www.iie.org/Why-IIE/Announcements/2019/11/Number-of-International-Students-in-the-United-States-Hits-All-Time-High.

50. In 2018, for example, a collaborative poll by the Chicago Council on Global Affairs and the Japan Institute of International Affairs indicated that 62 percent of Americans viewed Japan favorably, and 56 percent of Americans viewed South Korea favorably. Similar results prevailed in parallel polls in 2014. See Scott Snyder, "American Attitudes toward South Korea in 2014: Growing Support for a Solid Relationship," on the October 2014 Chicago Council on Global Affairs poll, https://www.thechicago council.org/sites/default/files/USSouthKorea_Snyder.pdf; also see Karl Friedhoff and Craig Kafura, "American Views toward US–Japan Relations and Asia-Pacific Security," April 17, 2018; and on the 2018 Chicago Council on Global Affairs poll, https://www.thechicagocouncil.org/publication/american-views-toward-us-japan-relations-and-asia-pacific-security.

51. E.g., the South Korean government offered packages with masks and other health-related items to elder Americans who had served as Peace Corps volunteers in South Korea, as a token of appreciation for their dedication to Korea. See Choe San-Hun, "South Korea Delivers 'Something Magical' to US in Time of Need," *New York Times*, November 21, 2020.

52. Estimated figures from US Census Bureau, 2018, drawn from the American Community Survey. See the US Census Bureau website, at https://data.census.gov/cedsci/table?q=asian%20alone%20or%20any%20&tid=ACSDT1Y2018.B02018&hide Preview=false.

53. Gustavo Lopez, Neil G. Ruiz, and Eileen Patten, "Key Facts About Asian Americans, a Diverse and Growing Population," Pew Research Center, September 8, 2017, https://www.pewresearch.org/fact-tank/2017/09/08/key-facts-about-asian-americans/.

54. In 2018, the US military created an Indo-Pacific Command, while in November 2020, US secretary of the Navy Kenneth Braithwaite proposed a US First Fleet, to be based around Singapore, at the intersection of the Indian Ocean and the Pacific. See Megan Eckstein, "SECNACV Braithwaite Calls for New US 1st Fleet Near Indian, Pacific Oceans," *USNI News*, November 17, 2020, at https://news.usni.org.

55. See the JHU coronavirus website, at https://coronavirus.jhu.edu/region/japan. Japan had 1930 fatalities as of November 20, 2020.

56. See https://coronavirus.jhu.edu/region/south-korea. South Korea had 503 fatalities as of November 20, 2020.

57. China also holds a 10 percent share of the global breathing apparatus market, manufacturing respirators, ventilators, and other essential hospital equipment for combating COVID-19. See World Trade Organization, "Trade in Medical Goods in the Context of Tackling COVID-19," April 3, 2020, https://www.wto-org/english/news_e/news20_e/rese_03apr20_e.pdf.

58. US Senate Committee on Finance, "Strengthening America's Supply Chain and National Security Act (S 3538)," March 19, 2020, https://www.congress.gov/bill/116th-congress/senate-bill/3538.

59. US Congress, Senate Committee on Finance, "Protecting Our Pharmaceutical Supply Chain from China (S.3537)," March 19, 2020.

60. The International Development Finance Corporation, in cooperation with the Defense Department, agreed, e.g., to jointly administer $100 million in supply chain reshoring funds, as an element of early $2.3 billion coronavirus legislation in March 2020. See David Lawder, "Exclusive: New US Developmental Agency Could Loan Billions for Reshoring, Official Says," Reuters, June 23, 2020, https://www.reuters.com/article/us-usa-trade-reshoring-exclusive/exclusive-new-u-s-development-agency-could-loan-billions-for-reshoring-official-says-idUSKBN23U31F.

Two
The Negative Feedback Loop of United States–China Relations

DAVID M. LAMPTON, *FOREIGN POLICY INSTITUTE, JOHNS HOPKINS UNIVERSITY, SCHOOL OF ADVANCED INTERNATIONAL STUDIES*

The conditions and processes described in this chapter, beginning in the Obama administration and gaining a full head of steam under President Donald Trump, have continued, and in some sense worsened, under President Biden since January 20, 2021.[1] President Xi Jinping has been a constant, aggravating central player through all three US administrations. The prospects are for a continued downturn for the foreseeable future. From the vantage point of the fall of 2021, one of the new factors in Chinese thinking is that they hoped (perhaps almost expected) that the Biden administration would to seek to ease pressure soon after entering office. In fact, in many respects the Biden policy has a sharper, military and alliance edge than was the case under Trump. Disappointment has given rise in Beijing to anger, a tougher foreign policy, and tightening down on "subversion" at home and in Hong Kong.

The United States–China relationship is now in a condition analogous to an airplane with a faulty gyroscope, in which each drop of the nose does not produce an offsetting correction upward but, instead, inclines the nose to a yet steeper angle and accelerating rate of descent. Each iteration of this negative feedback loop moves the aircraft ever closer to disaster—the ground. Security responses by Beijing produce countervailing security responses by Washington, whether it be new weapons systems, adjusted doctrines, or altered deployments abroad. Impediments to trade imposed by one side elicit countermeasures by the other. And constraints on civil society and diplomatic interactions imposed by one side generate aggravating responses by the other, whether it be greatly diminished dialogue, limiting visas, closing consulates, or ferreting out spies. Each side sees itself as responding to the other. Each perceives itself as defensive, as the aggrieved party. COVID-19 did not create this condition, but it has exacerbated it.

Layered on top of all this, the Biden administration assumed office in January 2021, and, far from breaking with the central features of Trump policy, it has maintained them, not moving to lower tariffs. Biden's Washington has also been more forward leaning in dealings with Taiwan. With domestic gridlock so apparent in Washington, it is easier to promote legislation aimed at China than exhaust oneself in domestic partisanship. There is an avalanche of bills working its way through Congress to enhance American competitiveness with the People's Republic of China (PRC) in all dimensions.

Even as recently as 2010, it was not like this. The global financial crisis of 2008–9 led Beijing and Washington to cooperate in stabilizing the world economy through enhancing the role of the Group of Twenty and stimulating aggregate demand in both countries. However, it was not long before Beijing began to criticize Washington for having catalyzed the global financial crisis, a charge signaling that Beijing no longer saw America as a model to be emulated and, instead, a society with which it could compete. In 2010, issues existed in the East China Sea and South China Sea, but these problems rapidly became more acute after 2012, when newly installed Chinese leader Xi Jinping anchored his growing power in a nationalistic agenda. Even before Xi, Washington saw these changing trends and attitudes and responded with a strategic "pivot" (later "rebalance") under President Obama in 2011, and then a much greater strategic departure occurred under President Trump, with his America First Policy in the latter half of the decade. In short, as recently as slightly more than a decade ago, the United States and China had dissatisfactions with one another, but combinations of leadership change in both countries, rising nationalism, and a sense in China that the American sun was setting have combined to produce what became a rapidly deteriorating bilateral relationship in the 2010–20 period. The Chinese narrative became "China Rising, America Declining."

In the run-up to the 2020 US general election, there was some expectation that if Biden were to prevail, he would restore a more predictable policy process, one that was data based and developed in a careful interagency process. This expectation has been fulfilled to a considerable extent, but it has not produced an actual policy toward Beijing that breaks with some central features of the Trump policy, or the Obama policy before that. Biden is emphasizing democracy versus autocracy, arguing for deeper interaction with Taiwan;

building more strategically significant relations with Australia, Britain, Japan, and India; and using China's competitiveness as a driver for his effort to "build back better" at home. To Beijing, Trump's policy was fickle in a way that Biden's does not appear to be.

Three fundamental changes have occurred in the Sino-American relationship, starting before the Trump-Xi era, but greatly accelerated after these two leaders rose to power and carried into the Biden era. There is not much to be gained by asking "who started" these trends, because each capital has the frame of mind that it is responding to the actions of the other—a classic action/reaction cycle: (1) Strategically, United States–China relations have moved from *reassuring* each other (from about 1972 until 2010) to *deterring* each other thereafter. (2) There has been a shift toward *more managed economic relations* in both Beijing and Washington for reasons of both security and industrial policy, rather than striving toward market-driven United States–China economic and financial systems. And (3), *ideology is playing* an increasingly prominent role in bilateral ties. Words like "hegemony," "democracy," and "authoritarian" are ideological ordnance lobbed across the Pacific by each power to portray the other one as a fundamental to threat to core values and interests. In 2020, the Trump administration replaced "China" with "Chinese Communist Party (CCP)" as its name of choice when speaking of its strategic competitor, harkening back to the Cold War vocabulary of "Red China." Under the Biden administration, the words are different, but the meaning the same—democracy versus authoritarianism is the frame.

After briefly describing the deterioration of United States–China relations that antedated the Donald Trump–Xi Jinping era, this chapter examines the current domestic drivers of China policy in the United States; the way in which the COVID-19 pandemic exacerbated almost all bilateral frictions; and future prospects for bilateral relations. The chapter concludes by assessing the implications of all this for policy.

The Trump-Xi Era Downturn in United States–China Relations and Its Antecedents

We date the beginning of a significant downslide in United States–China relations to about 2010. In 2009 Beijing began to assert that the South China Sea was a "core interest" (like Taiwan and Tibet) and to speak of the waters within the 1947 "Nine-Dash Line" (a claim Chiang Kai-shek made and that originally was made up of eleven dashes) in terms that indicated the PRC considered itself sovereign. Under President and General Secretary Hu Jintao, Beijing became more assertive in maritime claims in the East China Sea and South China Sea, by grabbing rocks and reefs in the area, gradually transforming them into permanent features, which Beijing then claimed were entitled to control surrounding waters and resources, raising freedom of navigation and other issues. Most fundamentally, all this heightened concern about how China would use its growing naval power. For its part, Beijing observed that rival claimants in the Nanyang (Southern Seas) already had been consolidating their control over disputed land features, so the PRC was responding to the actions of others.

Secretary of State Hillary Clinton began what became a progressively more robust US pushback on Beijing's assertions and actions at the mid-2010 meeting of the Association of Southeast Asian Nations' Regional Forum in Hanoi. Beijing reacted furiously. Over the next year and a half, through presidential and cabinet-level visits to the region, Washington rolled out its "pivot" (later "rebalance") policy, stating the intention to augment the deployment of US naval and other forces in the Pacific, thereby aiming to reduce Washington's traditional force weighting in the transatlantic, Gulf, and Mediterranean theaters to a relatively heavier emphasis on the Western and South Pacific. Economic initiatives were planned to augment the force repositioning, the most potent being Washington's promotion of a twelve-nation (excluding Beijing) Trans-Pacific Partnership (TPP); but in the 2016 election campaign, the combination of Hillary Clinton's fear of being identified with a free trade proposal, the Republican Party opposition, and then President Trump's outright opposition to the effort doomed US participation. Washington withdrew from negotiations, which Tokyo carried on. Eventually the eleven-nation Comprehensive and Progressive Agreement for Trans-Pacific Partnership was established without US participation.

The initial interaction between Beijing and Washington in 2010 and 2011 set the context for Xi Jinping's assumption of power in 2012–13. Immediately building on themes of "the China Dream" and "National Rejuvenation," in 2014 President Xi articulated an "Asia for Asians" position, rejected the Permanent Court of Arbitration at The Hague's July 2015 ruling on land features in the South China Sea, and converted small land features there to platforms with military utility, contrary to Xi's personal pledge to President Obama. Domestically, Xi simultaneously sought to strengthen the CCP leadership, prevent foreign ideological contamination through Central Committee ideological directives, and to create the National Security Commission to stop foreign "subversion."[2] Contemporaneously, Beijing became progressively more rigid in its dealings with Hong Kong and Taiwan. By 2017, US public opinion concerning China began to dramatically deteriorate as these trends became unmistakable.³ This deterioration in public opinion has continued into the Biden era.

With the ascension of Donald Trump to the US presidency in January 2017, a series of strategic documents were quickly issued by the new administration: "The National Security Strategy" (December 2017); "The National Defense Strategy" (January 2018); "The Nuclear Posture Review" (February 2018); and "The United States Strategic Approach to the People's Republic of China" (May 2020). "The Nuclear Posture Review" put it bluntly: "Global threat conditions have worsened markedly since the most recent 2010 NPR."⁴ These documents cumulatively defined the PRC as the principal, long-term, state-level security threat to the United States. Moreover, in May 2018, the Trump administration built upon the earlier Obama strategic reorientation toward the Pacific with its own "Indo-Pacific Strategy" and renamed the Pacific Command the "United States Indo-Pacific Command," signaling a more regionwide approach to addressing a rising China. What is notable is that the Biden administration has not changed any of this strategic guidance; indeed, it has proceeded vigorously along the same path. For its part, Beijing has done nothing to make it easier for Washington to change its course.

These developments have occurred for several reasons, the first of which is an increase in Chinese power and confidence. For its part, Washington has been distracted and gridlocked at home and overcommitted abroad, gradually coming to realize that the transformation occurring in China's comprehensive national power had important regional and global implications, not all of which were positive for US interests and not all of which were military in character, including the Belt and Road Initiative.⁵

As expressed in the Trump administration's strategic documents, the United States came to perceive that it faces two hostile powers—China and Russia—with China overall seen as the more capable of the two over time. This is a specter that US foreign policy has sought to avoid since Thomas Jefferson—domination of the Eurasian landmass and the Pacific Ocean by a power or coalition of powers hostile to American interests. Indeed, carrying this theme forward, the Biden administration in the summer of 2021 used the pressing strategic challenge from China as part of its rationale to rapidly exit Afghanistan. This would allow the United States to refocus from a war that was not advancing its interests to focus on a theater of growing strategic importance and perceived danger.

Moving beyond strategic considerations to the business and civic society dimensions of United States–China relations, an increasingly deep array of American institutions and business entities are acclimating to a world of increasing strain with Beijing. There is diversification of some supply chains away from China (and vice versa, with Beijing calling for "self-reliance" and a "dual circulation system"). Over the last decade, Washington and Beijing each has alienated key domestic constituencies in the other society, constituencies that used to be supportive of productive bilateral ties. The business communities in both countries have become far less vocal advocates for constructive bilateral ties. With respect to civic organizations, in the pages of *Foreign Affairs* and the programs of its parent organization, the Council on Foreign Relations, one sees sporadic calls for containment of the PRC and abandonment of the policy of "strategic ambiguity," the latter having been an enduring feature of Washington's policy with respect to maintaining cross–Taiwan Strait stability. There is greater risk that the Taiwan issue now could quickly erupt as a source of conflict than at any time in the last quarter century (since 1995–96).

In Taiwan, the autonomy-oriented Democratic Progressive Party has been institutionalizing its role noticeably since the 2016 election (and the 2020 reelection) of Tsai Ing-wen as president. The historically more accommodating (on cross-Strait issues) Nationalist Party on Taiwan is also trying to figure out how to adjust its posture to win more popular support given, the Democratic Progressive Party's strength.[6] The democratic character of Taiwan, along with its important geographic location, assumes almost strategic importance in the United States, particularly as ideological and military frictions between Washington and Beijing grow. Washington is incrementally making changes in the way it deals with Taipei that would have, in Beijing's eyes, the cumulative effect of boosting the "official" character of Taipei–Washington links. This, in my view, is dangerous.

As for China, economic growth has gradually slowed by virtue of natural long-term processes; declining total factor productivity because of misallocated capital; mounting domestic (corporate) debt; the United States–China trade war begun in 2018; and the COVID-19-induced global economic slowdown. More recently, the underpinnings of China's real estate industry look increasingly shaky, a development with consequences beyond China's borders.

As the United States applies more comprehensive pressure to the PRC, Xi has adopted the strategy of a tough external policy to consolidate the domestic regime's support and to deter Washington and others. Xi Jinping increasingly uses Leninist instruments to prevent subversion and mobilize nationalism as a regime support. So, for example, there is a crackdown on the internet, tighter control over school curricula, a cult-like campaign to study Xi Jinping's Thought, and a campaign against "sissy culture," including K-Pop. In turn, this intensifies United States–China frictions and gives an ever-more-ideological tone to interactions. Former US secretary of state Mike Pompeo referred to

China by emphasizing the role of the Chinese Communist Party. The US Congress in the late Trump era was considering legislation that would no longer refer to Xi Jinping as "president" but instead authorize the use of only Communist Party titles (e.g., general secretary) for US interaction with him. The bill's title leaves little to the imagination: "Name the Enemy Act." The late-Trump policy of limiting access to visas for members of the Chinese Communist Party and family members has thus far continued into the Biden era.

This tendency to domestically mobilize against outside forces is exacerbated by the fact that July 2021 was the one-hundredth anniversary of the founding of the CCP and Xi was under considerable pressure to show what a hundred years of the party's existence has brought in terms of China's power and status in the world and internal welfare. Moreover, China was moving toward its Twentieth Party Congress and accompanying People's Congress in 2022–23, a process characterized by intense internal jockeying for power. From the vantage point of early 2021, it looked inevitable that President Xi would extend his period in the presidential office indefinitely. There is no likely successor visible on the horizon.

Of course, these expectations could be in error if Xi believed that some accommodation with the United States and reassurance in the region were pluses for him, or if power were to slip from his hands to more reform-oriented individuals, both of which seem highly unlikely contingencies. But the current downward move of Sino-American relations is generating further negative opinion toward the United States in China and seemingly more support for Xi. How deeply embedded those negative sentiments toward the United States may be, and how firm Xi's domestic support is, are important uncertainties. If Xi were to develop new, welcome initiatives at home and abroad, this could positively shape American thinking. It is hard to say, however, how responsive Washington would be and what PRC behaviors could most change the trajectory. A change in strategic tone and behavior in Beijing would be key. But the longer the current direction persists in each country, the more entrenched becomes this action-reaction dynamic. In my interactions with Chinese diplomats since the 2020 election, the uniform message they deliver is: "You [the United States] tied the knot; you untie it."

The Domestic US Context: Fundamental Drivers of US China Policy

The hardening of US policy toward China since at least 2010 has been driven by increasingly negative American views on China, with an unfavorable reassessment of its economic and trade policies, human rights violations, and military challenges to the United States. The weakening of mutually beneficial security, economic, and societal/diplomatic interaction between the two countries has reinforced the negative trends.

The Domestic Political Context

Against the just-recounted backdrop of the deterioration of the United States–China relationship extending back to at least 2010, history brought the United States to a landmark juncture in its own history: the general election of November 2020. In terms of domestic policy, the transition from Trump to Biden has been important, but, with respect to China policy, the changes are more of style and process than policy outcomes. Trump may have lost the election, but "Trumpism" is far from dead, as witnessed by the events of January 6, 2021, on Capitol Hill.

The US electorate is deeply divided, with President Trump still having a notably committed support base (i.e., about 30 percent of the electorate). His supporters are spread across states so that in the 2016 general election he gained a majority in the all-important Electoral College, even though he lost the popular vote. The shock of that unanticipated Trump victory in 2016, and his divisive governance after January 20, 2017, energized the Democratic Party in 2020.

In many of the key battleground states—such as Michigan, Ohio, Wisconsin, Pennsylvania, and Florida—one finds that China, by reason of its economic and trade policies, human rights behavior, and security challenges to the United States (indeed, all these together) has become a target for both the left and right. Nationally, disapproval of China is at 73 percent, with Republican disapproval somewhat higher than among Democrats (figures 2-1 and 2-2).

Nonetheless, as attractive a punching bag as China may be in American politics, Democratic Party Nominee Joe Biden in the 2020 election campaign did differentiate himself somewhat from the hardest edges of Trumpism. What has so disconcerted Beijing is that after his election victory, he has not really moved away from Trump-like policies. Indeed, early on, Biden's secretary of state, Antony Blinken, accused Beijing of "genocide" in Xinjiang, something that even Trump did not do.

Rather, during his relatively balanced election campaign, Biden recognized that the *domestic* concerns of Americans eclipse their foreign policy anxieties (the pandemic, the economy, and social justice and stability issues). Second, Biden recognized that he would have to deal with Beijing should he win and he avoided painting himself into a corner. And finally, Biden believed (and still does believe), like Deng Xiaoping at the dawn of the reform era in China

Figure 2-1. Unfavorable Views of China Reach New Highs in the United States

Percentage who say they have a(n) __ opinion of China

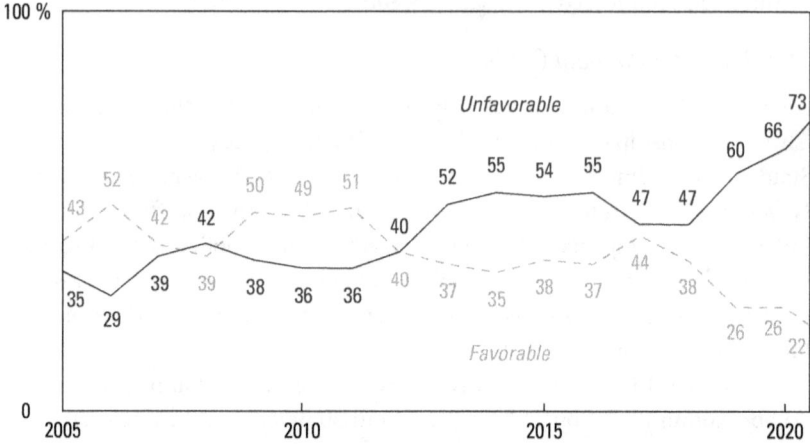

Sources: Laura Silver, Kat Devlin, and Christine Huang, "Americans Fault China for Its Role in the Spread of COVID-19," Survey of US adults conducted June 16–July 14, 2020; Q8b, "Americans Fault China for Its Role in the Spread of COVID-19." Pew Research Center; https://www.pewresearch.org/global/2020/07/30/americans-fault-china-for-its-role-in-the-spread-of-covid-19/. Used by permission.
Note: "Don't know" responses are not shown.

Figure 2-2. Republicans Remain More Unfavorable Toward China, but All Partisans Are Increasingly Negative

Percentage who say they have an unfavorable opinion of China

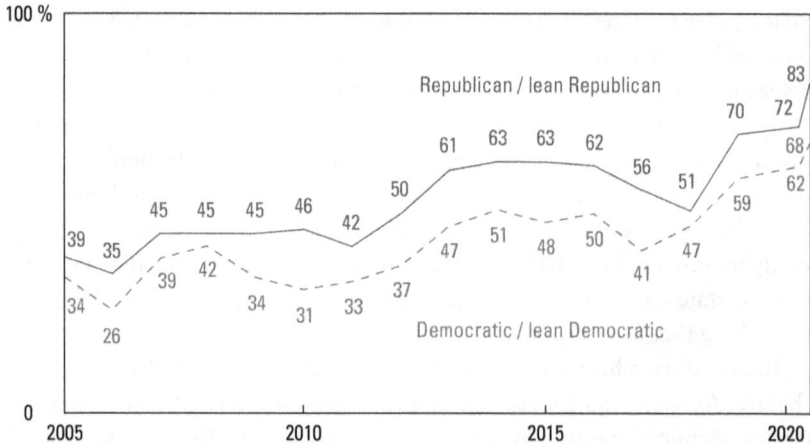

Sources: Laura Silver, Kat Devlin, and Christine Huang, "Americans Fault China for Its Role in the Spread of COVID-19," Survey of US adults conducted June 16–July 14, 2020; Q8b, "Americans Fault China for Its Role in the Spread of COVID-19." Pew Research Center; https://www.pewresearch.org/global/2020/07/30/americans-fault-china-for-its-role-in-the-spread-of-covid-19/. Used by permission.

in the late 1970s, that his primary task is to "build back better," not get still more overcommitted abroad. Parenthetically, that is why Biden pulled out so fast from Afghanistan—to get out of "endless wars." Given these predispositions, Beijing had some hope that if Biden were to win the election, the new US president would settle into a more balanced policy. This has not happened and, to put it bluntly, there are some in Beijing who have "cast away illusions" about Washington.

Beyond electoral politics and public opinion, there are several other enduring drivers of United States–China policy.

Three Core Domestic Drivers

The United States–China relationship from 1972 to 2010 rested upon a diversified tripod of variably positive security, economic, and societal/diplomatic legs. During this era, there were important interest groups giving strength to each leg of this tripod. When one leg of the tripod became weaker, the other two were able to bear increased weight. Today, however, all three tripod legs have dramatically weakened simultaneously. Many of the previously supportive interest groups associated with each leg during the engagement period have become dissatisfied with bilateral ties and less willing to expend political or economic capital to support the relationship, especially when public and congressional opinion has turned so negative. This is not to say that all support has vanished (the business community still, overall, makes money in China and grosses more than it actually withdraws[7]), but each leg has weakened considerably and the still-remaining latent support is much less vocal, for reasons explained below. An analogous process is under way in the PRC.

In the United States, particularly harmful has been the declining support among American business, finance, and high-tech interests and the growing antagonism within security-related bureaucracies and interests in *both* countries—the military-industrial complex, for short. Moreover, the economic and diplomatic/cultural aspects of the relationship are increasingly filtered through a *hard security lens*. This is what I call *the securitization of the entire relationship*.

For example, while a few short years ago, Chinese students studying in the United States were portrayed as full tuition payers and science and tech assets in American universities; now, in many quarters, they are painted as spies and points of leakage of American intellectual property. American universities and other entities dependent on federal research dollars are particularly sensitive to not jeopardizing the pipeline of money coming through government contracts and research grants by ignoring Washington's security cautions. We see this, for example, in the Defense Department urging universities to dismantle Confucius Institutes, the National Institutes of Health's more vigorous vetting of China-connected researchers, and in the Department of State's and Department of Homeland Security's restricting visa issuance to Chinese students studying sensitive areas and/or from security-related institutions in the PRC.[8] The Justice Department initiated a "China Initiative" to ferret out Chinese spies.

Moreover, since early 2020, overlaying this multidimensional deterioration has been the COVID-19 pandemic, a development that exacerbates every other friction. Ironically, in a different context, this global health challenge could have (should have) provided a rationale to reduce and deescalate tensions and enhance cooperation on existential transnational threats. Beijing has unwisely turned its foreign policy guns on countries like Australia, which have called on the World Health Organization to conduct an inquiry into the origins of COVID.

Driver one: the weakened security pillar. All societies privilege physical security over other objectives. The combination of growing Chinese power of all sorts,[9] more muscular PRC interaction with its extensive periphery (the East China Sea, the Taiwan Strait, the South China Sea, the Sino-Indian border, and tougher policies in Tibet and Xinjiang), and Beijing's sense that America's weakened domestic governance and protracted wars abroad have considerably sapped US power and will to resist, feed American defensiveness and embolden the PRC, itself a dangerous brew. American defensiveness, in turn, stokes a technological *action/reaction cycle* (an arms race) and a repositioning of military assets to deter one another, thereby increasing the probability of accident or miscalculation. The September 2021 announcement of an Australian–US–British initiative to build nuclear-powered submarines for the Australian Navy is just the most recent manifestation of this effort.

Predictably, the closer alignment of China's neighbors with Washington, the more counterpressures Beijing exerts on countries such as Australia, Japan, South Korea, New Zealand, and even Lithuania. Further, China reacts by trying to deepen its strategic ties with Russia. This entire security dynamic becomes grist for domestic politics in both the United States and China.

Driver two: the weakened economic, trade, and finance pillar. Long a mainstay leg of the tripod holding up the United States–China relationship, economic interests in America have become visibly less robust in supporting productive ties with the PRC. One indication of this softening support is an August 2020 American Chamber of Commerce in Hong Kong survey of member firms. The survey found that about 40 percent of its member firms were contemplating leaving Hong Kong. Americans had traditionally considered Hong Kong by far the best and most secure place to do business among PRC cities.[10] As mentioned above, however, firms continue to make money in China overall, and what has happened to US business support is best described by the American Chamber of Commerce in Shanghai: "China's relative importance in companies' global investment plans fell across industries" in 2020.[11] It is not that China is unimportant or that there is a stampede out, but rather that the PRC simply is becoming relatively less attractive to companies, with firms steering marginal new attention away from the mainland. Moreover, American firms are averse to being viewed as defending the United States–China relationship at home.

With respect to China, the PRC's share of US goods imports has declined from 45 percent to about 40 percent. Nonetheless, at the same time, China's share of global exports rose from 12.8 percent in the first quarter 2018 to about 20 percent in the same period of 2020, indicating that Beijing has been remarkably adept at finding new markets.[12] This relatively reduces PRC firms' interests in the United States and presumably their incentives to defend the relationship in Beijing. Finally, Chinese foreign direct investment in the United States dropped from $40 billion in 2016 to below $5 billion in 2019. This weakens US locality support for China ties inasmuch as local job creation declines as the PRC's foreign direct investment drops.

All this indicates that each country is diversifying away from the other; both are being hurt. Put in political terms, each country is alienating potential supportive constituencies in the other country. For example, farming states in the United States historically were stabilizers in United States–China relations, dependent as they were on exports to the PRC. There were dramatic declines in US farm sales to China in 2018–19, but farmers were resistant to breaking with the Trump White House, despite the pain they felt from the president's policies.[13]

More broadly, there is a growing, tightening web of investment and technology export restrictions being imposed on Beijing by Washington. The United States went after China's national champion firms—Huawei, ZTE, and WeChat, among others. More recently, the US "Competitiveness Act" is winding its way through the legislative process. In short, the most fundamental underlying transformation of the United States–China economic relationship has been *the securitization of economic relations.* By this I mean that the exporting and importing of goods, foreign direct investment, services like education, and financial ties of all sorts are now being judged in both societies by their actual and feared effects on national security, broadly defined. This dynamic has changed not at all under Biden, at least thus far.

In January 2020, Beijing and Washington signed the "Phase One Trade Deal," which held out the prospects of China buying more US exports (especially farm and other commodities).[14] However, the deal substantially left unaddressed underlying US business concerns—such as intellectual property protection, market access, and an array of other impediments to foreign firms seeking to do business in China. These issues were deferred to a mirage-like future, when there was to be a "Phase Two" trade deal. Consequently, each side has become increasingly frustrated with the other and, inexplicably, Washington has failed to enlist allied and friendly countries in a multilateral effort to achieve commonly desired economic and trade outcomes.

For President Trump, there really was only one economic indicator (beyond the US stock market) that he tracked—the bilateral trade deficit in goods with deficit-running countries. Comparing the US trade deficit in goods (in 2016) with China just before Trump came into office with the United States–China trade deficit in goods at the end of 2019, there was virtually *no change*, while total bilateral trade in goods is *less than when Trump came into office.* Put another way, the goods deficit situation for the United States showed virtually *no* improvement; total bilateral trade *dropped*; and US exports to China *dropped by a bigger share* (about 8 percent) than Chinese exports dropped to the United States (2.33 percent).[15] As the US–China Business Council reported in 2020, "Goods exports to China have fallen to their lowest level since 2011. US goods exports to China contracted 11.4 percent in 2019 to $104.8 billion after contracting by more than 7 percent the year prior. Only two-fifths of [US] states saw growth in goods exports to China last year."[16] Concisely, the deficit situation did not improve, total trade fell, and US economic interests became increasingly dissatisfied and reticent to be seen as a defender of the relationship. Moreover, with rising labor costs in China, and growing middle classes in places such as Southeast Asia, US business is eyeing opportunities elsewhere, but the pandemic and corporate reticence to take financial risks at this moment may have slowed down actual relocations from the PRC. What is notable is that upon his election, Biden did not immediately move to try to revivify the trade relationship.

China suffered, too, with slowed export growth and reduced overall economic system efficiency—lower total factor productivity and growing debt. Overall, the United States–China economic interaction was managing to hurt everyone, but perhaps the United States most.

Driver three: the weakened diplomatic and cultural pillar. In the 1970s, when China and America built their "relationship restored," it was cultural, societal, and diplomatic instruments that led the way.[17] Ping-Pong teams in

1971–72, and rapidly accelerating scientific, student, and scholarly exchanges in the second half of the 1970s, all were undergirded by supportive and active elite diplomacy. President Jimmy Carter explicitly decided to allow virtually unlimited numbers of Chinese students to come to America, university-to-university ties exploded, and nongovernmental organizations and similar institutions in both countries rapidly established ties.

Nearly fifty years later, with the *securitization* of all Sino-American ties, as mentioned above, such interconnections now are filtered through a hard security lens in both societies. Xi Jinping in 2014 established the National Security Commission to stanch "subversion" from abroad; in 2017, Beijing implemented its Foreign NGO Law, which moved oversight of civic organization ties from a civilian regulatory agency to the Ministry of Public Security; the US FBI director called for a "whole of society response" to Chinese influence operations, spying, and theft of intellectual property (2018); the US Department of Defense now forces American universities and colleges to choose between some Defense Department grants and having Confucius Institutes on their campuses; and the Justice Department launched its "China Initiative." Moreover, visas for some military-affiliated Chinese students and persons in selected high-tech fields are either denied or subject to increasingly arduous review. In terms of leadership statements, in the space of a mere two months (June–July 2020) three American cabinet-level officials and the director of the FBI delivered major speeches designed to further dampen civic society and other technological and business interactions.[18] In a 2018 speech at the Hudson Institute, then–vice president Mike Pence explicitly warned against subnational and civic organization linkages, seeing them as avenues of Chinese subversion and influence. The Biden administration has done virtually nothing to ease up in these areas.

While considerable latent grassroots and locality support for civic society linkages remains in both societies, and recently a large number of Stanford University professors spoke out against of many of these restrictions, the national security overlay in each national capital has made the implementation of programs increasingly difficult. The COVID-19 pandemic, and ensuing travel bans and suspicions stoked by the virus's spread, have further weakened society-to-society interaction. A thin tissue of Zoom meetings keeps some civic society connections alive. Another factor is becoming ever more apparent—it is going to be progressively more difficult for American and other Western scholars to do the kind of field and archival research characteristic of the last thirty or forty years, in both Hong Kong and on the mainland.

The Aggravating Effects of COVID-19 and Opportunity Lost

COVID-19 did not cause the problems identified above, but it has accelerated and exacerbated all of them. This was not inevitable. Different national leaders in both countries, in a different context, could have seized the COVID-19 outbreak as a potent rationale for bilateral cooperation to solve existential transnational issues. Instead, each leadership sought to turn the disease outbreak to its own domestic purposes and advantage, each blaming the other. A jarring and damaging aspect of this discord over the pandemic has been its hypernationalistic and blame-shifting overtones in both countries. These developments ignore the long history of critical and productive United States–China biomedical cooperation dating back to the nineteenth and twentieth centuries. It is fair to say that the Biden administration has avoided inflammatory/nearly racist language in connection with the COVID pandemic, but it is vigorously (and appropriately, in my view) trying to get Beijing's cooperation in an effort to ascertain exactly how this pandemic came about.

Considering Sino-American health cooperation only in the new millennium, in 2005, Washington and Beijing inaugurated the Collaborative Program on Emerging and Reemerging Infectious Diseases and, thereafter, the Centers for Disease Control and Prevention's (CDC's) China Center was established. In 2009, the H1N1 Swine flu erupted, with its epicenter in the United States and Mexico. Sino-American cooperation on this outbreak "proved useful when a new strain of avian flu, H7N9, emerged in China in March 2013," a virus strain that had a 30 percent mortality rate, according to a Georgetown University report. China helped dramatically reduce the virus's spread and shared its vaccine with the world. In short, the United States and China have had a long and mutually (indeed, globally) beneficial history of biomedical and public health cooperation in the post-1979 period.[19] In 2014–15, the United States and China powerfully cooperated on the Ebola outbreak in West Africa.[20]

Now, the barbarians are at the gates of medical science and public health cooperation in both countries. Forces in both societies express mutual hostility that ignores the positive and strategically significant health cooperation since the mid-1970s. We hear absolutely groundless charges coming from both societies suggesting the current pandemic had its origins in our respective militaries and intentionally pernicious actions. President Trump initially was more interested in assigning blame to foreigners, notably China, than taking the advice of his science and security advisers. For its part, China was slow in affording transparency and in responding to CDC requests for access and information. Some PRC military officers and Foreign Ministry voices have suggested intentional spread by American forces, echoing similar accusations in US civil society and the US Senate against the PRC.[21] The core reason for the lack of cooperation on COVID-19, as compared with previous instances of mutual assistance, was that both societies mishandled their opening moves in the pandemic and each leadership sought to find an excuse for its own missteps and incompetence in the other's deficient behavior.

In fact, what do we actually know about the origins and early course of the COVID-19 outbreak? A dangerous pathogen struck the first known patient (in Wuhan) on December 1, 2019; medical Dr. Li Wenliang in Wuhan on December 30, 2019, announced on social media that a dangerous SARS-like pathogen was spreading in the Wuhan area; Dr. Li, an ophthalmologist, was subsequently arrested for "spreading rumors" (he died of the disease on February 7, 2020); scientists in China released to the global scientific community the genetic sequence of the virus on the weekend of January 11–12, 2020; and, we know that China's national leaders did not make public announcements on the gathering storm in Wuhan until January 20 (Premier Li Keqiang) and January 25, 2020 (President Xi Jinping). Part of the delay had to do with the reluctance of local officials to send bad news up the hierarchy. Moreover, a key delay was in alerting the world to the reality of person-to-person transmission, a critical fact that only obliquely and gradually was officially acknowledged in the second half of January.

Evaluating the system's response, a *Chinese* judge said the following on the PRC Supreme Court's own social media account on January 28: "If the public listened to this 'rumor' [Dr. Li] at that time [December 30, 2019], and adopted measures such as wearing a mask, strict disinfection, and avoiding going to the wildlife market based on panic about SARS, this may have been a better way to prevent and control the new pneumonia.... As long as the information is basically true, the publishers and disseminators are not intentionally malicious, and the behavior objectively has not caused serious harm, we should maintain a tolerant attitude towards such 'false information.'"[22] This statement speaks for itself. If Chinese authorities had been more honest with themselves and their citizens, even though everyone had less than perfect information, they would have been more transparent with the world, and thereby would have allowed other localities in China and the world beyond to get a quicker start on addressing what quickly became a worldwide public health emergency.

Nonetheless, even once at least imperfect knowledge was globally available by late January, some political authorities around the world were slow to act and were not entirely honest with their own citizens, a notable example being President Trump, who on March 10 argued that "it will go away. Just stay calm. It will go away. . . . Be calm. It's really working out."[23] This, despite Trump having told investigative reporter Bob Woodward about a month earlier (on February 7, 2020), that this was a much more deadly virus than the seasonal flu and that it was spread through airborne transmission. Also, in March Trump revealed to Bob Woodward that he (Trump) was "downplaying" the virus so as not to cause "panic."[24]

To make matters worse, in July 2020 Trump withdrew the United States from the World Health Organization (WHO), which, despite shortcomings, was and is the most effective medical organization with global reach, a span that matches the reach of the disease. Trump's stated reason for doing so was that, in his view, WHO was too responsive to Beijing and had in the early days of the outbreak helped obscure the PRC's responsibility. All this notwithstanding, throughout 2020 the US federal government had no cohesive, effective, and funded strategy to deal with the virus beyond a highly effective effort to accelerate vaccine development. In terms of prevention, the Trump administration did not rein in (or coordinate) the fifty-plus US states and territories to tackle the onslaught—each went its own way, and Trump, himself, promoted a non-science-based approach. All this the new Biden administration did address, with a first rapid move to rejoin the World Trade Organization and get shots into arms.

So what impact has the coronavirus had on United States–China relations? Or, one could also ask, What impact has the deteriorating United States–China relationship had on pandemic cooperation? Ask either question and the answer is the same. The current insufficiency of essential United States–China health cooperation exacerbates the deterioration of broader bilateral ties, and the deterioration of bilateral ties further hampers Sino-American (and multilateral) public health cooperation.

Beijing's initial lack of transparency, in part, reflected the reluctance of lower-level officials to truthfully pass early warnings up the system, and there also was a reluctance in Beijing to publicly act on the worrisome news bubbling up from below, for economic and other reasons. Beijing presumably expected that, in the current setting of United States–China friction, Washington would use any PRC shortcomings to embarrass the regime. All this was reflected in a lack of timely and transparent information and Beijing's reluctance to cooperate sufficiently with WHO and the CDC. Nothing in Beijing's behavior has changed with the arrival of the Biden administration.

Americans also need to recognize that the Trump administration's response was woefully inadequate (as Biden has done), irrespective of China's missteps. President Trump's repeated mention of the "kung flu," the "foreign," and the "China" virus, along with the lack of domestic preparation organizationally (he did away with the National Security Council Office that would have focused on, and coordinated, a science-based response to the pandemic), poor budget priorities (the US administration lowered relevant CDC spending), the president's protracted resistance to doing anything to dramatically increase mask wearing, domestic testing, or contact tracing, his failure to get personal protective equipment production and orderly distribution of it up and running, his statements that contradicted the advice of his science advisers and included flogging fatuous "cures," and his early statements indicating that the outbreak would be abbreviated, collectively converged to drive Trump into a corner where he blamed his predecessor (President Obama), selected state governors, and local governments, "Democrat cities," China, and even his own experts—all the while the bodies piled up at home. With 4 percent of the world's population, the United States under Trump endured more than 20 percent of global fatalities (as of September 2020). Once again, with the arrival of the Delta variant of COVID, the United States had a very alarming death rate, this time fed by the refusal of many US citizens to get vaccinated.

This still-unfolding episode reveals that so-called soft security issues (e.g., global public health) can teach lessons as bitter and costly to human life as those taught by "hard security" failures—war. This experience should compel both Beijing and Washington to recognize that "decoupling" and "self-reliance" are dangerous aspirations in an interconnected world. The failure to achieve Sino-American cooperation on this issue not only has been hugely expensive in human and economic terms; it has magnified mutual distrust and diminished cooperation across all United States–China issues.

Implications

The drivers of current conflict in Sino-American relations are strong in both countries, and the global COVID-19 pandemic has further embedded mutual distrust. Though there had been hope on the eve of the inauguration of the Biden administration that these negative trends would be slowed or reversed, that has not occurred. Beijing has made virtually no positive moves, and President Biden has continued many of his predecessor's policies. The broad, negative consensus about China in the United States, and the unlikelihood that Xi Jinping will radically alter his course any time soon, means that Washington–Beijing ties will require careful management and be precarious (at best) for the indefinite future. Taiwan is daily becoming a more sensitive, indeed explosive, issue. That in the waning days of the Trump administration the chairman of the US Joint Chiefs of Staff felt it necessary to call his People's Liberation Army counterpart in Beijing to reassure Beijing that a US attack was not contemplated or imminent, tells you a lot.

Preelection expectations that a Biden victory would produce a more orderly, fact-based policy process in Washington have largely been borne out. Key foreign policymaking positions have been filled with competent persons. Nonetheless, there are genuine issues and trends in bilateral relations that are proving to be very difficult to address. Managing competition for dominance in the technologies and industries of the future is one. Dampening the already robust arms race now includes a PRC commitment to double its inventory of nuclear warheads "as soon as possible."[25] And there are differences concerning international norms, law, and values, as manifest in the PRC's treatment of Tibetans, Muslims in Xinjiang, and Hong Kong citizens. Moreover, the Taiwan issue is only one significant misstep away from becoming a major conflict. Looking regionally, US friends from India, through Southeast Asia, and to Japan have territorial and maritime frictions with China that, if they were to erupt, would entangle Washington to various extents.

For US allies and friends in Asia and around the world, the preceding means that they will have navigate between their desire to avoid conflict with the PRC and economically prosper from productive ties with China, and their parallel need to enhance their security by seeking some refuge in ties with the United States. In the circumstance of more Sino-American conflict, Washington will push its friends and allies to more closely align with America, as we now see Australia doing out of its own concerns. China's neighbors and US friends and allies may often feel they have to urge restraint on both Beijing and Washington in an effort to avoid their own entrapment. Most recently, for example, we have seen that as Australia, the United States, and Britain move toward tighter alignment against Beijing, the French for both commercial and strategic reasons become more dissatisfied with US alliance management.

Now, with the Biden administration in office, *job one is to keep the many hot spots and friction points in United States–China relations from escalating.* The restoration of bilateral dialogue, an expeditious Sino-American summit, and the creation or reinvigoration of mechanisms for crisis management are essential. We now have a new Chinese ambassador, Qin Gang, in Washington, and it is imperative that Washington get an ambassador approved and off to Beijing. Both sides need envoys who carry as much clout as possible with their respective supreme leaders. Beijing would be making a huge mistake if it were to seize the moment of transition in the United States to use muscular means.

New administrations reflexively will react strongly to provocation or aggression, feeling that their future credibility at home and abroad is on the line.

Job two is to develop tangible proposals for stabilizing and advancing ties. Opportunities for strengthening ties might include cooperating with Beijing to complete the provisions of the Phase One Trade Deal and moving on to Phase Two; restarting Bilateral Investment Treaty talks; beginning to explore how China and the United States could both join the Comprehensive Progressive Agreement for Trans-Pacific Partnership (which would be controversial in both US political parties); rekindling cultural and educational exchanges (including the Fulbright Program); resuming and strengthening intergovernmental dialogues; and reopening the Chengdu and Houston consulates. With respect to the toughest nut to crack, the security relationship, the two sides should start talking about what our respective strategic needs are, what we both could define as a mutually acceptable strategic end state or equilibrium, and initiate discussions on how arms control might help stabilize things (something that Beijing has been reluctant to do until it achieves what it sees a some degree of parity with the United States or Washington commits itself to sizable weapons reductions). I must observe, however, that the two first attempts at dialogue between the United States and China under Biden, first in Anchorage and then later in Tianjin, were not encouraging for those hoping dialogue would help.

Concluding this research with the aircraft metaphor with which it began, the United States–China relationship is in a nosedive, in which attempts to correct the altitude perversely steepen the angle and rate of descent. Now is the time for change. Taking actions such as those outlined above will be difficult, politically expensive, and perhaps impossible. One thing, however, is certain: failure to move in such directions will impose future costs that dwarf those we already can see. As Henry Kissinger usefully analogized: If key European leaders on the brink of World War I had understood the full costs of their actions in 1914, history thereafter might have been quite different from the catalytic war into which the world was plunged.

Notes

1. David M. Lampton is professor and director of China studies emeritus at Johns Hopkins–SAIS, where he now is senior research fellow at its Foreign Policy Institute. Previously, he was president of the National Committee on US–China Relations and chairman of the Asia Foundation. His most recent book, coauthored with Selina Ho and Cheng-Chwee Kuik, is *Rivers of Iron: Railroads and Chinese Power in Southeast Asia* (University of California Press, 2020). The author thanks Zoe Balk for her research assistance.

2. David M. Lampton, "Xi Jinping and the National Security Commission: Policy Coordination and Political Power," *Journal of Contemporary China*, published online, March 18, 2015, 759–77.

3. Laura Silver, "Republicans See China More Negatively Than Democrats, Even as Criticism Rises in Both Parties," July 30, 2020, https://www.pewresearch.org/fact-tank/2020/07/30/republicans-see-china-more-negatively-than-democrats-even-as-criticism-rises-in-both-parties/.

4. US Department of Defense, *Nuclear Posture Review 2018*, v, https://fas.org/issues/nuclear-weapons/nuclear-posture-review/.

5. David M. Lampton, Selina Ho, and Cheng-Chwee Kuik, *Rivers of Iron: Railroads and Chinese Power in Southeast Asia* (University of California Press, 2020).

6. David G. Brown, "Can the KMT Reform—and Remain Relevant?" *Diplomat*, September 11, 2020, https://thediplomat.com/2020/09/can-the-kmt-reform-and-remain-relevant/.

7. US Chamber of Commerce in Shanghai, *2020 China Business Report*.

8. A US State Department official confirmed that as of September 8, 2020, certain Chinese graduate students and researchers (often visiting scholars) with ties to China's "fusion strategy" had had their visas cancelled. All this was compounded by the dramatic slowdown to a trickle in visa issuance, partly because of COVID-19-induced travel obstacles and partly because of Department of State budgetary problems. In July 2019, there had been 21,781 F1 visas issued to "China mainland," and a year later, that number was 145; https://www.reuters.com/article/us-usa-china-visas/us-has-canceled-more-than-1000-visas-for-chinese-nationals-deemed-security-risks-idUSKBN2602OO. All this will have an enormous and enduring effect on American tertiary teaching and research institutions and on the attitudes of Chinese students (and probably those of other nationalities around the world) about coming to the United States for study.

9. As in the Cold War experience with the Soviet Union, it may well be that Washington will come to be seen by future historians as having overestimated the People's Republic's power, notwithstanding the fact that now, in certain settings such as the Taiwan Strait, China may already enjoy crucial local power asymmetries.

10. Cannix Yau, "Some Four in 10 Amcham Members Considering Leaving Hong Kong Over National Security Law Fear, Survey Finds," https://www.scmp.com/news/hong-kong/politics/article/3097257/some-four-10-us-businesses-considering-leaving-hong-kong?utm_medium=email&utm_source=mailchimp&utm_campaign=enlz-agah_hong_kong_national_security_law&utm_content=20200817&tpcc=enlz-hong_kong_national_security_law&MCUID=a9e4ca70d2&MCCampaignID=896a92f53f&MCAccountID=7b1e9e7f8075914aba9cff17f&tc=22. Only time will tell whether this fraction of businesses leaves Hong Kong, given its still strategic location, comparatively strong infrastructure, and its long history of competence.

11. American Chamber of Commerce in Shanghai, *2020 China Business Report*, 4.

12. Keith Bradsher, "Trump's Tariffs? Coronavirus? China's Exports Are Surging Anyway," https://www.nytimes.com/2020/08/31/business/trumps-tariffs-coronavirus-china-exports.html.

13. David M. Lampton, "Engagement with China: A Eulogy and Reflections on a Gathering Storm," in *Engaging China: The Making and Unmaking of Sino-American Relations*, edited by Anne F. Thurston (Columbia University Press, 2022).

14. In fact, however, the onset of the COVID-19 pandemic and the ensuing global economic slowdown meant that China did not initially meet even the purchase targets of the Phase One Trade deal.

15. US Census Bureau, "Trade in Goods with China," https://www.census.gov/foreign-trade/balance/c5700.html. This figure is "trade in goods"; it does not include trade in "services," where the United States runs a surplus.

16. US–China Business Council, "2020 State Export Report," https://www.uschina.org/reports/2020-state-export-report

17. David M. Lampton, with Joyce A. Madancy and Kristen M. Williams, *A Relationship Restored: Trends in US–China Educational Exchanges, 1978–1984* (Washington: National Academy Press, 1986).

18. Then–secretary of state Mike Pompeo delivered the fourth of the four policy addresses at the Nixon Library on July 23, 2020. Ironically, a Republican secretary of state went to the memorial library for a past Republican president—an institution that houses the records of the signature foreign policy achievement of that president—to try to bury the opening to China. Other extremely tough remarks were delivered by then–vice president Mike Pence, National Security Adviser Robert O'Brien, Attorney General Bill Barr, and FBI director Christopher Wray in the period leading up to Pompeo's remarks. Paul Heer, "Mike Pompeo Challenges China's Governing Regime," https://nationalinterest.org/feature/mike-pompeo-challenges-china%E2%80%99s-governing-regime-165663.

19. Interview by US–China Perception Monitor, "David 'Mike' Lampton on COVID-19: 'Decoupling' or 'Self-reliance' in US–China Relations Are Dangerous Delusions,"https://uscnpm.org/2020/03/16/david-mike-lampton-covid-19-demonstrates-that-decoupling-or-self-reliance-in-u-s-china-relations-are-dangerous-delusions/

20. Callie Aboaf, *US-China Collaboration on Combatting the 2014 Ebola Outbreak in West Africa*, Carter Center, Trilateral Cooperation Research Series, no. 3.

21. "Senator Tom Cotton Repeats Fringe Theory of Coronavirus Origins," *New York Times*, February 7, 2020, https://www.nytimes.com/2020/02/17/business/media/coronavirus-tom-cotton-china.html.

22. Tripti Lahiri and Jane Li, "China's Top Court Says It Was a Mistake to Quell Early 'Rumors' About the Wuhan Virus," *Quartz*, https://qz.com/1793764/china-court-says-wuhan-coronavirus-rumors-might-have-helped/.

23. White House, "Remarks by President Trump After Meeting with Republican Senators," March 10, 2020, https://www.whitehouse.gov/briefings-statements/remarks-president-trump-meeting-republican-senators-2/.

24. Bob Woodward, *Rage* (New York: Simon & Schuster, 2020), xviii-xx, 242. In a February 6, 2020, telephone call between Trump and Xi, the Chinese president asked Trump "not to take excessive actions that would create further panic."

25. Eyal Propper, "Possible Changes in China's Nuclear Policy and the Significance for Arms Control," https://www.inss.org.il/publication/china-nuclear-strategy/.

Three

The Postpandemic Order
CHINA, THE ASEAN, AND THE FUTURE
OF THE INDO-PACIFIC

RICHARD JAVAD HEYDARIAN, *UNIVERSITY OF THE PHILIPPINES,
ASIAN CENTER*

This chapter examines the emerging geopolitical order and strategic balance of forces in the Indo-Pacific, especially in East Asia, amid the COVID-19 pandemic. The chapter traces and analyzes China's growing maritime assertiveness as its rivals and neighbors scramble to contain epidemic outbreaks, prevent economic meltdowns, and helplessly overstretch their strategic resources to deal with the full-spectrum crisis triggered by the Wuhan-originated virus that rapidly spread across the world in early 2020. The chapter looks at how "middle" and small powers in the region, particularly in Southeast Asia, are coping with a new age of Chinese assertiveness and a festering Sino-American geopolitical competition, the so-called New Cold War. I provide an analysis of (1) the New Cold War and China's revanchist ambitions, (2) the increasingly determined pushback by the United States and its key allies across various arenas of strategic competition, and (3) the need for the Association of Southeast Asian Nations (ASEAN) to step up to the plate and embrace an institutional and strategic reset.

Thus, this chapter, in an effort to trace the emerging contours of the postpandemic regional order, examines the complex, dynamic, and mutually constitutive interaction by the ASEAN as a middle power, its key members nations as smaller powers, and the Sino-American superpower rivalry—most poignantly expressed in the precarious naval showdown in the South China Sea but also increasingly turning into a full-fledged trade and technology warfare on a global scale. Since cold war–style containment is both counterproductive and infeasible, the chapter recommends a strategy of "constrainment" by the United States and like-minded regional partners—namely, a multilateral, calibrated, and decisive deployment of a combination of diplomatic, economic, and military tools to check Beijing's worst instincts as well as lay down the foundation for an inclusive and ASEAN-driven postpandemic security architecture.

The Real Cold War

Reflecting on the dizzying speed and devastating turn of his era, the Russian revolutionary Leon Trotsky once remarked,[1] "Anyone desiring a quiet life has done badly to be born in the twentieth century." A century later, his eloquent foreboding is even more resonant, given the concatenation of existential crises facing humanity, with no less than planetary climate change casting a long shadow over our future as a species.[2]

The ongoing COVID-19 pandemic, which originated in China amid a massive coverup and oversight by local officials, will likely only accelerate structural contradictions and preexisting fissures within the international system.[3] To be clear, history has often revealed itself as nonlinear and as filled with detours and surprises, whereby at times major events (*événementielle*) could supersede the Braudelian impersonal and long-term forces (*longue durée*) that primarily shape the course of civilization. As Francis Fukuyama correctly observes, "major crises have major consequences," which are "usually unforeseen." The Great Depression, for instance, best captures this ontological indeterminacy, since it was an event that reinforced preexisting trends, namely, rise of Fascism in Europe, but also spurred progressive outcomes such as the New Deal and, within less than a generation, the birth of the liberal international order under the aegis of a preeminent America.[4]

So far, however, the COVID-19 pandemic seems to have only reinforced preexisting trends, namely, the shift in material power from West to the East, as well as exacerbated structural tensions in the international security system.[5] Thus, we have found ourselves in the midst of the most consequential geopolitical showdown in history, as the United States and China try to shape and reshape the contours of a new brave world on the ruins of the devastating pandemic. If one were to believe pundits and policymakers, what we are confronting is the latest iteration of the bipolar Cold War, with resurgent China supplanting the once-mighty Soviet Empire. As Henry Kissinger warned, an existing order—namely, a set of commonly shared written rules and unwritten norms governing interstate affairs—is in danger of disintegration when there is "either a re-definition of legitimacy or a significant shift in the balance of power."[6] In many ways, this geopolitical showdown has been long in the making, with eerie elements of the so-called Thucydides trap.[7]

Throughout the past decade, China has leveraged a rapid shift in Asia's balance of power to challenge the broader the United States–led liberal international order.[8] The COVID-19 pandemic, which hit Western and Japanese economies much harder than China's, the only major economy to still grow in 2020, will only reinforce the seismic shift in the global balance of economic power.[9] Dispensing with Deng Xiaoping's advice to "hide our capabilities and bide our time, [and] never try to take the lead," Xi is calling for a "Chinese Dream" of "great rejuvenation," which, in the case of this former empire and resurgent superpower, is most likely a euphuism for primacy, especially in East Asia.[10] The upshot is naked strategic opportunism, which was on full display during the the first half of 2020. Beginning in March, China began conducting large-scale wargames, fortified its military facilities in the Spratlys, deployed large coast guard vessels to Philippine-claimed Scarborough Shoal, and announced two new administrative regions cutting across much of the South China Sea Basin. The "Nansha District" covers the Spratly Islands, which are also claimed by Taiwan, Vietnam, the Philippines, and Malaysia, and the "Xisha District," which covers the Vietnam-claimed Paracel Islands and the Macclesfield Bank. Within a span of months, smaller claimant states in the South China Sea faced China's harassment of their fishermen (Vietnam), warships (the Philippines), and oil exploration activities (Malaysia).[11]

In the past, China exhibited a similar kind of opportunism whenever it sensed a power vacuum in adjacent waters. After the defeat of Imperial Japan, which occupied much of the South China Sea during World War II, China quickly seized control of large number of contested islands in the area. Decades later, when the Soviet Union wavered on its alliance with Vietnam, China seized Vietnamese-claimed land features in the Spratlys after violent clashes. Years earlier, it also consolidated its control over the Paracels, when the then–South Vietnam government was embroiled in a devastating war with the communist north. The twilight of Cold War, and America's withdrawal of military bases in the Philippines, was followed by China's seizure of the Philippine-claimed Mischief Reef in the early 1990s. Two decades later, China seized the Philippines-claimed Scarborough Shoal as the West struggled with the aftermath of the Great Recession in the late 2000s.

In response, the United States has seamlessly embraced the logic of Cold War competition. In a searing address, which evoked Reagan's "evil empire" speech, the then–US secretary of state, Michael Pompeo, accused Beijing of seeking "global hegemony" and criticized its fatuous fidelity to a "bankrupt totalitarian ideology." Experts were quick to point out the eerie similarity with President Harry Truman's 1947 speech to the US Congress, where he warned of an existential struggle between "alternative ways of life," namely, between democratic freedom and the Soviet Union's totalitarianism, which "relies upon terror and oppression, a controlled press and radio; fixed elections, and the suppression of personal freedoms." While it is true that Xi is no Stalin, the Chinse leader oversees a far more capable, nimble, and well-endowed imperium, which is challenging, and in some cases has even surpassed, the West at the frontier of science and technology, a dynamic that has been most pronounced in artificial intelligence, quantum communications, and 5G network development. If anything, the pandemic accelerated this trend in favor of China.

In retrospect, one could argue that the Soviet challenge to the liberal international order was simply a dress rehearsal for what awaited the so-called free world in the twenty-first century: the world's most powerful and sophisticated authoritarian empire. One could argue that, unlike the US-Soviet competition that claimed as many as 20 million lives throughout 130 proxy wars across the postcolonial world, this is the real Cold War, since both Washington and Beijing have studiously avoided either direct or indirect armed conflict. Unlike the largely impoverished and isolated Soviet Union, today's China cannot be "contained" in ways George Kennan envisioned throughout the mid–twentieth century.[12] The dynamic Asian powerhouse has become so integral to the global (and American) economy that Niall Ferguson and Moritz Schularick have coined the term "Chimerica,"[13] namely, the virtual entwinement of American and Chinese economies.[14]

Thus, the new virtual cold war—or rather "cold peace"—requires a new strategy, where the United States and its key allies and partners can employ an optimal "Goldilocks approach" that combines just the right amount of meaningful engagement with decisive and firm deterrence. This is even more poignant in the postpandemic era, where strategic uncertainty combined with China's growing sense of insecurity is the new name of the game. In the words of Xi, China confronts a "period of turbulent change."[15] Perhaps no strategist better encapsulated this approach than the political scientist Gerald Segal, who, at the dawn of the post–Cold War era, envisioned a "constrainment" strategy, which "is intended to tell [China] that the outside world has interests that will be defended by means of incentives for good behavior, deterrence of bad behavior, and punishment when deterrence fails."[16] This approach, Segal argues, will work if the United States and its key partners in Asia "act in a concerted fashion both to punish and to reward China."[17] The stakes are high, since, as Graham Allison correctly observed, the two powers are trapped in a structural predicament, where "fear, insecurity, and determination to defend the status quo" rises in proportion to "the rising power's [China] growing entitlement, sense of its importance, and demand for greater say and sway."[18]

The Art of Constrainment

The Trump administration's response employed certain elements of the "constrainment" strategy, namely, the calibrated deployment of economic sanctions, military countermaneuvers and diplomatic pressure to check China's worst instincts. While there was a misguided abandonment of the Obama administration's economic initiatives, most notably the Trans-Pacific Partnership deal, comprehensive pushback against China has ramped up, most notably in Freedom of Navigation Operations (FONOPs), which have become more regular, more aggressive, and more geographically expansive.[19] In a sense, what we have seen is a revamped version of the much-anticipated military Pivot to Asia policy, which suffered from strategic reticence under the Obama administration. China's brazen opportunism amid the COVID-19 pandemic only reinforced American pushback. In particular, the US "Free and Open Indo-Pacific" strategy employs elements of "constrainment" on three levels.

First, there has been a major policy reformulation, especially on the military front. The Trump administration provided "total authorizations" to the Pentagon, which has brought "a new calculus to global politics, in which the use of force plays a more prominent role, and that [senior Pentagon officials such as former defense secretary] Mattis may be the policy's principal driver."[20] As early as March 2017, just few months into the then-new administration, the *New York Times* reported that the US president began "shifting more authority over military operations to the Pentagon, according to White House officials, reversing what his aides and some generals say was a tendency by the Obama White House to micromanage issues better left to military commanders."[21] These regulatory shifts empowered the Pentagon to adopt more robust countermeasures to Chinese maritime assertiveness. During the first year of the Trump administration, the Pentagon conducted four FONOPs within the span of only five months (an unprecedented record).[22] In early 2019, it deployed, for the first time in history, two pairs of nuclear-capable bombers within a span of just over a week alone to challenge China's excessive maritime claim to the detriment of freedom of overflight in the South China Sea.[23] In contrast, the previous administration failed to conduct regular, quarterly FONOPs as promised, while centralizing the decision-making process in the White House, which reportedly had to give prior clearance for each maneuver. But under Trump the Pentagon regularly deployed, often two at the same time, warships to the disputed island chains as well as the Scarborough Shoal in the South China Sea.[24]

Second, there has been a greater commitment to frontline allies, particularly the besieged island nations of Taiwan and the Philippines in the "first island chain." In the first months of 2019, the Pentagon deployed the guided-missile destroyers USNS *Walter S. Diehl* and USS *McCampbell* in January and, the next month, the ammunition and cargo vessel USNS *Cesar Chavez* and the destroyer USS *Stethem* through the Taiwan Strait in a show of force against escalating Chinese threats to the island nation. The Trump administration also authorized a $1.3 billion arms sale to Taiwan to help it quell any coercive reunification efforts by China. Conversations with senior Tsai administration officials, including the country's national security adviser and foreign minister, suggest Taipei's growing confidence in the American commitment—a far cry from more reticent views expressed by the Ma administration.[25] Interestingly, Washington is finally integrating the US Coast Guard into the FONOPs equation. In March 2019, it deployed among America's biggest and most advanced Coast Guard cutters, the USCGC *Bertholf,* through the Strait.[26]

Despite uneasy diplomatic relations since the beginning of the Duterte administration in the Philippines, the Trump administration nevertheless stepped up its security commitment to its oldest regional ally and former sole Asian colony. Despite all his "Pivot to Asia" rhetoric, President Barack Obama repeatedly refused to clarify the precise extent of the US commitment to allies such as the Philippines. Adding insult to injury, during a 2014 visit to Manila, he dismissed Philippine-claimed islands as "a bunch of rocks" not worth fighting over. This is precisely the context within which one should understand Philippine president Rodrigo Duterte's penchant for questioning America's sincerity and commitments and accordingly, efforts to diversify the country's relations in favor of China short of fully severing ties with traditional allies per se.[27]

In contrast, during his surprise visit to Manila in March 2019, the US secretary of state, Mike Pompeo, made the unprecedented move of clarifying, on the most senior level and in public, the precise extent of American commitment to its treaty ally under the 1951 Mutual Defense Treaty, a major departure from the equivocations of the Obama administration.[28] "As the South China Sea is part of the Pacific, any armed attack on any Philippine forces, aircraft, or public vessels in the South China Sea will trigger mutual defense obligations under Article 4 of our Mutual defense treaty," the US chief diplomat said, confidently stating: "We have your back," Pompeo reportedly told Filipino leaders.[29] Following an April 2019 visit by Philippine defense secretary Delfin Lorenzana to Washington, the two allies also discussed potential purchase of the High Mobility Artillery Rocket System as deterrence against Chinese militarization of the South China Sea.[30]

When a suspected Chinese militia vessel rammed a Filipino boat later that year, the US ambassador to the Philippines warned Beijing that the US-Philippine treaty alliance will apply to "any armed attack" by "government-sanctioned militias." Again, this was the first time ever that top US officials were so open and specific in reassuring about the American military commitment. In 2019, the Philippines and United States conducted 280 joint exercises, the highest number of joint exercises on the record and highest among any of the Pentagon's Indo-Pacific partners.[31] The aim of expanded joint military activities is to enhance military interoperability in response to shared strategic threats, including China. The Trump administration further raised the stakes in July 2020, when it released a policy statement on the South China Sea disputes. Invoking the 2016 Arbitral Tribunal award at The Hague, which rejected much of China's expansive claims in adjacent waters, Pompeo's latest statement has practically placed the United States behind Philippine claims across the Spratlys and the Scarborough Shoal, which fall "in areas that the Tribunal found to be in the Philippines' EEZ or on its continental shelf."[32]

This was even more explicit with respect to Manila's claims over the Second Thomas Shoal, where it maintains a military presence, and China-occupied Mischief Reef, because "both of which fall fully under the Philippines' sovereign rights and jurisdiction." The top US diplomat also warned China against "any unilateral . . . actions to exploit" natural resources, as well as "harassment of Philippine fisheries and offshore energy development" in Philippine waters. The United States' latest statement may have undercut its claims to neutrality, but it has provided desperately needed assurance of American military assistance if China were to take aggressive actions against Philippine troops, vessels, and aircraft in the Scarborough Shoal, Second Thomas Shoal, and the Spratlys. This is the reason why the Philippines' top defense official was among the first to openly welcome the United States' latest statement. In short, the Trump-Duterte populist tandem has overseen the strongest ever security alliance, as both countries grapple with a resurgent China, albeit with difference diplomatic cadences.[33]

Bolstered by the multi-billion-dollar Asia Reassurance Initiative Act,[34] the Trump administration has also doubled Foreign Military Financing to key regional allies like the Philippines,[35] while contemplating ways to optimally deploy the $60 billion Better Utilization of Investments Leading to Development

(BUILD) for high-quality strategic investments in the Indo-Pacific, especially in Southeast Asia.[36] Rightly, the Trump administration also called for a *reversal* of China's militarization of the disputed islands, and highlighted threats posed by Beijing's activities to global economic interest, especially energy security in sea lines of communication.[37]

Third, the Pentagon has now adopted a more comprehensive approach to China's "People's War at Sea" strategy in the South China Sea. In early 2019, Admiral John Richardson, chief of US naval operations, announced a bolder strategy to combat so-called "gray zone" or "short of conflict" operations in contested seascape. He accused China of deceptively employing paramilitary forces to swarm, intimidate, and even threaten the disruption of supply lines of other claimant states short of triggering direct conflict. The Pentagon has begun to rightly treat China's People's Armed Forces Maritime Militia, and other corollary paramilitary forces, as extensions of the People's Liberation Army Navy, thus treating them with uniform rules of engagement. In June 2019, shortly after releasing its Indo-Pacific Strategy paper and after the ramming of a Filipino fishing vessel by a suspected Chinese militia, the United States made it clear that the Mutual Defense Treaty could apply to cases involving Chinese militia attacks on Philippine assets in the South China Sea.[38] Senior Philippine officials, including Defense Secretary Delfin Lorenzana, have confirmed to the author[39] that the two allies could revise guidelines in their existing treaty in order to deal with new and emerging threats from China.[40] Later that year, the coast guard forces from both the Philippines and United States also conducted exercises in the South China Sea,[41] the first visit by the US Coast Guard in almost a decade. In November 2019, Admiral Karl Schultz told the author that he envisions a greater role for the Coast Guard to address threats post by China's paramilitary forces in the South China Sea under so-called gray zone operations.[42] Postpandemic geopolitical tensions are expected to further reinforce America's comprehensive pushback against China.

Middle-Power Diplomacy

While the Trump administration corrected the excessive reticence of its predecessor, it suffered from its own excesses as well as shortcomings. Washington's Indo-Pacific strategy has, for instance, lacked any substantial economic element, while being perilously confrontational vis-à-vis China—to the consternation of many Southeast Asian nations that count Beijing as a major trade and investment patron, if not defense partner.[43] Moreover, the Trump administration's strategy on China carried immense risks of unintended consequences, especially his trade war, which sent shockwaves across global markets.

While some countries such as Vietnam have been benefiting from the ongoing tariff escalation between the world's two biggest economies, the threat to highly integrated global supply chains and investment linkages is serious. If we were to confront an all-out global trade war, leading economists predict up to a 70 percent contraction in international trade,[44] which, in turn, could trigger a global depression, with a 2 to 3 percent contraction in the world's gross domestic product.[45] Southeast Asian leaders, such as Prime Minister Mahathir Mohamad, have openly opposed the trade war, arguing,[46] "[President] Trump is unusually aggressive and inconsistent, we don't really know what he is going to do next," warning that the trade war could easily morph into a cold war at the expense of regional prosperity, hard-earned stability, and the welfare of smaller nations.

Meanwhile, there is also the growing fear of a technological iron curtain,[47] if not full decoupling in global production networks,[48] with the Trump administration presenting a Manichean position on adoption of Chinese 5G network technology. During his high-profile speech at the 2019 Munich Conference, Vice President Mike Pence openly warned against the perils embedded in welcoming cutting edge Chinese telecom technology.[49] Less belligerently, the Trump administration stepped up its criticism of the Belt and Road Initiative (BRI), with Pompeo describing it as a nefarious "debt [trap] diplomacy," which is "almost certainly designed for foreclosure."[50] But what is America's tangible alternative, aside from criticizing China's tantalizing economic initiatives?

The Trump administration's "Indo-Pacific" strategy is often seen across the region and beyond, especially by smaller states in Southeast Asia, through the prism of a new, dangerous superpower rivalry. As Barbara Tuchman explains in her magisterial *The Guns of August*, nations can sleepwalk into cataclysmic wars, since "in the midst of . . . crisis nothing is as clear or as certain as it appears in hindsight."[51] And this is where the middle powers, including the ASEAN, play a critical role.

Nonetheless, there have also been positive externalities, namely, the rise in "middle power diplomacy."[52] Without question, Japan, the true progenitor of the "Indo-Pacific" strategic concept, has been leading parallel efforts to promote a "free and open Indo-Pacific" beyond the dictates of superpower rivalry. On the trade front, Japan, together with Australia and other Indo-Pacific partners, has effectively rescued the Trans-Pacific Partnership under the rebooted Comprehensive and Progressive Agreement for Trans-Pacific

Partnership;[53] facilitated, in conjunction with Indonesia and the ASEAN, the Regional Comprehensive Economic Partnership negotiations,[54] the biggest of its kind anywhere in the world; and has secured trade deals with the European Union, including the world's biggest bilateral free trade agreement on record, pushing back against Trump's populist protectionism. On the infrastructure front, Japan, under the "Asia connectivity" strategy, has been the leading investor in Southeast Asia, where there are growing worries about debt sustainability and corrosive investments under China's BRI.[55]

According to the latest data from Fitch Solutions, Japanese infrastructure investments (worth $230 billion)[56] overshadow China's (worth $155 billion) across Southeast Asia.[57] In the Philippines, the margin is even more significant, with Tokyo pledging twenty-nine infrastructure projects worth $43.5 billion, compared with Beijing's eight key projects in the pipeline worth $7.4 billion, only a fraction of Japanese investments. Most recently, it also signed an infrastructure deal with the European Union amid rising fears over Eastern Europe's potential fall into China's debt trap.[58] At the heart of Japan's infrastructure vision is not matching China's pledges on a dollar-to-dollar (or yen-to-renminbi) basis, but instead advocating transparent, sustainable, high-quality infrastructure across the Indo-Pacific and Eurasian landmass. And this has gone hand in hand with Japan's tightening maritime security partnership with the ASEAN members,[59] especially the Philippines and Vietnam, and to a lesser degree Malaysia, which have benefited from Japanese assistance in the realm of domain awareness and the development of nascent coast guard forces across maritime Southeast Asia.

Meanwhile, Australia has recalibrated its China policy, tightening scrutiny over "influence operations"[60] and Chinese "sharp power" in domestic politics and policy circles; imposed restrictions,[61] on national security grounds, vis-à-vis the entry of Chinese companies in strategic sectors, namely, the 5G network telecommunications infrastructure; and adopted an openly skeptical position on the BRI and "debt trap" risks. Closer to home, Canberra blocked entry of Huawei in its strategic depth in South Pacific islands by subsidizing an alternative underwater internet cable project as well as a cybersecurity center for the Solomon Islands;[62] lobbied Fiji to block Chinese plans of developing a regional military hub, particularly in the Fiji Military Forces' Black Rock Camp in Nadi;[63] leveraged concerns over the Chinese "debt trap"[64] by securing its position as the biggest source of development aid in the region;[65] and, together with the United States, agreed to develop a vital naval base on Manus Island in Papua New Guinea, a poignantly strategic site that served as the Allied forces' resistance base against Imperial Japan's expansion during World War II.[66]

Similar to Japan, Australia has also upgraded its strategic ties with the ASEAN, with the inaugural 2018 Australia–ASEAN summit underscoring the depth of their burgeoning strategic partnership. The two sides have, inter alia, signed an investment agreement, which aims to "develop a pipeline of high-quality infrastructure projects, to attract private and public investment."[67]

Separately, India, which held its own inaugural bilateral summit with the ASEAN in early 2019, has been expanding its technical and developmental assistance to the ASEAN and its key countries, especially Vietnam.[68] This has coincided with expanding defense and maritime security ties with key ASEAN countries, from traditional partners in Hanoi to new defense partners in Manila, which has eyed, among others, closer naval exercises with and advanced cruise missiles from New Delhi to enhance its minimum deterrence capabilities.[69]

For its part, South Korea, another middle power in the region, has launched its own "New Southern Policy," with a growing focus on expanded trade and investment ties with key ASEAN nations. In the Philippines, South Korea is not only a top trading and investment partner but also a leading source of advanced military hardware, from fighter jets to frigates. With improved prospects of inter-Korean peace, and given South Korea's increasingly formidable naval and defense capabilities, Seoul could increasingly play a key role in upholding basic freedoms in the South China Sea and other sea lines of communication in the Indo-Pacific.

Strategic Soul-Searching: ASEAN and the Future of Asia

It is often hard to discern what exactly Southeast Asian countries seek from external powers, especially the United States. One must ask if regional leaders even know what they truly seek from outside powers, aside from their instinctive preference for being left to govern as they wish and, accordingly, extract maximum benefits from all major powers for collective or personal interest. During the Obama administration, countless pundits and policymakers across the region bemoaned the supposed lack of American wherewithal and, accordingly, sufficient pushback back against China. Under the succeeding American administration, regional leaders sang a different tune, fretting over supposedly excessive pushback against China. The Pivot to Asia policy was criticized for lacking teeth and vigor, while the "free and open Indo-Pacific" was met with fear and foreboding.

The Trump administration's Indo-Pacific strategy is largely dismissed as a thinly veiled containment strategy[70] by the so-called Quad (Quadrilateral)[71] grouping of the major, like-minded powers of Australia, Japan, India, and the United States against a rising China. Accordingly, there is growing fear over the ASEAN's "centrality" in shaping the regional order.[72] It is hard to blame the ASEAN, after all, when the Trump administration's National Security Strategy openly embraces "great power competition" and classifies China as a "revisionist" power that seeks to "challenge American power, influence, and interests" across the Indo-Pacific and beyond "to erode American security and prosperity."[73] The same tone is evident in the "National Defense Strategy" of the Pentagon, which accuses Beijing of "leveraging military modernization, influence operations, and predatory economics to coerce continues its neighboring countries to reorder the Indo-Pacific region to their advantage" and "continu[ing] to pursue a military modernization program that seeks Indo-Pacific regional hegemony in the future" through the "displacement of the United States to achieve global preeminence in the future."[74]

On the most basic level, the ASEAN is opposed to "great power competition," and it is staunchly opposed to any geopolitical formula whereby it has to choose between competing powers.[75] To this end, Indonesia, the cradle of the "third way" Non-Aligned Movement (NAM), has led intra-ASEAN efforts at developing an alternative regional vision,[76] culminating in the 2019 ASEAN Outlook on the Indo-Pacific (AOIP).[77] Under this vision, the ASEAN rejected any categorical portrayal of China as a hegemonic threat to the region, instead welcoming the Asian powerhouse as a responsible stakeholder in shaping the future of the Indo-Pacific. The problem, however, is that the AOIP is more an *assertion* of centrality rather than its *demonstration*. If anything, it sounds, at best, defensive and, at worst, desperate. It offers no road map to achieving ASEAN "centrality"; nor does it address the elephant in the room: China's revanchist ambitions in the South China Sea and, accordingly, its nefarious influence through "debt trap" practices and potentially risky technological investments in critical infrastructure of regional states.

What Southeast Asian commentators and leaders tend to miss is this: By refusing to support efforts at securing a "free and open" regional order, they are effectively enabling Chinese threats to its neighbors and broader liberal international order in Asia. In a way, it is even disingenuous for the ASEAN to claim neutrality, since consistently opposed, among others, the Trump administration's trade protectionism.[78] On a fundamental level, the ASEAN suffers from what I have called the "middle institutional trap," namely, the unanimity-based decision-making procedures that worked in the past, among the ten diverse members, which are no longer up to the task, especially in light of the reemergence of China as a potential regional hegemon.[79] To disrupt the

ASEAN's unity, and undermine its "centrality," Beijing can simply lean on one or two regional "weak links," since each member—regardless of the degree of interest, size, or contribution—has de facto veto-power over ASEAN statements and, more broadly, its overall strategic direction. No wonder, until this date, the regional body has failed to issue even a single openly critical statement condemning China's aggression against its Southeast Asian neighbors; nor has there been any substantial movement toward a legally binding Code of Conduct in the South China Sea. In short, the ASEAN's multilateralism on the defining geopolitical challenge of our era has reached a deadlock, if not institutional paralysis.

As Vladimir Lenin once asked: What is to be done? The good news is that the ASEAN is not a monolithic geopolitical entity, and that the "ASEAN Way" is not set in stone. On the most fundamental level, the ASEAN is going through its "fourth reset," or moment of truth. The Konfrontasi era of the 1960s paved the way for the creation of MAPHILINDO and, not long after, the ASEAN. The late 1970s and 1980s saw another moment of soul searching, as archipelagic Southeast Asian nations, together with the United States–allied Thailand, contemplated the admission of communist-leaning Indo-Chinese nations, including Vietnam. The end of Cold War presented the third and most promising reset for the regional body, which saw a distinct opportunity to create an ASEAN-led regional security architecture based on the norms of multilateralism, conflict prevention, and peaceful management of disputes. Today, the ASEAN is facing its fourth moment of reckoning, as it grapples with the post-American era and the rise of China as a global superpower. In short, the ASEAN is dynamic, and it has to be remain so in the rapidly shifting geopolitical landscape lest it risk, at the very least, total irrelevance in shaping the postpandemic, long-term security architecture in twenty-first-century Asia.

In the future, the ASEAN should embrace three major reforms. First and foremost, it has to seriously contemplate a more extensive and judicious adoption of the "ASEAN Minus X" formula;[80] namely, majority-based voting (X being a dissenting member or two), which proved effective in facilitating intraregional trade negotiations and the vision of the ASEAN Economic Community. Alternatively, the ASEAN could even embrace the European Union's qualified majority voting modality,[81] which takes into consideration differential (demographic, geopolitical) weights of member states, ensuring fair and commensurate reflection of the will of the majority of Southeast Asian peoples.

Second, the ASEAN should embrace "minilateralism," namely, ad hoc and issue-specific cooperation among key member states. In the past, we saw how minilateral efforts led by individual or a few key members led to "osmotic integration" on the ASEAN level: the Counter-Terrorism Convention is the best example of this.[82] In the South China Sea, for instance, claimant states and like-minded ASEAN members such as the Philippines, Malaysia, and Vietnam, together with Indonesia and Singapore, have developed the intra-regional Code of Conduct,[83] which is consistent with international law and the 2016 arbitral tribunal at The Hague under the aegis of the United Nations Convention on the Law of the Sea. Indonesia has, for instance, proposed joint patrols in contested areas of the South China Sea as another way to deescalate tensions and manage disputes effectively.[84]

While the ASEAN, as a regional organization, has struggled to play a key role in the South China Sea disputes, key members are beginning to push back against China's excesses. In fact, during the final months of 2019, the Asian powerhouse faced simultaneous pushback from its neighbors in adjacent waters. In a dramatic departure from its long tradition of "quiet diplomacy," Malaysia launched bolt-from-the-blue legal warfare in the South China Sea. Long seen as Beijing's most quiescent rival, Kuala Lumpur directly challenged Beijing's expansive claims in the area through submission of a claim for an extended continental shelf in the southern portions of the disputed waters. This coincided with the deployment of the *West Capella* drill ship to southwestern portions of the South China Sea, sparking a three-way showdown with both China and Vietnam. Then–Malaysian minister Saifuddin Abdullah did not shy away from a diplomatic showdown, dismissing China's claims as "ridiculous" and even threatening international arbitration to reassert his country's claims in the area. Soon after, Jakarta followed suit, with the Indonesian Foreign Ministry accusing China of a "violation of [its] sovereignty" off the coast of the resource-rich Natuna Islands, which overlap the southernmost tip of China's Nine-Dashed-Line. Dismissing China's expansive maritime claims as having "no legal basis" in modern international law, Indonesia upped the ante by dispatching President Joko Widodo to the contested area, where he warned China: "We have a district here, a regent, and a governor here. There are no more debates. De facto, de jure, Natuna is Indonesia."[85]

But Indonesia went beyond empty rhetoric, scrambling jet fighters and bolstering its military position in the Natuna area. The most decisive pushback, however, was expected to come from Vietnam, the rotational chairman of the ASEAN that year. In late 2019, the Southeast Asian country, which has most decisively contested China's claims in the South China Sea, publicly warned Beijing of potential legal action. Hanoi also stepped up its efforts to rally its neighbors, advocating for a tougher common stance on the maritime disputes. Even the Beijing-friendly Duterte administration in the Philippines took an ever-tougher stance in the South China Sea, insisting on the finality of the 2016 arbitral tribunal award, which nullified much of China's expansive claims in the area; standing in solidarity with Hanoi after Chinese harassment of Vietnamese fishermen in the Paracels area; and publicly reiterating the importance of its military alliance with the United States as a hedge against Beijing's aggression.[86]

Finally, the ASEAN, whether as a whole or on a minilateral level, should expand cooperation with like-minded external powers. On one hand, middle powers such as Australia, Japan, South Korea, Germany, and India—as well as Indo-Pacific resident powers such as France, the United Kingdom, and the United States—should step up strategic ties with the ASEAN as well as key Southeast Asian nations, especially those on the frontline of the South China Sea disputes such as the Philippines and Vietnam. Instead of an "Asian NATO," perhaps it is much better to discuss a Quad Plus minilateral regime, whereby key ASEAN nations and like-minded external powers jointly check China's worst instincts as well as explore cooperation in the realm of nontraditional security threats, including terrorism, maritime piracy, transnational crime, and pandemic-related public health crises. Capacity building is the name of the game, and middle powers can go a long way in enhancing strategic confidence and minimum deterrence capability among key ASEAN members. Down the road, the ASEAN should even contemplate the prospect of closer cooperation with its "far neighbors," including the proposal for associate membership for Australia and New Zealand, which have a lot to offer in terms of resources, diplomatic capital, and institutional capacity-building.[87]

Joseph Biden's presidency has presented a unique opportunity to not only fine-tune the shortcomings of its predecessors but also to reset broader strategic relations between Southeast Asia and major powers. Most likely, the current US administration will continue stepping up its diplomatic engagement, in tandem with other like-minded powers, with the ASEAN; advocate for free trade and expanded investment ties; and adopt more sophisticated countermeasures against China that shun Cold War–style rhetoric but firmly support the sovereignty of smaller states and the liberal international order in tangible military, diplomatic, and economic commitments on the ground.

A more coherent, compelling, and compartmentalized Asia policy under Biden is providing significant space for preserving a "free and open" order in the Indo-Pacific based on partnerships between the ASEAN and like-minded major powers across the Indo-Pacific, most especially fellow members of the Quadrilateral Security Dialogue (QUAD) as well as major European powers such as Britain, France and Germany, which have stepped up their naval deployments in the area. The Biden administration has also, in a nod to its predecessor's regional policy, steadily expanded the United States' naval deployments across Asia's contested waters to reassure allies, signal strength and determination to China, and deepen military-to-military relations with likeminded regional powers.[88] After a relatively slow start, the Biden administration stepped up its regional diplomacy by deploying US defense secretary Lloyd Austin and vice president Kamala Harris for back-to-back visits to key Southeast Asian capitals in August, 2021, in a strong show of strategic reassurance to frontline states such as the Philippines and Vietnam as well as new strategic partners such as Singapore. In one of the Biden administration's greatest strategic breakthroughs in its first few months in office, Austin's visit to Manila coincided with Duterte's decision to fully restore the all-crucial Visiting Forces Agreement, which facilitates large-scale entry of US troops on Philippine soil, a key element of broader efforts to check China's maritime ambitions in the South China Sea. The Biden administration's "vaccine diplomacy"—with Southeast Asian countries of Indonesia, the Philippines, and Vietnam among the largest recipients—has strengthened America's strategic position in the region.[89]

However, much is to be desired, if the United States is intent on effectively competing against China. The "exit without strategy" debacle in Afghanistan, which saw a United States–backed regime collapsing within weeks, has only reinforced the need for a proactive regional policy, which reassures Asian allies and partners wondering about America's reliability and commitment to stand by them in the darkest hour. To begin with, Washington is yet to crystalize its regional economic diplomacy, which requires a clear trade and investment alternative to China's Belt and Road Initiative—other than the tepid Indo-Pacific Economic Framework. Details of a proposed "digital trade" pact in Asia are still murky; down the road, a full-fledged, panregional trade and investment deal (i.e., Trans-Pacific Partnership Plus / Trans-Pacific Partnership 15, with Indonesia, Thailand, the Philippines, and South Korea as additional partners) is indispensable to the Biden administration's efforts to effectively and credibly compete with China.[90] Over all, the Biden administration should adopt more sophisticated countermeasures against China that shun exclusionary and provocative cold war–style rhetoric while firmly supporting the sovereignty and legitimate interests of smaller states as well as the foundations of the International Labor Organization through tangible military, diplomatic, and economic commitments on the ground. There need to be tangible initiatives to establish "integrated deterrence" as well as deeper economic integration between the United States and likeminded powers in the region. A more coherent, compelling, and compartmentalized Asia policy provides significant space for preserving a "free and open" order in the Indo-Pacific based on partnerships between the ASEAN and likeminded major powers. Ultimately, the goal must be to establish a robust and sustainable United States–led "constrainment" strategy to check China's worst instincts and encourage the better angels of its nature.

Notes

1. Isiah Berlin, "Political Ideas in the Twentieth Century," *Foreign Affairs,* April 1950.

2. David Wallace-Wells, *The Uninhabitable Earth: Life After Warming* (New York: Tim Duggan Books, 2019).

3. Minxin Pei, "The Coronavirus Is a Disease of Chinese Autocracy," Project Syndicate, January 28, 2020.

4. Francis Fukuyama, "The Pandemic and Political Order: It Takes a State." *Foreign Affairs,* July–August 2020.

5. Graham Allison, "The Thucydides Trap," *Foreign Policy,* June 9, 2017.

6. Henry Kissinger, *World Order* (London: Penguin Books, 2014), 365.

7. Allison, "Thucydides Trap."

8. Jeffrey Anderson, G. John Ikenberry, and Thomas Risse, eds., *The End of the West? Crisis and Change in the Atlantic Order* (Cornell University Press, 2008).

9. CGTN News, "China to Be the Only Economy with Positive Growth in 2020, Says IMF Report," October 19, 2020.

10. Elizabeth Economy, *The Third Revolution: Xi Jinping and the New Chinese State* (Oxford University Press, 2018).

11. Richard Javad Heydarian, "Opportunism and Opportunity: Responding to Beijing's Push in the South China Sea," Asia Maritime Transparency Initiative, June 17, 2020.

12. George Kennan, "Containment: 40 Years Later—The Sources of Soviet Conduct," *Foreign Affairs,* March 1987, https://www.foreignaffairs.com/articles/russia-fsu/1987-03-01/containment-40-years-later-sources-soviet-conduct.

13. Yuan Li, "In China, Some Fear the End of 'Chimerica,'" *New York Times,* May 14, 2019.

14. Niall Ferguson and Xiang Xu, "Make Chimerica Great Again," Hoover Institution, May 3, 2018.

15. Reuters, "China's Xi warns 'Period of Turbulent Change' as External Risks Rise," August 24, 2020.

16. Gerald Segal, "East Asia and the 'Constrainment' of China," *International Security* 20 (1996): 107–35.

17. Segal.

18. Allison, "Thucydides Trap."

19. Tom Squitieri, "On Sea and in Air This Week, US Reminds China the South China Sea Is International and Open," Talk Media News, March 15, 2019.

20. On Trump's empowering of the Pentagon, also see Dexter Filkins, "James Mattis, A Warrior in Washington," *New Yorker*, May 22, 2017.

21. Michael Gordon, "Trump Shifting Authority Over Military Operations Back to Pentagon," *New York Times*, March 19, 2017.

22. Ankit Panda, "US Secretary of State Criticizes China's South China Sea Practices," *Diplomat*, March 14, 2019.

23. Caitlin Doornbos, "US Sends B-52 Bombers Over South China Sea for Second Time in a Week," *Stars & Stripes*, March 15, 2019.

24. Based on conversations with former senior Obama administration senior defense officials in Washington, 2017–18.

25. Based on conversations with senior Taiwanese officials, including Presidents Ma and Tsia, in August 2015 and June 2019. See also Bethany Allen-Ebrahimian, "Trump Comes Through for Taiwan with $1.3 Billion Arms Sale," *Foreign Policy*, June 29, 2017.

26. Jesse Johnson, "Pentagon Sends Ships Through Taiwan Strait for Third Time in Three Months." *Japan Times*, March 25, 2019.

27. Richard Javard Heydarian, "Duterte's Dance with China," *Foreign Affairs*, April 2017.

28. Pia Ranada, "South China Sea Covered by PH-US Mutual Defense Treaty— Pompeo," *Rappler*, March 1, 2019.

29. Ranada.

30. Rosie Perper, "The US and Philippines Are Reportedly Discussing Deploying a Rocket System in the South China Sea to Fend Off China," *Business Insider*, April 3, 2019.

31. US Department of Defense, *Indo-Pacific Strategy Report*, 2019.

32. Richard Javad Heydarian, "The True Significance of Pompeo's South China Sea Statement," Asia Maritime Transparency Initiative, August 4, 2020.

33. Heydarian.

34. Panda, "US Secretary of State."

35. Paternon Esmaquel II, "China Chopper Harasses PH Rubber Boat in Ayungin Shoal—Lawmaker," *Rappler*, May 30, 2018.

36. Josh Zumbrun and Siobhan Hughes, "To Counter China, US Looks to Invest Billions More Overseas," *Wall Street Journal*, August 31, 2018.

37. Reuters, "US Presses China to Halt Militarization of South China Sea, Drawing Rebuke from Beijing," CNBC News, November 10, 2018.

38. Janvic Mateo, "Sea Militia Attacks Could Trigger US Obligations under Defense Treaty," *Philippine Star Global*, June 16, 2019.

39. GMA News, "FYI with Richard Heydarian: Exclusive Interview with Defense Secretary Delfin Lorenzana," May 28, 2019.

40. GMA News; Bill Hayton, *The South China Sea: The Struggle for Power in Asia* (Yale University Press, 2014).

41. Virgil Lopez, "Duterte Considers Setting Aside Arbitral Ruling for Economic Gain," GMA News, September 11, 2019.

42. This is from exchanges with the author during the Halifax International Security Forum, November 17.

43. Philip Hejmans, "The US Fears This Huge Southeast Asian Resort May Become a Chinese Naval Base," Bloomberg, July 19, 2019.

44. Paul Krugman, "Supply Chains and Trade War (Very Wonkish)," *New York Times*, August 10, 2018.

45. Krugman.

46. Interview with the Malaysian prime minister; GMA News, "FYI with Richard Heydarian: Interview with Malaysian Prime Minister Mahathir Bin Mohamad," March 8, 2019.

47. Adam Segal, Cobus Van Staden, Elsa Kania, Samm Sacks, and Elliott Zaagman, "Is an Iron Curtain Falling Across Tech?" *Foreign Policy*, February 4, 2019.

48. Uri Friedman, "Donald Trump's Real Endgame with China," *Atlantic*, October 4, 2018.

49. Mike Pence, "Remarks by the Vice President at the 2019 Munich Security Conference in Munich, Germany," February 16, 2019.

50. Mike Pompeo, "Keynote Address at CERA Week," March 12, 2019.

51. Barbara Tuchman, *The Guns of August* (New York: Macmillan, 2009; orig. pub. 1962), 1199.

52. For a more detailed analysis of what "middle power" means as well as its contested definition, see, e.g., Willem Oosterveld and Bianca Torossian, *A Balancing Act: The Role of Middle Powers in Contemporary Diplomacy*, 2019, https://www.hcss.nl/pub/2018/strategic-monitor-2018-2019/a-balancing-act/; also see Richard Javad Heydarian, "The Post-American World: Middle Powers and the Coalition of Deterrence," in *The Indo-Pacific: Trump, China, and the New Struggle for Global Mastery* (Berlin: Springer, 2019).

53. Daniel Hurst, "Amid US Trade Tensions, Japan Formally Completes TPP-11 Entry," *Diplomat*, July 13, 2018.

54. Anton Hermansyah, "Indonesia Targets to Conclude RCEP Negotiations This Year," *Jakarta Post*, April 24, 2018.

55. Emil Kirchner, "EU–Japan Trade Deal Comes into Force to Create World's Biggest Trade Zone," *Conversation*, January 21, 2019.

56. John Garnaut, "How China Interferes in Australia," *Foreign Affairs*, March 9, 2018.

57. Michelle Jamrisko, "China No Match for Japan in Southeast Asia Infrastructure Race," Bloomberg, June 23, 2019.

58. Joanna Eva, "Japan and the EU Sign Infrastructure Deal to Rival China's Belt and Road," *European Views*, September 30, 2019.

59. This is from the Mission of Japan to ASEAN, 2016.

60. Garnaut, "How China Interferes."

61. Christopher Walker, "What Is 'Sharp Power'?" *Journal of Democracy*, July 2018.

62. Tom Westbrook, "Australia, ASEAN Agree to Start Regional Infrastructure Cooperation," Reuters, March 19, 2018.

63. Christopher Mudaliar, "Australia Outbids China to Fund Fiji Military Base," Lowy Institute, 2018.

64. Stephen Dziedzic, "Tonga Called on Pacific Islands to Band Together Against China—Then Had a Sudden Change of Heart," ABC News, August 20, 2018.

65. Matthew Dornan and Philippa Brant, "Chinese Assistance in the Pacific: Agency, Effectiveness and the Role of Pacific Island Governments," *Asia & The Pacific Policy Studies*, June 11, 2014.

66. Jonathan Barrett, "US Joins Australian Plan to Develop New Pacific Naval Base," Reuters, November 17, 2018.

67. Westbrook, "Australia, ASEAN Agree."

68. Harsh Pant, "The Future of India's Ties with ASEAN," *Diplomat*, January 26, 2018.

69. Army Technology, "India and Philippines to Sign BrahMos Cruise Missile Deal," November 13, 2020.

70. George Kennan, "The Sources of Soviet Conduct," *Foreign Affairs*, July 1947, https://www.foreignaffairs.com/articles/russian-federation/1947-07-01/sources-soviet-conduct.

71. Tanvi Madan, "The Rise, Fall and Rebirth of the 'Quad,'" *War on the Rocks*, November 16, 2017, https://warontherocks.com/2017/11/rise-fall-rebirth-quad/

72. Hoang Thi Ha, "ASEAN Outlook on the Indo-Pacific: Old Wine in New Bottle?" https://www.iseas.edu.sg/wp-content/uploads/pdfs/ISEAS_Perspective_2019_51.pdf.

73. "National Security Strategy of the United States of America," 2017, https://www.whitehouse.gov/wp-content/uploads/2017/12/NSS-Final-12-18-2017-0905.pdf.

74. "Indo-Pacific Strategy Report," US Department of Defense, 2019, https://media.defense.gov/2019/Jul/01/2002152311/-1/-1/1/DEPARTMENT-OF-DEFENSE-INDO-PACIFIC-STRATEGY-REPORT-2019.PDF.

75. Jonathan Stromseth, "Don't Make Us Choose: Southeast Asia in the Throes of US-China Rivalry," Brookings, October 2019, https://www.brookings.edu/research/dont-make-us-choose-southeast-asia-in-the-throes-of-us-china-rivalry/.

76. Agnes Anya, "East Asia to Hear About Indo-Pacific Idea," *Jakarta Post*, May 9, 2018, https://www.thejakartapost.com/news/2018/05/09/east-asia-hear-about-indo-pacific-idea.html; Nyshka Chandran, "As Pence kicks Off His Asia Tour, Other Countries Have Their Own Ideas for the 'Indo-Pacific,'" CNBC News, November 11, 2018, https://www.cnbc.com/2018/11/12/us-japan-and-indonesia-set-their-sights-on-the-indo-pacific-region.html.

77. "ASEAN Outlook on the Indo-Pacific," ASEAN, June 2019, https://asean.org/storage/2019/06/ASEAN-Outlook-on-the-Indo-Pacific_FINAL_22062019.pdf.

78. Kim Jaewon, "South Korea and ASEAN Vow to Resist Trump-Style Protectionism," *Nikkei Asian Review*, November 26, 2019, https://asia.nikkei.com/Economy/Trade-war/South-Korea-and-ASEAN-vow-to-resist-Trump-style-protectionism.

79. Richard Javad Heydarian, "ASEAN Needs to Move to Minilateralism," *East Asia Forum*, December 5, 2017.

80. Ralf Emmers, "ASEAN Minus X: Should This Formula Be Extended?" *RSIS*, October 24, 2017, https://www.rsis.edu.sg/rsis-publication/cms/co17199-asean-minus-x-should-this-formula-be-extended/#.XZ_2EFUzbIU.

81. "Voting System: Qualified Majority," European Council, https://www.consilium.europa.eu/en/council-eu/voting-system/qualified-majority/.

82. Emmers, "ASEAN Minus X."

83. Tashny Sukumaran, "Mahathir to Update Malaysia's Foreign Policy, Including on South China Sea and International Muslim Cooperation," *South China Sea Morning Post,* September 19, 2019, https://www.scmp.com/week-asia/politics/article/3027949/mahathir-update-malaysias-foreign-policy-including-south-china.

84. "Jokowi to Discuss S. China Sea Joint Patrols with Turnbull," *Today Online,* February 25, 2017, https://www.todayonline.com/world/asia/jokowi-discuss-s-china-sea-joint-patrols-turnbull.

85. Richard Javad Heydarian, "Could Europe's Reemergence in Asia Be a Win-Win This Time?" *National*, April 8, 2021.

86. Heydarian.

87. Graeme Dobell, "Australia as an ASEAN Community Partner," Australian Strategic Policy Institute, February 20, 2018, https://www.aspi.org.au/report/australia-asean-community-partner.

88. Heydarian, "Could Europe's Reemergence."

89. Richard Javad Heydarian, "In US–China Tussle over Southeast Asia, America Must Do More Than Speak Softly and Carry a Big Stick," *South China Morning Post*, August 3, 2021.

90. Richard Javad Heydarian, "Why the US-Led Response to China's Belt and Road Is a Cause for Celebration, Not Alarm," *South China Morning Post*, June 25, 2021.

Four

Europe and the World after COVID-19

HOW THE EU'S INTERNAL DYNAMICS WILL SHAPE ITS EXTERNAL RELATIONS

MATTHIAS MATTHIJS, *JOHNS HOPKINS UNIVERSITY, SCHOOL OF ADVANCED INTERNATIONAL STUDIES*

The COVID-19 global pandemic hit the European Union at a time when it was still reeling from a decade of crises. In March 2020, the EU had not yet fully recovered from its euro challenges or migration woes, had recently said good-bye to the United Kingdom as a member, and had continued to hesitate about how to cope with democratic backsliding among some of its newer members. But COVID-19 proved to be the catalyst for a German shift vis-à-vis European integration, in which Berlin embraced financial solidarity and the French notion of "EU sovereignty"—in trade and financial affairs, in health, and in the green and digital economy—that could be the beginning of a more coherent EU foreign policy. The fact that the United Kingdom can no longer act as a veto player, plus Democrat Joe Biden's victory in the United States, are proving to be key factors. That said, the EU's internal divisions (both North/South and East/West) remain significant and are likely to slow down progress along the way. In the future, the EU will continue its careful balancing act in dealing with Putin's Russia, with sanctions staying in place but the Nord Stream 2 pipeline going ahead. The EU is likely to take a firmer line toward Xi's China, despite the signing of the new landmark investment treaty, with closer scrutiny of its inward direct foreign investment. We could see closer relations between the EU and the United States in dealing with China but ongoing transatlantic tensions when it comes to EU–Russia relations.

Introduction: The Initial COVID-19 Response Was Marred by Hesitation and Internal Tensions

The COVID-19 pandemic caught the European Union off guard in early March 2020. The project of European integration had been badly bruised by the euro zone debt crisis, which exposed the differences in economic philosophy between Northern creditors and Southern debtors, and the migration crisis, which underscored the chasms between more progressive Western and more conservative Eastern member states.[1] The United Kingdom's vote in June 2016 to leave the EU ("Brexit") was a reminder that there was nothing irreversible about the integration process, while the growing autocratic tendencies of the governments in Hungary (since 2010) and Poland (since 2015) underlined that democracy and the rule of law could not be taken for granted.[2] On top of those internal crises, the EU had to find its way in a more complicated, multipolar world. It had to cope, across the Atlantic, with the openly hostile US administration, after the election of Donald Trump to the American presidency in November 2016; to its east, with Vladimir Putin's revanchist Russia, which had annexed Crimea and provided covert military support to Ukrainian rebel forces in the Donbass region; and with Chinese president Xi Jinping's aggressive courting of Eastern and Southeastern EU members and aspirant members through the Belt and Road Initiative.[3]

The pandemic also hit Europe's shores when its main political and economic institutions had just undergone important leadership transitions. Former Belgian prime minister Charles Michel took over from Donald Tusk as president of the European Council on December 1, 2019, while Ursula von der Leyen, the former German defense minister, took the helm of the European Commission from Jean-Claude Juncker that same day. Just a month earlier, former managing director of the International Monetary Fund Christine Lagarde had taken over as president of the European Central Bank (ECB) from the Italian Mario Draghi. All three leaders had barely been in office for a few months, and hence were largely untested in their new functions when they had to cope with the breakout of a major public health crisis and an unforeseen economic and financial shock. Further complicating things was that both public health and fiscal policies are national rather than EU competencies.

In an almost cruel twist of fate, in March 2020, the first EU member states to be badly hit by COVID-19 were Italy and Spain, the same two big states that had struggled the most during the sovereign debt crisis that had started a decade earlier. As the rest of Europe watched the local quarantine in the Northern Italian region of Lombardy turn into a nationwide lockdown, and the number of Italian infections and deadly casualties steadily rise, the initial response in most EU member states was to close their borders while issuing travel and export bans to places where the virus was spreading at an alarming rate. The EU was struggling to come up with a collective response, as von der Leyen pleaded with EU members—to no avail—not to close their borders.[4] National export bans of ventilators, masks, medicine, and personal protective equipment were eventually changed into EU export bans, which left those European countries in the Western Balkans, which were aspiring to one day join the EU, out in the cold. With no EU response, and Trump's US administration preoccupied by the rapid spread of the virus, Russian and Chinese humanitarian planes landed in Rome and Madrid with medical assistance. The Serbian president, visibly frustrated, even went as far as to say that "European solidarity does not exist. That was a fairy tale."[5] All this was happening before China had lifted its own lockdown in Wuhan on April 8 and was still fighting itself to overcome the crisis, making Chinese humanitarian help to Europe all the more remarkable.

By mid-April, the contours of the EU's coordinated response were emerging on the economic and strategic fronts. After Lagarde's initial mistakes—in which, as a lawyer by training, she had claimed that the ECB's role was *not* to close the spreads in yield between German and Italian bonds, sending financial markets into a tailspin—the ECB's Governing Council quickly responded with overwhelming monetary firepower.[6] On the fiscal front, the idea of a recovery fund to deal with the economic fallout from COVID-19 gained ground.[7] The public health response stayed with the national governments, but they agreed to coordinate on international travel and supply chains. Also, thanks to the coronavirus, the idea of the need for EU "sovereignty" would gain traction, and a more assertive trade and industrial policy was put on the negotiating table.[8]

The joint EU recovery fund came together rather quickly in the summer of 2020. This was partially due to the fact that the United Kingdom had left the bloc on January 31, 2020, and because EU leaders understood the urgency, were willing to compromise, and agreed to paper over their differences, be they along North/South or East/West lines. The EU's longest-serving national leader—German chancellor Angela Merkel, who was holding the rotating EU presidency for Germany starting July 1—proved crucial in using her political capital to bring the EU together. However, the EU's unity and sense of purpose would quickly be tested again later in the year, with Hungary and Poland ready to veto the EU recovery fund, along with the EU's 2021–27 Multiannual Financial Framework, over "rule of law" conditionality in November 2020. Also, about the same time, politicians in Germany and the Netherlands, with national elections in 2021 in mind, started to wonder for how long exactly the EU's fiscal rules could be suspended and how much more public debt could be piled on.

COVID-19 was a stark reminder for many Europeans that they were vulnerable in key sectors, that globalization might have gone too far in certain fields, and that they could no longer count on the power and resources of the United Kingdom as a member state or hope for the United States to come to the continent's rescue.[9] Even after Joe Biden's inauguration as US president, transatlantic relations would not go back to the status quo ante Trump, as Biden's unilateral withdrawal of US troops from Afghanistan underscored in the summer of 2021. The relatively benign world in which the EU made its most important integration steps—between the mid-1980s and mid-2000s—has changed dramatically in the past fifteen years. Relations with Russia will remain a difficult balancing act. Relations with China are likely to get tenser despite the signing of the landmark investment treaty right before the end of 2020.[10] As a consequence of COVID-19, the EU is likely to chart a more independent though not necessarily more coherent path in world affairs. As long as the unanimity rule holds in foreign policy decisions, it remains doubtful whether there will be real consequences in geopolitical terms in the short to medium terms. But the EU is serious about "strategic autonomy" in key sectors and will be more willing to use trade and market access for leverage in world affairs. While the EU has in theory always had those powers, the combination of four years of Donald Trump and the global pandemic have made it much more likely in practice for Brussels to actually do so.[11]

Responding to COVID-19: The EU Gets Its Act Together, but Doubts Remain

While the individual member states of the European Union kept complete control over the public health response to COVID-19—including serious curbs on individual freedoms through regional and national lockdowns—the ECB and EU finance ministers started acting resolutely starting in mid-March 2020. The initial missteps in communication with financial market participants were quickly rectified by Christine Lagarde herself, when the ECB's Governing Council lifted all self-imposed constraints on bond purchases by rolling out the bold, €1 trillion euro Pandemic Emergency Purchasing Program that immediately calmed down jittery financial markets.[12] That action alone eased borrowing constraints on Italy and other Southern European countries in one fell swoop. Given that the EU and national fiscal authorities were relatively slow to respond, the ECB acted once again as the "leader" of last resort, just as the Federal Reserve stabilized US and international markets in late March.

On April 10, the euro zone finance ministers agreed to a financial package worth roughly €540 billion to fight the pandemic, on top of the €37 billion Coronavirus Response Investment Initiative and Support Instrument set up by the European Commission a few weeks prior. That package had three additional elements. First, the euro group agreed to a €100 billion in loan guarantees for the European Commission to set up the instrument for temporary Support to Mitigate Unemployment Risks in an Emergency (known as SURE). Second, they agreed to an additional €200 billion in loan guarantees for the European Investment Bank in Luxembourg to set up the European Guarantee Fund. Third, they approved an extra €240 billion in pandemic crisis support through the European Stability Mechanism, also based in Luxembourg.[13]

The problem with the euro group's proposals was that all the financial support the EU was giving to individual member states was through loans and loan guarantees. Given that the ECB had just committed to buying unprecedented amounts of sovereign debt through its pandemic emergency purchasing program, there was absolutely no shortage of liquidity. However, there was little desire on the part of heavily indebted euro zone members that were badly hit by COVID-19—especially Italy and Spain—to go even deeper into sovereign debt. The calls to take the next step in completing the Economic and Monetary Union by introducing euro bonds (or "coronabonds") were getting louder, especially from France and Mediterranean member states. A major EU fiscal package in the form of grants was clearly needed, buttressed by the Northern members' creditworthiness and in solidarity with their suffering Southern counterparts.[14]

In May 2020, German chancellor Angela Merkel would let go of her long-standing opposition ("No Eurobonds as long as I live!" she had stated back in 2012) and make a U-turn on jointly issued EU bonds.[15] By doing so, Merkel's Germany broke ranks with fellow Northern euro zone travelers like the Netherlands, Finland, and Austria. On May 18, together with French president Emmanuel Macron, she put her shoulders under the "French-German Initiative for the European Recovery from the Coronavirus Crisis."[16] While most of the attention went to the second point of the proposal—the setting up of the ambitious Recovery Fund at the EU level worth €500 billion in grants, to be distributed by the European Commission and financed through jointly issued bonds—the other three points were potentially more important for the future strategic direction of the European Union. They included the joint Franco-German call for the

EU to develop strategic health sovereignty with a joint "health strategy," speeding up both green and digital transitions, and enhancing EU economic and industrial resilience by giving a new impulse to the single market.[17] This joint statement put Merkel's Germany quite a bit closer to Macron's France in the latter's vision for the EU's future. Indeed, Macron hailed the Franco-German initiative as a "profoundly unprecedented step."[18]

Just over a week later, the European Commission built on the Franco-German momentum by rolling out an EU stimulus plan of €750 billion, calling it "Next Generation EU," that would consist of €500 billion in grants and €250 billion in loans. The centerpiece of the Commission's plan was the €560 billion Recovery and Resilience Facility to address the economic fallout from the pandemic, consisting of €310 billion in grants and €250 billion in loans. Another €50 billion was proposed for the REACT-EU cohesion fund, in order to guarantee a green and digital recovery. The other €140 billion was earmarked to pad key existing programs in the EU budget, including for research, rural development, a just transition, solvency support, strategic investment, health, and humanitarian aid.[19] This hugely ambitious package was hailed by some observers as a potential "Hamiltonian moment" for the European Union, in which the seeds of a future fiscal union were being planted.[20] While undoubtedly significant, Merkel herself was quick to point out that this was a "one off" gesture of solidarity and should not be interpreted as the beginning of the EU taking on its member states' national debts.

To many EU observers' surprise, the European Council's meeting of heads of state or government in mid-July 2020 agreed to a compromise proposal that stuck to the substantial headline figure of €750 billion. After significant pressure from the so-called Frugal Five member states—Austria, Denmark, Finland, the Netherlands, and Sweden—the total amount in grants was cut back from €500 billion to €390 billion, while the total amount of loans was raised from €250 billion to €360 billion. The Frugal Five also negotiated substantial budget rebates for themselves as part of the final package. Clearly, Next Generation EU did not completely lay to rest the differences in economic philosophy between North and South. Another divide in the EU, between East and West—even though it was really Poland and Hungary versus the other twenty-five member states—was papered over with the vague principle that the funds would be tied to a member state's adherence to the rule of law.[21]

However, the summer's euphoria would be short-lived. Just as the number of COVID-19 cases started to go up all over Europe as the weather was getting colder in October 2020, and as new national lockdowns followed, old divisions began to creep back into the arduous negotiations between the European

Commission, European Parliament, and European Council on the implementation details of the overall budgetary package. While the Commission and Parliament could agree on a strict rule-of-law mechanism to go along with the generous funds of Next Generation EU, this would be vetoed by Hungary and Poland. By December, this put in doubt the rapid implementation of the fund. While the Southern member states were desperate for corona cash, the Northern member states, led by the Frugal Five, were not willing to water down their commitments to democratic principles for all EU member states. This put Merkel, who still held the rotating EU presidency, in the tough spot trying to find a compromise.[22] Eventually, she would succeed.

But 2021 and 2022 had dark clouds on the horizon for European fiscal policy, as both German and Dutch politicians started to question for how long the euro zone could maintain its loose fiscal policy. The fact that both the Netherlands (in March) and Germany (in September) held inconclusive general elections in 2021 with long coalition negotiations between multiple parties made things even more complicated. In effect, while the pandemic created the conditions for the European Union to take a big step forward in fiscal solidarity and integration by establishing Next Generation EU, all was not well in Brussels.

The economic differences between North and South—temporarily bridged by Germany's U-turn in accepting a one-off issuing of joint debt by the European Commission—did not go away and will come back to haunt Europe in the years to come. However, the steady democratic backsliding in Hungary (since 2010) and Poland (since 2015) will prove to be the most difficult crisis for the EU to deal with, given that it goes to the heart of the EU as a union of values. Furthermore, while member states can choose to leave the EU, there is no actual mechanism to expel a member state. Both Hungary and Poland are willing to use their vetoes to halt major leaps forward in integration and will not hesitate to do so on important foreign policy issues if they can use them as leverage.[23]

The Impact of Brexit on the EU's Global Role

One of the consequences of the United Kingdom leaving the European Union on January 31, 2020, is that Next Generation EU—the EU's ambitious fiscal instrument to deal with the economic fallout from COVID-19—would probably never have come together as fast (or at all) if the United Kingdom had still been a formal member of the EU in that turbulent coronavirus spring of 2020. The emphatic victory of Boris Johnson's Conservative Party during the UK general elections of December 2019 settled the Brexit question once and for all in Westminster and Whitehall. Starting in February 2020, the United

Kingdom was no longer a member of the political institutions of the EU, and as of January 2021, it left the EU's single market and customs union, with a new (and relatively thin) free trade and cooperation agreement in place.

But while the United Kingdom was steadfastly the EU's most reluctant member state between 1973 and 2020, with many opt-outs, including from the euro and the Schengen free passport zone, its exit from the EU was undoubtedly a serious blow to the prestige of the European project.[24] Brexit put into doubt the irreversibility of EU integration, and though unlikely in the near future, it creates a precedent for other member states to leave in the more distant future. While it is true that future steps toward integration may be easier without the potential of a British veto, most of the EU's problems have actually very little to do with UK intransigence, and the EU's internal fault lines—whether they are North versus South, West versus East, large versus small, or intergovernmental versus supranational—will endure and are usually the real causes of the EU's strategic inaction or passivity.

When it concerns the EU's ambitious plans to play a more active role in world affairs, the loss of the United Kingdom will be felt for a long time to come. With the UK gone, the EU has lost its largest military power, one of its two nuclear member states, one of its two veto-wielding Permanent Five members of the UN Security Council in New York, a member of the Group of Seven, its second-biggest economy, some of its most prestigious universities and most important cultural institutions, and its only truly global financial center.[25] The UK is one of the few countries in the world that have truly "global" reach, and it is also the birthplace of the English language and culture, and continues to possess vast reserves of soft power around the world. Anglo-French defense and security cooperation has always been at the heart of the EU's common defense strategy, along with NATO membership, just as the Franco-German engine was the driving force behind economic and monetary union.

In the short to medium terms, therefore, the United Kingdom's exit seriously limits what the European Union can collectively achieve in international affairs. While the exact framework of the future post-Brexit relationship between the UK and the EU, as well as the UK's relationship with the United States, remain to be determined at the time of writing, and will undoubtedly evolve, it is clear that while there will be cooperation on foreign and security affairs between Brussels and London, there will be much less coordination than before, and there will be more times when the UK and EU will be on the opposite sides of the issue at hand. While the UK is closer to the EU when it comes to dealing with climate change, terrorism, and the peace process in the Middle East, it does not always look eye to eye with Germany or France on how to handle Putin's Russia or Xi's China, and there may be divergence on how to manage transatlantic relations as well, no matter which political party—Democratic or Republican—holds the presidency in the White House.

The rest of the world will also need to adjust to a European Union that no longer has the United Kingdom as a member state. From an economic point of view, this will mean that the UK can no longer be treated as a gateway or first entry point into the EU's single market and customs union. Inevitably, this will divert foreign direct investment and international trade away from the UK and toward Ireland, the Netherlands, Germany, and other business-friendly EU destinations. From a political point of view, it also has the consequence that the "special relationship" between the United States and the UK will no longer serve as a bridge to the rest of Europe, if it ever did. It will put Germany more securely in the position of Washington's privileged and preferred European partner, if it had not been for a while already. But it also means other powers—including China, Russia, and India—will look to Paris and Berlin to bolster their political ties with the EU, especially if Brussels proves to be serious about building up its "strategic autonomy."

The EU as a Geopolitical Actor Post-COVID: "Open Strategic Autonomy" in Practice

The COVID-19 pandemic proved to be a catalyst for the European Union to focus on its own vulnerabilities and strengths and how to address and bolster them. After the election of Donald Trump to the White House in November 2016, it had become painfully obvious to many Europeans that they could no longer rely on the United States for their own security and protection. This was given additional urgency every time Trump called into question the future of NATO.[26] The 2020 buzzwords in Brussels and other EU capitals that excited think tankers and tried to give a common purpose to the EU in a more unpredictable multipolar world were "EU sovereignty" and "strategic autonomy." The EU Commission prefers the term "open strategic autonomy" as it tries to find a balance between a Europe that is open for international commerce and ideas but that also protects its own businesses from unfair competition and global threats like pandemics, cyberattacks, and environmental disasters.[27]

Josep Borrell, the EU's high representative for foreign affairs and security policy, started using the term "open strategic autonomy" in late June 2020 as a way of framing the European Union's choices in foreign affairs. For Borrell, the "open" modifier signaled the EU's belief in the value of cooperation among countries and competition among firms in producing progress and prosperity.

Borrell sees the "strategic" part of the term as a key element in defining the EU's unsentimental understanding of the range of policies and relationships necessary to shape the global economic environment in its favor.[28] The EU Commission's June 2020 paper on "Open Strategic Autonomy" called for strengthening the EU's capacity to assert its own interests while working with allies around the world. For Sabine Weyand, the director-general for trade at the European Commission, open strategic autonomy will become a reality after a fundamental review of the EU's trade policy in light of the disruptions to international supply chains due to COVID-19, the loss of the EU's manufacturing prowess, the changing orientation of EU external trade vis-à-vis East Asia, and the United States–China trade war that was started in earnest by the Trump administration in 2018. For Weyand, the transatlantic relationship should remain the crux of the world economy's global value chains and the World Trade Organization should remain the centerpiece of international trade, even though she also admits that its dispute settlement system needs fundamental reform.[29]

Charles Michel, the president of the European Council of Heads of State or Government, in a major speech at the Brussels Economic Forum in September 2020, also put his shoulders under the idea of European strategic autonomy, boldly stating that these were "not just words" and that the "strategic independence of Europe is our new common project for this century."[30] This is actually a significant break from the views of EU founding fathers like Jean Monnet, Robert Schuman, and Konrad Adenauer, who envisioned Western Europe strategically aligned with the United States for the foreseeable future. So what does this mean in practice for the European Union and the post-COVID-19 world? Let me focus on key relationships for the EU with three major global powers: Joe Biden's United States, Vladimir Putin's Russia, and Xi Jinping's China.

First, European–American relations have substantially improved since Joe Biden took office as forty-sixth president of the United States. Not only is Biden a committed "Atlanticist' who believes in NATO as the bedrock of Western security; he is also committed to ending the trade tensions that had developed during the Trump administration with the EU by lifting a whole series of punitive tariffs. Unlike Trump, Biden also looks favorably on the project of European integration and probably welcomes more EU strategic autonomy, assuming it will be largely in line with US interests, especially if the EU takes on more of the burden of defending itself and its own near abroad. The United States and the EU worked closely together on ending the COVID-19 pandemic, and have been much more in tune when it comes to fighting climate change and terrorism and renewing their joint commitment to democratic norms and human rights. Closer transatlantic coordination on how to jointly deal with rising China is also on the cards.

However, transatlantic relations have not returned to the status quo ante. Tensions remain over the relatively low levels of defense spending in the EU and how much money different EU member states are contributing to their collective security. Differences remain on how to regulate and tax big tech companies and data privacy. The EU and United States also do not see eye to eye on how to deal with Putin's revanchist Russia. While Germany especially continues to believe in positive engagement with Russia through trade and investment and joint energy projects, the United States is keen to have the EU take a firm line with Moscow, keep sanctions in place, and avoid appeasement.

Second, EU relations with Russia will continue to be complicated as long as the military conflict in Eastern Ukraine is frozen and Crimea remains annexed to Russian territory. Russia's active involvement in cyber warfare and election manipulation in many EU member states and occasional poisoning of Russian opposition figures on EU soil will convince a majority of EU member states to keep its sanctions, which were initiated in 2014, firmly in place. The fact that the UK left the EU, however, is taking one staunch opponent of Putin's Russia out of the game, and it has been well documented that not all EU countries—including Hungary, Italy, and Greece—are as hostile to Russian interests as, for example, are the Netherlands or Scandinavian countries.

Germany especially will continue its careful balancing act of keeping sanctions in place but push ahead with the completion of the Nord Stream 2 pipeline, which bypasses the Baltic states and Poland to bring Russian natural gas directly into Germany via the Baltic Sea. It is worth noting that the EU itself is divided on this issue, with the Baltic states and Poland firmly against the project. Opposition to Nord Stream 2 is shared broadly in the United States, which is eager to boost its exports of liquefied natural gas to the EU. While the issue of how to deal with Putin's Russia is likely to cause further tensions between Washington and Berlin, it is also clear that the Biden administration is keen to restore close ties with Berlin and is willing to let Nord Stream 2 go ahead. But the EU's quest for strategic autonomy will be aimed less at containing Russian aggression and more at trying to deal with the challenge of the increasingly assertive rising power in the East.

Third, relations between the European Union and China have become more antagonistic and tense since COVID-19. While the EU traditionally has had a more benign, even sympathetic, view of China's rise, seeing it as a great civilization finally taking its rightful place again in the world, the last five to ten years have been a rude wake-up call for many European capitals. Clearly, from the EU's point of view, China has been acting more like an aspiring global hegemon and "Middle Kingdom" for the world rather than a nation content to be a regional power. Not only is there an increased sense of vulnerability to globalization because of the pandemic, there is also a heightened awareness in many EU member states that they are almost entirely dependent for certain necessary goods—be they medical supplies or services of a sensitive national security nature—on Chinese imports.

China has also been very active on the foreign direct investment front in the European Union and is likely to face much more scrutiny in considering the security implications of those investments. The case of the role of 5G in future data transmission and the Chinese conglomerate Huawei as a key provider of those services underscores the EU's renewed sensitivity to inward Chinese investment. While the EU and Russia complement each other in trade relations, the EU and China compete more directly with one another. Strategic autonomy is likely to see the EU cooperate much more closely with the United States in meeting the competitive challenges posed by more confident China, even though differences in approach will remain. Washington and Brussels are likely to find common ground on climate change and human rights when it comes to confronting Beijing. Also, China's active involvement through the 17+1 Process and the Belt and Road Initiative with Central and Southern European countries and the Balkans, including many EU member states, is worrying Brussels, because EU officials interpret the forum as an effort by Beijing to sow division in Europe.[31]

Though the post-COVID world is eventually likely to see the EU forge a more coherent foreign policy and enjoy better relations with the United States, complicated by its reluctant engagement with Russia and bolstered by its much tenser relationship with China, the EU will continue to be bogged down by its internal disagreements. While the EU can flex its muscles as an economic and trading power, when it comes to foreign policy, it still relies on unanimity among its member states. Even if France and Germany manage to coordinate their positions in international affairs, they still need buy-in from other EU member states as diverse as Poland and Hungary, the Netherlands and Sweden, and Portugal and Greece. If these existing tensions cannot be overcome, the EU's strategic autonomy will continue to be severely handicapped.

Conclusion

The COVID-19 pandemic brought the European Union closer together after a decade of crises. The loss of the United Kingdom was compensated for by the

German U-turn on issuing joint "corona" bonds and making the first steps toward fiscal solidarity and increased EU sovereignty in the areas of health, a greener economy, the digital transformation, and industrial policy. While "open strategic autonomy" remains a vague and somewhat confusing concept, France and Germany (and most of the other EU member states) are serious about the Old Continent's strategic independence in today's world, where the international liberal order, along with US leadership of this order, can no longer be taken for granted. The EU's somewhat naive commitment since 1989 to free trade and an enthusiastic embrace of global interdependence has been replaced by a more realistic view that certain types of economic protectionism are necessary to neuter certain vulnerabilities and make the EU's strategic autonomy a reality. But it is still too early to tell whether EU sovereignty will make the EU a more powerful actor on issues of hard military and economic power.

The European project over the past seventy years has taken big steps in regional integration at those times when national elites could coalesce on a jointly shared vision. The organizing principle of the early postwar European Economic Community was "embedded" liberalism—combining increased economic openness with strong welfare states and domestic discretion over economic policy—but it ran into trouble in the 1970s as stagflation and "eurosclerosis" haunted Europe's capitals. The project was relaunched in the 1980s and 1990s by embracing the "neoliberal" organizing principle, including the creation of the European single market and single currency, the euro, managed by an independent central bank focused almost exclusively on price stability and strict fiscal rules. But the new European "Union," as it was rebranded in Maastricht in 1992, would run into trouble in the 2010s, with multiple crises calling its very existence into question. Since Brexit, and triggered by the COVID-19 pandemic, EU elites have been trying to come up with a new organizing principle, focused on EU sovereignty or open strategic autonomy. Whether this can prove as durable or successful as the two previous principles, however, remains to be seen.

Notes

1. For North/South divisions in the euro crisis, see Matthias Matthijs and Kathleen McNamara, "The 'Euro Crisis' Theory Effect: Northern Saints, Southern Sinners, and the Demise of the Eurobond," *Journal of European Integration* 37, no. 2 (2015): 229–45; for East/West divisions in the migration crisis, see Ivan Krastev and Stephen Holmes, *The Light That Failed: Why the West Is Losing the Fight for Democracy* (New York: Pegasus, 2019).

2. See Matthias Matthijs, "Europe After Brexit: A Less Perfect Union," *Foreign Affairs* 96, no. 1 (2017): 85–95.

3. On China–EU relations, see Yixiang Xu, "From 16+1 to 17+1: The EU's Challenge from the Rebranded China-CEEC Initiative," *AICGS Economics*, 2019, https://www.aicgs.org/2019/04/from-161-to-171-the-eus-challenge-from-the-rebranded-china-ceec-initiative/.

4. For an overview, see David Herszenhorn and Sarah Wheaton, "How Europe Failed the Coronavirus Test," *Politico*, April 7, 2020, https://www.politico.eu/article/coronavirus-europe-failed-the-test/.

5. Vuk Vuksanovic, "China Has Its Eyes on Serbia," *Foreign Policy*, April 8, 2020, https://foreignpolicy.com/2020/04/08/china-serbia-aleksander-vucic-xi-jinping-coronavirus/.

6. Martin Arnold, "Christine Lagarde Apologizes for Botched Communication of ECB Strategy," *Financial Times*, March 15, 2020, https://www.ft.com/content/ce39716e-66c0-11ea-a3c9-1fe6fedcca75.

7. Zsolt Darvas, "The EU's Recovery Fund Proposals: Crisis Relief with Massive Redistribution," *Bruegel*, June 17, 2020, https://www.bruegel.org/2020/06/the-eus-recovery-fund-proposals-crisis-relief-with-massive-redistribution/.

8. Mark Leonard and Jeremy Shapiro, "Strategic Sovereignty: How Europe Can Regain the Capacity to Act," *ECFR Policy Brief*, June 25, 2020, https://ecfr.eu/wp-content/uploads/1_Empowering_EU_member_states_with_strategic_sovereignty.pdf.

9. Matthias Matthijs, "The Right Way to Fix the EU: Put Politics before Economics," *Foreign Affairs* 99, no. 3 (2020): 160–70.

10. Jim Brunsden, Mehreen Kahn, and Michael Peel, "EU and China Agree New Investment Treaty," *Financial Times*, December 30, 2020, https://www.ft.com/content/6a429460-4bfb-42d4-9191-73ba97dde130.

11. Henry Farrell and Abraham Newman, "Weaponized Interdependence: How Global Economic Networks Shape State Coercion," *International Security* 44, no. 1 (2019): 42–79.

12. European Central Bank, "ECB Announces 750 Billion Euro Pandemic Emergency Purchase Programme (PEPP)," press release, March 18, 2020, https://www.ecb.europa.eu/press/pr/date/2020/html/ecb.pr200318_1~3949d6f266.en.html,

13. Viktoria Dendrinou, Nikos Chrysoloras, and Milda Seputyte, "EU Finance Chiefs Dodge Coronabonds in $590 Billion Rescue," *Bloomberg Economics*, April 10, 2020, https://www.bloomberg.com/news/articles/2020-04-10/eu-finance-chiefs-dodge-coronabonds-in-590-billion-rescue-deal.

14. Kathleen McNamara and Matthias Matthijs, "Europe's Leaders Meet This Week to Confront the Coronavirus," Monkey Cage, *Washington Post*, April 21, 2020, https://www.washingtonpost.com/politics/2020/04/21/europes-leaders-meet-this-week-confront-coronavirus/.

15. "Keine Eurobonds solange ich lebe"—see the video footage at https://www.youtube.com/watch?v=p2s0bGq-bTI.

16. German Federal Government, "*Pressemitteilung*: A French–German Initiative for the European Recovery from the Coronavirus Crisis," May 18, 2020, https://www.bundesregierung.de/breg-en/news/dt-franz-initiative-1753890.

17. German Federal Government.

18. Mark Copelovitch, "No, This Isn't Europe's 'Hamiltonian Moment,'" *Monkey Cage*, *Washington Post*. May 27, 2020, https://www.washingtonpost.com/politics/2020/05/28/no-this-isnt-europes-hamiltonian-moment/.

19. European Commission, "Recovery Plan for Europe," May 27, 2020, https://ec.europa.eu/info/strategy/recovery-plan-europe_en#:~:text=On%2027%20May%202020%2C%20in,EU%20budget%20for%202021%2D2027.

20. Not everyone agreed, of course. For a great discussion of this moment in EU history, see Copelovitch, "No."

21. For details, see European Council, "European Council Conclusions, 17–21 July 2020," https://www.consilium.europa.eu/media/45109/210720-euco-final-conclusions-en.pdf.

22. R. Daniel Kelemen, "Time to Call Hungary and Poland's Bluff," *Politico*, xxxxbluff/.

23. R. Daniel Kelemen, "The European Union's Autocratic Equilibrium," *Journal of European Public Policy* 27, no. 3 (2020): 481–99, https://www.tandfonline.com/doi/abs/10.1080/13501763.2020.1712455?journalCode=rjpp20.

24. Matthias Matthijs, "Europe After Brexit: A Less Perfect Union," *Foreign Affairs* 96, no. 1 (2017): 85–95.

25. Matthijs, 85.

26. See, e.g., Eileen Sullivan, "Trump Questions the Core of NATO: Mutual Defense, Including Montenegro," *New York Times*, July 18, 2018, https://www.nytimes.com/2018/07/18/world/europe/trump-nato-self-defense-montenegro.html.

27. Phil Hogan, "Opening Statement at CETA Hearing," speech to the Dutch Senate, May 12, 2020, https://ec.europa.eu/info/news/opening-statement-ceta-hearing-2020-may-12_en.

28. See Peter Rashish, "EU Strategic Autonomy: Opening Up?" American Institute for Contemporary German Studies, July 7, 2020, https://www.aicgs.org/2020/07/eu-strategic-autonomy-opening-up/.

29. Sabine Weyand, "EU Open Strategic Autonomy and the Transatlantic Trade Relationship," paper for Delegation of the European Union to the United States, September 17, 2020, https://eeas.europa.eu/delegations/united-states-america/85321/eu-open-strategic-autonomy-and-transatlantic-trade-relationship_en.

30. Charles Michel, "Recovery Plan: Powering Europe's Strategic Economy," speech delivered at Brussels Economic Forum, August 9, 2020, https://www.consilium.europa.eu/en/press/press-releases/2020/09/08/recovery-plan-powering-europe-s-strategic-autonomy-speech-by-president-charles-michel-at-the-brussels-economic-forum/.

31. On the 17 + 1 Process, see Xu, "From 16+1 to 17+1."

Five

The Transformation of Eurasia in the Post-COVID World
THE END OF THE SINO-CENTRIC CONTINENT?

JACOPO MARIA PEPE, *GERMAN INSTITUTE FOR INTERNATIONAL AND SECURITY AFFAIRS*

Long before the COVID-19 pandemic's outbreak, geoeconomic and technological factors proved conducive to China's rise as the driving force beyond the reconfiguration and integration of the Eurasian continent. At the transcontinental level, with supply and value chains moving from Europe (EU enlargement) and China (Go West strategy) respectively eastward and westward, transcontinental production networks have emerged, strengthening the EU–China economic relationship and paving the way for China's Belt and Road Initiative (BRI). Meanwhile, at the transregional level, China has been keen to diversify its final markets beyond the West and its energy supply beyond the Middle East. By doing so, it has forged an economic and political axis with Moscow, which for its part has increasingly estranged itself from the West and Europe. This chapter analyzes how the COVID-19 pandemic will presumably alter this equation and affect political and economic relations among the three biggest Eurasian players: the European Union, Russia, and China. The chapter asks whether COVID-19 will eventually lead to a less Sino-centric Eurasian continent, opening up space for maneuvering for the EU, Russia, and other powers in both Asia and Europe beyond and besides China. Accordingly, the chapter is structured in two sections. The first section sketches the long-term trends and drivers of the Eurasia's transformation and specifically the evolution of the EU–Russia–China relationship before the COVID-19 pandemic. The second section discusses the impact of COVID-19 on this triangular relationship and on postpandemic Eurasia. The conclusion briefly sums up the results and offers an outlook on the evolution of the EU–Russia–China triangular relationship.

Before the COVID Pandemic: Long-Term Trends and Drivers of Eurasia's Transformation

The COVID-19 pandemic represents a major disruptive event set to further alter the configuration of Eurasian geopolitical and geoeconomic relations as they have been evolving in the past fifteen years.[1] It is not, however, an epochal game changer. In fact, the COVID pandemic has much more proved to be a transforming accelerator of trends already unfolding both globally and continentally long before its outbreak: *a fragmentation of the global liberal economic and political order, a regionalization and continentalization of value and supply chains, a geopoliticization of trade,* and *a shift from a Western-centered transatlantic order to a more Sino-centered Eurasian-Pacific system, which, however, lacks a common security architecture and economic governance.*

In fact, these trends have all started unfolding since the 2008 financial and economic crisis, a turning point in reconfiguring Eurasia as a more Asia- and Sino-centered continent. Doubtless, the eastward shift in the world's center of economic gravity (from the "great divergence" to the "great convergence"[2]) predates even the 2008 global financial and economic crisis and has roots deep in major historical junctures like the economic boom of Japan and East Asia, the opening up of China, the democratization of India, and the end of the Soviet Union. Since the 1980s, the industrial and economic rise of Asia allowed for the slow emergence of a large middle class, which indeed did contribute to increased demand for exports from the United States and Europe in the 1990s and 2000s. Doubtless, its final benefits mostly accrued to shareholders and the global elite, not the middle and working classes of Western societies, whose relative decline, in addition to automation and globalization, had been precipitated by the neoliberal policies of Thatcher and Reagan of the early 1980s. However, these policies themselves represented—among others—also a response to the industrial-managerial and commercial competition coming from Asia when the second wave of globalization. This intracapitalist competition started with Japan in the late 1970s and 1980s and continued with China in the late 1990s and 2000s. Against this backdrop, the 2008 crisis somehow ratified both the rise of China as an alternative, dynamic economic-industrial model and of Asia's middle class as the driving engine of global demand. By doing so, however, the crisis has also shown that the globalization has eventually deepened the divide both inside Western societies and between

Asia's and Western middle classes rather than contributing to the convergence toward a global middle class with shared interests and perceptions, cultures, and values.

As a result, not only has Western-centered globalization slowed down but the liberal political order underpinning it has simultaneously shown the first signs of external contestation and internal fragmentation, favoring the emergence of alternative world order narratives. Against this backdrop, under the impulse of China's rapid recovery, particularly the Eurasian "super-continent" stretching from Central and Eastern Europe, Russia and Central Asia to Northeast Asia, and from the Mediterranean and the Arab Sea across the Indian Ocean to Indian and Southeast Asia, has slowly emerged as an economically and infrastructurally more interconnected and integrated space.[3] Across the continent, the functional distinction in subregions increasingly started to vanish. Geopolitically, however, the continent has also turned into a more diversified and competitive playing field, where a multitude of middle and great powers, being emerging or resurging, coexist and interconnect but lack shared "rules of the game."

At the very core of this double- and contradictory transformation—economic and infrastructural interconnectedness and geopolitical fragmentation—has been, and still is, the complex, triangular relationship between China, the European Union, and Russia. In the fifteen years before the pandemic's outbreak, different, chronologically nonsynchronized but deeply interrelated geoeconomic and technological factors shaped this relationship. They all contributed to China's emergence as the major—though not sole—driver of the Eurasian transformation and the cornerstone of the triangular relationship with the EU and Russia.

Geoeconomically, these factors are, first, the boom in EU–China trade and the related "continentalization" of Sino-European/German supply and value chains across Eurasia;[4] second, China's deepening bidirectional trade and energy ties with Eurasian (and Middle Eastern) producers beyond and besides Europe;[5] third, the emergence of a stronger, though asymmetric, Russian–Chinese relationship and of joint Russian–Chinese integration arrangements (the BRI and the Eurasian Economic Union); and fourth, the growing estrangement in the EU–Russia political and economic relationship, culminating in bilateral sanctions as consequence of the 2014 Ukraine crisis and in a drop in trade.

First, the globalization of trade, value, and supply chains during the first decade of the 2000s led to the boom in EU–China trade (roughly €560 billion in 2019), creating stronger interdependencies and enhancing political and diplomatic ties between the major powerhouses at the two edges of the

Eurasian megacontinent.[6] However, as opposed to common assumptions, the spread of elongated global value chains did not only mean a spatial dilution of production networks from domestic or regional to global networks.[7] In the case of the China–EU, the spread of global value chains has first and foremost triggered a shift in the localization of production activities across the continent, thus altering the geography of production. In fact, since 2004, internal developments in both the European Union (the EU's eastern enlargement) and China (the Go West strategy and the Central and Western Development Strategy) have almost simultaneously brought regional production networks at the two edges of the continent closer to each other across the Eurasian space, while increasing the level of economic activity concentration in both spaces.[8] The "continentalization" of trade, supply, and value chains has hence paved the way for establishing overland logistic services between inland production hubs in China (Chongqing, Chengdu, and Yiwu) and Europe (Southern Germany and Central and Eastern Europe) able to complement the booming seaborne trade, further deepening economic, political, and financial ties between China on the one side and—particularly—Germany and Central and Eastern Europe on the other.

The second major geoeconomics factor contributing to China's emergence at the center of Eurasian transformation has been Beijing's unprecedented deepening of bidirectional trade and energy ties at the intraregional and transregional levels, with Eurasian (and Middle Eastern) energy producers and markets.[9] As figure 5-1 shows, China's exports to broader, developing Eurasia, here defined as a supercontinent encompassing both the Commonwealth of Independent States member countries, the Middle East and developing Asia but excluding the EU and advanced Asian economies, have increased both in relative terms (twentyfold between 2000 and 2017) and absolute value (from less than $25 billion in 2000 to almost $523 billion in 2017), compared with a sevenfold to eightfold increase in exports to the United States and the EU. As figure 5-2 shows, in comparison with China's exports to Eurasia, the EU's exports to the broader region, which also includes exports to China, have experienced only a three-and-a-half-fold increase since 2000 (from $145 billion in 2000 to $660 billion in 2017). If considering the data net of export to China, the increase is only threefold.[10]

Otherwise, as figure 5-3 shows, the EU's increase in export to Eurasia and China (eightfold, from $20 billion in 2000 to over $200 billion in 2017) is significantly higher than the increase in EU's exports to the United States (twofold, from $175 billion in 2000 to $360 billion in 2017). From a European perspective, these data testify to a double shift: first, the increasing importance of China and

Figure 5-1. China's Exports to Eurasia (Aggregated), the United States, and the European Union, 2000–2017 (millions of dollars)

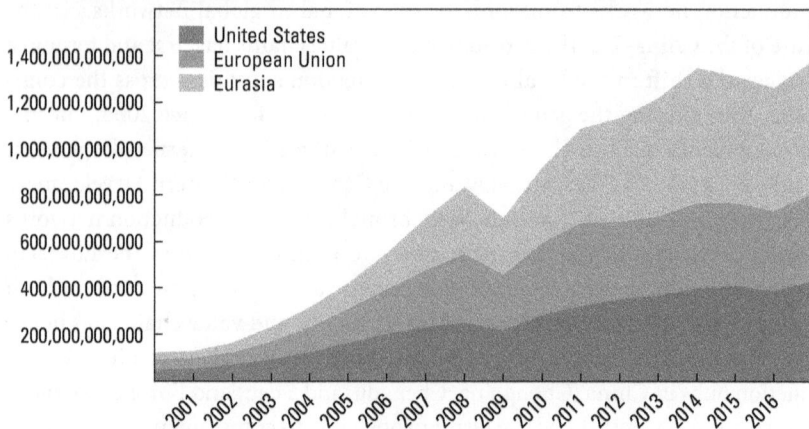

Sources: Direction of Trade Statistics, International Monetary Fund; author's calculations.

Figure 5-2. The European Union's and China's Exports to Eurasia, 2000–2017 (millions of dollars)

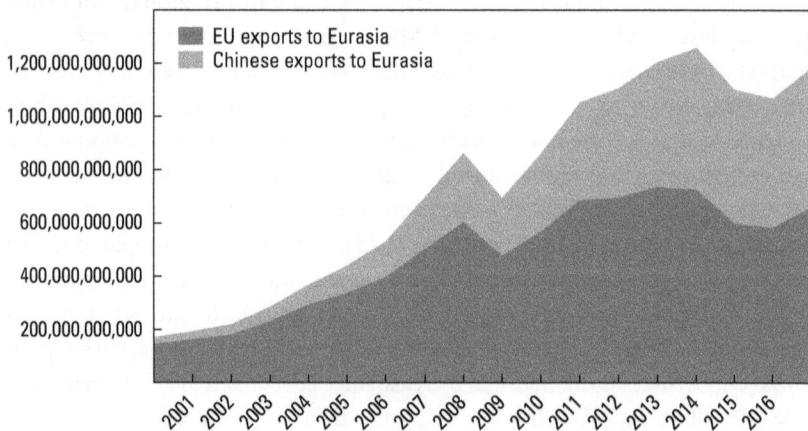

Sources: Direction of Trade Statistics, International Monetary Fund; author's calculations.

Figure 5-3. The European Union's Exports to Eurasia (Aggregated), the United States, and China, 2000–2017 (millions of dollars)

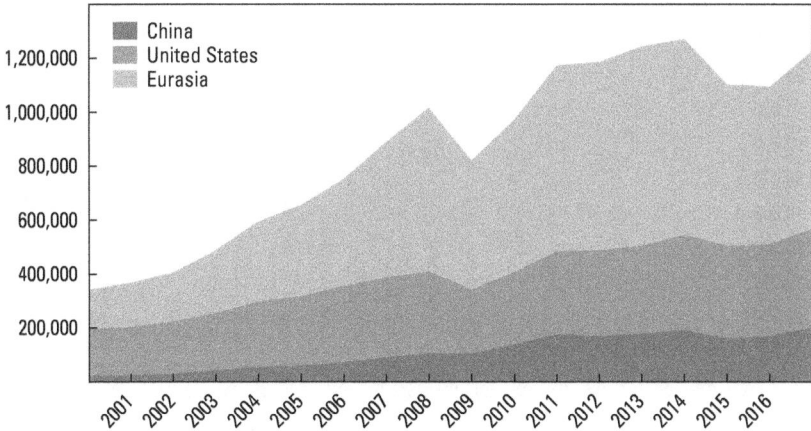

Sources: Direction of Trade Statistics, International Monetary Fund; author's calculations.

broader developing Eurasia for Europe's exports, with a growing centrality of trans-Eurasian as compared with the traditional transatlantic trade (still higher, but growing at a much slower pace); and second, a gradual loss of market share experienced by Europeans in Eurasia's developing markets.

Because of the increased economic ties between China and Eurasia, the Russian–Chinese relationship has emerged as the third geoeconomic factor: the relation has evolved from an economic one (trade between the two countries had reached over $100 billion in 2019, from less than $10 billion in 2000) to a more coherent, geostrategic, and geoeconomic axis (figure 5-4). A stable relationship with Russia secures China's continental periphery, legitimizes Beijing's actions, and rises globally.

The fourth major geoeconomic factor contributing to shifting the geoeconomic balance of the European–Chinese–Russian triangular relationship in Beijing's favor in the years before COVID has been the deterioration in the EU–Russia relationship. While the EU–China and Russia–China relationships unfolded, the relationships between Russia and the EU, on the contrary, gradually lost traction. While remaining strong trade and energy partners, neither Brussels nor Moscow gave a major impetus to renew their partnership. On the contrary, some of the factors facilitating the emergence of transcontinental geoeconomic ties between China and the EU—like the EU's and NATO's eastern enlargements—proved decisive to worsen geopolitical—and economic—relations between the

Figure 5-4. China's Trade with Russia, 2000–2019 (millions of dollars)

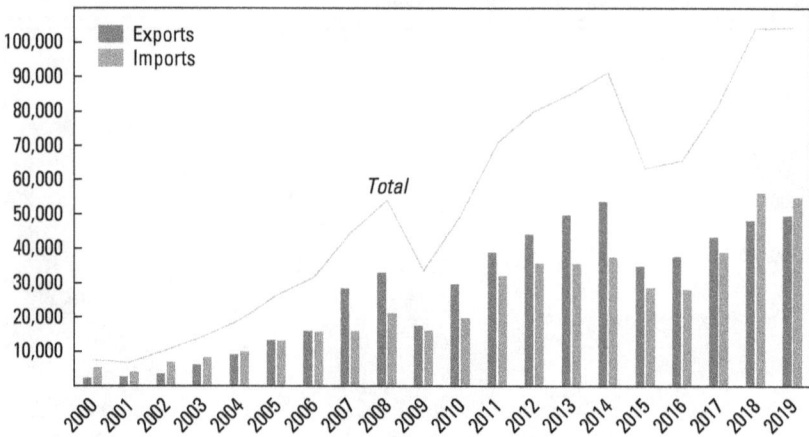

Sources: Direction of Trade Statistics, International Monetary Fund; author's calculations.

EU and Russia as Moscow increasingly looked eastward. Trade between the EU and Russia, which had steady increased until 2008 and is still three times as high as Chinese–Russian trade, dropped sharply after the crisis, rapidly recovered and then dropped again following the combined effect of declining oil prices and the sanction regime imposed after the Ukraine crisis in 2014 (figure 5-5). Since then, it has not yet recovered to the precrisis level. In 2019, the European–Russian trade volume was still below the 2007 level.

Along with these geoeconomic factors, *technological ones* added to and contributed to China's emerging centrality across Eurasia. First, the increase in the containerization pace during the 2000s has not only accelerated seaborne trade between China and Europe but also made overland transcontinental connections and transregional intermodal services to connect China with the rest of Eurasia a technically and economically viable solution. In the years before the BRI, China moved fast to control both long-distance shipping and rail services, creating major state-controlled shipping companies (COSCO) and vertically integrated rail companies (CRCC), acquiring critical ports and inland hubs across Eurasia.

Second, since the early 2010s, the digitalization of industrial production and logistics has than opened chances for moving production closer to final consumers, shortening supply and value chains. This has accelerated China's technological catch-up process and reinforced China's willingness to build global value chains in new manufacturing technologies like artificial intelligence and electric cars.

Figure 5-5. The European Union's Trade with Russia, 2000–2019 (millions of dollars)

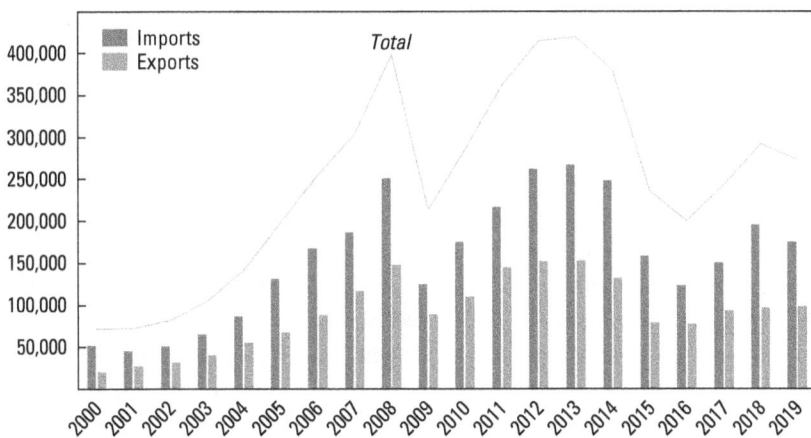

Sources: Direction of Trade Statistics, International Monetary Fund; author's calculations.

Third, more recently (since the 2015 Paris Agreement), the global transition to renewable energies has increased the role of electricity in national economies, fostering decentralized generation and regional cross-border electricity trade and connectivity but also paving the way for a restructuring of energy relationships, potentially affecting Eurasian traditional fossil fuels producers like Russia. China dominates smart grid technologies, ultra-high-voltage transmission lines, and engineering and renewable energy value chains—particularly photovoltaics, wind turbines, and the hydropower power plants equipment market—while financing the construction and exporting of coal-fired power plants abroad. Against this backdrop, the country's proposal to create a transcontinental supergrid based on an ultra-high-voltage direct current line and multiterminal connections to link regional electricity grids across Eurasia and with Europe has become a catalyst for China's manufacturing exports of both low-carbon and high-carbon technologies.[11]

The 2008 Global Financial and Economic Crisis as the Geopolitical Turning Point in the EU–China–Russia Relationship

Against this backdrop, before the COVID-19 pandemic, the 2008 economic and financial crisis proved to be the major event defining Eurasia geopolitics of the decade 2010–20. In fact, it has turned geoeconomic and technological factors already at work into major geostrategic assets, consciously exploited by Beijing-and to a lesser extent by Moscow, to durably redefine the relationship with Europe in the decade 2010–20.

From China's perspective, the significant slowdown in global trade and the first signs of a desynchronization of growth paths among the three major blocs of the EU, Asia, and United States, in the years after the crisis, augmented Beijing's perception that the economic foundation of Western-centered international governance and of liberal economic globalization was eroding. Henceforth, globalization with Chinese characteristics was set to emerge. This more self-confident strategic perception—the central and westward shifts in the localization of industrial production, and the need to both export overcapacity generated by the enormous stimulus package to counter the effects of the crisis and to create alternatives to the Western markets across Eurasia—is at the origin of the Belt and Road Initiative, which was launched in 2013. The years after 2013 and until 2020 witnesses the rise of China's as the major financial and political driver of Eurasian political-economic reintegration, and increasingly as a technological, industrial norm and standard setter for new technologies—Made in China 2025 and China Standards 2035. These years, however, also augmented the enormous diplomatic and political, open or hidden resistance that China's plans and actions have generated in several BRI countries, including in Europe and in Russia.

For its part, Moscow has perceived the 2008 economic and financial crisis as a chance to reassert itself as a major power in Eurasia. By engaging China as an alternative source of trade and finance, and as an alternative market for its energy resource, it would be able to rebuff Western expansion in the former Soviet space (the Georgia war and the Krim annexation) and foster its own regional integration schemes, like the Eurasian Economic Union.

As a result, while the Russian–Chinese relationship was already deepening before the 2008 crisis, in the years after it, it rapidly evolved into a quasi-alliance defined by the common interest in keeping the United States out of maritime and continental Eurasia and opposing the normative integration model of Europe across the continent. The relationship has not (yet) evolved toward an alliance and remains an asymmetric "axis of convenience," but Moscow has accepted China's new economic preeminence in the former Soviet space, particularly in Central Asia.[12] Until before the COVID-19 pandemic, Moscow—while increasingly uncomfortable with its role as junior partner and disappointed by China's geopolitical ambiguity—was convinced to be able to manage the relationship and keep sufficient space for maneuvering. As a result, the axis with Beijing until the outbreak of the pandemic proved to be solid and lasting.

Finally, in the decade 2010–20, the EU found itself—for the first time—increasingly confronted by three simultaneous, major geopolitical shifts: first, the reorientation of the United States toward the Asia Pacific region, followed by the global disengagement and renationalization operated by the new Trump administration in reaction to China's rise both in the Asia-Pacific region and across Eurasia; second, a resurgent and increasingly aggressive Russia; and third, an even more self-confident China, industrially and technologically rapidly catching up while still deeply interwoven with Europe's industrial value chains.

While Brussels originally ignored both the BRI and Russia's reintegration attempts (Eurasian Economic Union), after the Ukraine crisis and the deterioration of the relationship with Moscow, Brussels first hoped to leverage the commercial interdependence to engage China in an effort to isolate Russia. With Trump's election, the EU even turned to China as a potential partner in supporting multilateralism and open markets against the new administration's protectionist agenda and Russia's closed regionalism.

At least since China's Nineteenth Party Congress in 2017, however, the EU's perceptions of China have started to change. From a European perspective, while Russia is an economically declining power and only a short-term military challenge, it is now China—with its mix of assertive diplomacy, rapid technological-industrial development, and aggressive investments—that represents both a major opportunity in the short and middle terms, and the biggest systemic challenge in the middle to long terms. Given the United States' insulation and reorientation to Asia, however, Europe has concluded that it will presumably face the double Russian-Chinese challenge alone.

COVID-19's Impact on EU–Russia–China Relations and Postpandemic Eurasia

Since the COVID-19 pandemic started spreading in early 2020, its impact has therefore only accelerated—and partially modified—trends already unfolding across Eurasia, and specifically on the trilateral China–EU–Russia relationship, potentially turning technological and geoeconomic factors so far conducive to China's growing influence across Eurasia into elements that might in fact reverse this trend and in the long term lessen China's grip on the continent.

China: The Pandemic's Winner?

To be sure, while it is still too soon to say, there are signs that China might—again—emerge as the major economic, technological, and geopolitical winner of the COVID-19 pandemic, thus reinforcing the trends described in the previous paragraph. It could further tighten its grip over value and supply chains across Asia, Eurasia, the Middle East, and Africa; and it could increase its competitive advantage vis-à-vis Europe and the West at a time where the EU (and the United States) is still struggling to recover and now facing a second pandemic wave.

China's economy has indeed bounced back from the pandemic-induced shock sooner and faster than the United States and Europe. With COVID-19 almost having disappeared from the country, the recovery from the pandemic continued in the third quarter of 2020 and showed signs of even broadening in September and October, with a growth of 4.9 percent from 2019. Industrial production grew 6.9 percent and investment growth accelerated to 0.8 percent, signaling that the radical containment measures of the pandemic in early 2020 had borne fruit, and China's factories quickly reopened and profited from the global need for medical and chemical equipment. As a result, China's trade boomed in September, with imports rising 13.2 percent year on year, while exports rose 9.9 percent.[13] According to the Organization for Economic Cooperation and Development, in 2021 China was expected to grow by 8 percent, while the United States and Europe will experience a slower path to recovery, with growth of about 4–5 percent.[14] Against this backdrop, in Eurasia, particularly the Russia–China relationship could even deepen, leaving Russia with no alternative but accepting Beijing's embrace in an even more asymmetric relationship.[15]

Beijing will not give up on the BRI; nor will reduce its scope, as its very logic is linked to domestic calculations of political, ethnic, and economic balance. On the contrary, in the middle to long terms, the BRI will be streamlined, rationalized, and used as instrument to export both overcapacities and new technologies. It will focus more and more on digital technologies, on electricity grids, and on exporting low-carbon technologies and value chains, which will add to the still high level of high-carbon projects like coal-fired power plants.[16] For instance, across the BRI countries, China has so far financed more coal-fired power plants than renewable power plants, in an effort to allow state-owned enterprises to keep working on coal-fired projects overseas while opportunities on the domestic market are limited.[17] After COVID-19, this might have changed: in the first half of 2020, non-fossil-fuel-related energy investment (including solar, wind, and large hydropower) for the first time dominated BRI energy investments, making up fast 58 percent of them. In comparison, in the first six months of 2019 56 percent of energy investments were fossil fuel-related.[18]

While more attention will be given to economic profitability, the BRI will hence remain the principal instrument of China's action and influence across the continent, and even an instrument to export of Chinese industrial norms and standards attached to its technologies, as the new strategy "China Standards 2035" testifies.[19] This is also the sense of Xi Jinping's new concept of the "dual circulation economy" discussed and included in China's Fourteenth Five-Year Plan. While stressing the primary role of domestic production and "circulation" in a time of protectionism and decoupling attempts, China's new strategy will unlikely abandon the outward-looking policy of the past decades, but rather increase the aggressive promotion of its technology and high-value-added products abroad.[20]

Diplomatically and geopolitically, Beijing will try to capitalize on these adjustment, and it has already aggressively promoted its "mask diplomacy" vis-à-vis European countries and other Eurasian partners, including Russia, rebranding the BRI as the "Health Silk Road" to position itself as leader in the global fight against the pandemic. All this being said, the reality might be less clear-cut, and thus also might be the assumption of China's unstoppable recovery.

First, China's image as supplier of critical industrial goods, parts and components has dramatically suffered. Diplomatically, Chinese aggressive attempts to impose its post-COVID narrative has increased skepticism abroad, particularly in Europe, but also in East Asian countries like Japan and South Korea, historically interlinked with China supply and value chains but wary of China's more aggressive foreign policy attitude.

Second, also in the post-COVID-19 world, notwithstanding the immediate recovery, China's domestic economic situation remains strained, and under pressure from the United States' decoupling attempts. The new concept of dual circulation implies a prioritization of domestic production, consumption, and supply chains (internal circulation) in order to be less vulnerable to external shocks and disruption, while remaining engaged in global markets (external circulation). This might force Chinese companies to temporarily prioritize the domestic market over undifferentiated global expansion, while attempting to regain terrain in the immediate neighborhood, particularly in Southeast Asia, as part of the BRI. For instance, in the first six months of 2020, overall BRI-related investment dropped by about 50 percent, from $46 billion invested during the first six months of 2019 (and dropping by 60 percent compared with the first six months of 2018), with a particularly strong decline in West and East Asia.[21]

By doing so, however, they might experience greater opposition from the governments of the target countries, with Chinese mergers and acquisitions, and aggressive acquisition practices of local industrial know-how, increasingly under scrutiny, as well as by external competitors. Most important, the combined effect of foreign companies relocating production outside China and China's reshoring of own supply and value chains closer home might have a doubly negative impact for Beijing: first, it will accelerate already ongoing intra-Asia competition over relocalization of regional supply and value chains, especially in the Association of Southeast Asian Nations (ASEAN) countries, giving them leverage vis-à-vis Beijng; and second, it will make China less central in Asia's regional production networks—unless China expands its outbound foreign direct investment in these countries as well to establish China-centered value chains.[22] These countries are indeed set to become the next geoeconomic playing and battlefield, as Japan's relocation toward Southeast Asia,[23] South Korea's reshoring attempts,[24] the more recent EU–Vietnam free trade agreement,[25] and the renewed European interest for cooperation with ASEAN show.[26]

In this respect, the recent inception of the Regional Comprehensive Economic Partnership, while a clear geopolitical win for Beijing, comes at a geoeconomic price and is the result of a compromise, particularly with the advanced economies of Japan and South Korea. In fact, its streamlined and cumulative rules of origin provisions actually seems to offer many different possibilities for non-Chinese Asian companies to build their regional value chains independent from China's production networks, even though Chinese multinational corporations also can benefit from cumulative rules-of-origin provisions by establishing their value chains in the region. As a result, a less Sino-centered Asian production network in Asia and China's temporarily hold on major transcontinental BRI projects will leave room for a reconfiguration of value and supply chains for new technologies like hydrogen or battery cells that at least partially bypass China. This development might reverberate across Eurasia as well.

The EU's China Policy: From Growing Skepticism to Fierce Competition

Amid the COVID-19 pandemic, the EU has particularly grown even more skeptical about its relationship with China, including the BRI, as dramatic bottlenecks in the supply of medical equipment have exposed the fragility of European companies' overreliance on China supplies in the medical sector. European countries and the European Union have hence started openly questioning their dependence on China's supply chains, particularly in this critical sector, pledging a repatriation of production activities and greater supply chain resilience.

While the debate both inside national governments and in the European Commission about the necessity to reaffirm European industrial sovereignty did not start with the COVID pandemic outbreak, COVID-19 has exacerbated the

European discourse on China.[27] This has moved from Europe reflecting on the competitiveness of its own economic-industrial model vis-à-vis China to the need to nurture production at home to make itself more independent from China.

China is not only a major supplier of intermediate goods for European and German industries (particularly medical-pharmaceutical, electronic, and automotive) but also an increasingly competitive provider of new technologies, high-value-added manufacturing like renewable energies, battery cell production chains, raw mineral processing, and information technology. From a European perspective, the pandemic reinforces China's willingness to set own technological and normative standards in sectors where European businesses have lost competitive advantage and in some cases the technological edge (5G technologies) and to selectively exploit economic interdependencies.

To this add the increasingly insulated and aggressive trade policy of the former Trump administration, which will be presumably set to continue—though different in tone—under the Biden administration. This makes a joint transatlantic approach toward China difficult to realize and leaves the EU facing a dilemma: align with the more confrontational US stance or develop equidistance and strategic autonomy from both blocs, remaining the sole sponsor of a multilateral global political and economic order. In fact, the Trump administration's policy goal to decouple from China and reshore production has been aimed not only against Chinese producers but also against European manufacturers: the administration's willingness to use trade-distorting instruments like duties and the US pressure on European governments to align with Washington's newly assertive industrial, energy, and digital strategy vis-à-vis both China and Russia, has contributed to an increasing the perception among Europeans that their production model based on globally elongated, complex supply chains is particularly vulnerable to geopolitical shocks and needs to be rethought, also vis-à-vis a dramatic redefinition and reassessment of the transatlantic partnership. While the Biden administration might correct some of the excesses of the previous administration, it will not entirely change the course in the new, more robust approach to trade and industrial policies.

And here the COVID-19 pandemic has clearly acted once more as an accelerator in translating the already-ongoing European debate in an official, more self-confident, and active policy strategy. While further concrete steps on implementation are still lacking and we are at the very beginning of a long process, during the months of the pandemic, the EU Commission, under the impulse of the member states, and especially of the French–German initiative, approved two documents (the EU Industrial Strategy, approved by the Commission in March 2020;[28] and the Road Map to Recovery,[29] presented by the Commission after the Joint Statement of the Members of the European Council adopted on March 26) aiming to ensure what has been defined the EU's "strategic autonomy." This means (1) develop greater resilience in supply and value chains, (2) keep control over key infrastructure, and (3) repatriate the production of some critical goods back to Europe, where possible.

The two documents, whose goals and scope were eventually included in the grand EU budget deal reached by the European Council on July 21, 2020, which includes a one-time €750 billion recovery fund named Next Generation EU, mention five main instruments essential for enhancing European industrial production: the development of a new, more dynamic industrial policy to invest in strategic value chains, including in low-carbon and no-carbon technologies, in line with the Green Deal as well as in digital technologies and in the medical sector; the geographic diversification of supply chains, privileging nearshoring and—where possible—reshoring; the full realization of the potential of robotization and digitalization of production, enabling relocalization of activities; an effective screening of foreign direct investments, with the aim to harmonize national legislations at the European level (even though a unified, mandatory European screening procedure will not be implemented, leaving it to the single member states); and the support for small and medium-sized enterprises and start-ups in the high-technology sector. To this adds the willingness to develop connectivity partnerships across Eurasia to promote norms and standards for sustainable, green, and digital connectivity with new, like-minded partners beyond the transatlantic relationship, with a good example being the partnership on connectivity signed with Japan in September 2019.[30]

The evolving EU stance on China—in line with President von der Leyen willingness to forge a more "geopolitical" Europe that speaks the "grammar of power"—does not guarantee that the EU will be able to effectively decouple itself from China or stand up geopolitically against it. In fact, China will remain an important final market and production platform in Asia and increasingly a source of (digital) technology and raw material processing in the green energy sector across the continent. However, a more economically sovereign and self-confident EU, targeting the development of new technologies like hydrogen, might very well be able to diversify its supply chains and enhance partnerships with other Asian and Eurasian players, partially lessening its dependence on China. Moreover, by leveraging its market power, the EU might obtain concessions from Beijing at a moment where China still needs Europe in its conflict with the United States. This fact might become visible at the upcoming summit between China and the European Union–27 scheduled for December, which is set to finalize the long-awaited EU–China investment agreement on top of the German EU Presidency's agenda. Against this backdrop, also the EU's relationship with Russia, so far deeply damaged and "frozen," might also regain traction, even though under completely different premises.

Russia: Between China's Uncomfortable Embrace and a Long-Term, Pragmatic Rapprochement with Europe?

To be clear, the EU–Russia relationship will remain strained and difficult, with scarce chances in the short to middle terms to develop toward a more strategic partnership. The more so considering that the changing energy system will not favor the return to the old European-Russian energy axis.

Moreover, the COVID-19 pandemic has brought China and Russia even closer together, diplomatically, economically, and even in terms of alternative international norms, particularly in the cybersphere.[31] Under these circumstances, Moscow will not abandon its privileged relations with Beijing. The pandemic will not change the Kremlin's attitude in this sense; nor Moscow will concede much to the EU's vision of a multilateral liberal order. In the recent words of Foreign Minister Sergey Lavrov, Russia will even be ready to reduce the dialogue with the EU to a minimum and to work together only on selected issues, if tensions since the poisoning of the opposition leader Alexey Nawalny will keep rising.[32] Moreover, Moscow will further try to prioritize economic, industrial, and geostrategic sovereignty, at both the national and regional levels.

However, the pandemic has shown that Russia—weakened by the combined effects of collapsing oil prices, reduced energy demand in Europe, and economic lockdown—is set to become even more dependent on China as a fossil fuels final market and as a source of investments in its digital and physical infrastructure and energy and nonenergy sectors. And this in a time when China might try to more aggressively tighten up control over regional value and supply chains and energy resources in its immediate neighborhood in Asia and Eastern Eurasia.

As the pandemic is strengthening China's economic-technological grip on Russia, particularly in the energy and telecommunications sphere (5G), it has also increased Moscow's foreign policy dependence on China, reducing its strategic options.[33] While, after the Ukraine crisis in 2014, Russia's pivot to Asia was an expression of a sovereign and independent foreign policy, now the pandemic has forced Moscow more deeply into Beijing's arms, causing an increasing sense of unspoken discontent.

The latent though growing discomfort with Beijing is better expressed by two signals barely noticed in the West, sent by Moscow at Beijing's address: first, in June 2020, Moscow for the first time lowered the level of diplomatic participation in the digital BRI forum chaired by China's foreign minister, Wang Yi.[34] Second, the new nuclear strategy published at the beginning of June 2020, while not explicitly referring to China as a potential threat, however affirms that Moscow might employ nuclear weapons to defend Russia or its allies even in case of a conventional attack causing mass destruction, and that could inflict damage comparable to nuclear strikes. Considering that China's People's Liberation Army represents the biggest and geographically closest conventional army and the difficulty of defending the Far East regions in case of China's rapid troops deployment, this passage of the strategy can be understood as an encrypted warning to Beijing.[35] More recently, Moscow has also refused to openly align with China in the escalating Indo-Chinese conflict, keen to keep equidistance in order not to alienate New Delhi.[36]

In fact, as Moscow's policentric vision of the international system is based on the assumption that there are no stable alliances and that only flexible, fluid, and interest-driven relations allow for the greatest level of foreign policy autonomy, unilateral dependence on China is now becoming unacceptable.[37] To be clear, the axis with Beijing will remain paramount for Moscow's foreign policy, and no open conflict can be expected in the post-COVID world. However, the more the asymmetric dependence on China increases, the less Moscow will be willing to enter an exclusive alliance with China and the more it will consider more than in the prepandemic time the need to economically and diplomatically diversify its relations both within Asia and with Europe. As Russia's relationship with China becomes less exclusive, Moscow will in fact represent a factor of increasing strategic uncertainty for Beijing.

Conclusion: Toward a Less Sino-Centric, More Diversified and Competitive Eurasia?

Because of these COVID-induced changes in the China–EU–Russia trilateral relationship, Eurasia's geoeconomic and geopolitical transformation will be readjusted along four major lines, even though its logic and the long-term trends shaping it will not fundamentally change. First, the persisting decoupling at the global level between the United States and China will not necessarily lead to continental decoupling between the EU and China.[38] Trade relations between the two major manufacturing powerhouses at the two edges of Eurasia will remain strong, as both still need each other as sources of industrial know-how and technology, and as final markets. The need for greater resilience and diversification will, however, lead to greater EU-China competition over norms, standards, and control over new and emerging value and supply chains in critical new sectors like green energy and hydrogen and digital technologies (artificial intelligence), and over critical infrastructure like power grids, ports, and dry ports in Europe, Asia, and in Africa.

Second, while Moscow will not question the axis with Beijing, it will be more willing to seek alternatives to China, making the Chinese–Russian partnership more fluid. For Europe, given the relevance which geographic proximity will have for production networks and final consumers markets, the immediate neighborhood, starting with Eastern Europe but also including Russia, will regain strategic relevance. Against this backdrop, the relationship between the EU and Russia might evolve toward a more pragmatic and ad hoc form of cooperation, less than a strategic partnership but more than the current estrangement. To this presumable development will contribute not only China's rising political-economic-technological influence but also the digitalization and regionalization of production and the Green Transition, as new low-carbon value and supply chains (hydrogen and e-cars) will require a redefinition of the traditional gas and energy relationship in the transition period.

Third, for the EU a complete reshoring or even near-shoring of production back to Europe or its immediate periphery will prove an illusion in the long term, if the EU attempts to disguise economic autarchy with "strategic autonomy." Paradoxically, with the United States' insulation presumably set to continue under the Biden administration, the EU will be called to balance between domestic reshoring aspirations and the need for an even greater involvement in different regional Asian production networks, including but also transcending China. In fact, as growth, technological innovation, industrial development, and consumer markets will still gravitate around the macroregion of Eastern Eurasia–Asia–the Pacific and eventually along the nexus Southeast Asia–India–West Asia–Africa, competition over supply, value chains, markets, technologies, connectivity, and regional integration initiatives—even in more detached regions like Central Asia or the Russian Far East and Northeast Asia—is set to increase.

Fourth, and directly deriving from the first three factors, post-COVID connectivity across Eurasia will presumably be less Sino-centric and BRI-driven and more diversified and competitive. China will remain central in Eurasian integration. However, with the shifting political interests and perceptions in both Russia and Europe, their quest for alternative sources of investments, technology, and production—combined with the regional diversification and localization of new green and digitalized supply and value chains, and the emerging new role of middle powers—might represent a major obstacle to the creation of a Sino-centered political-economic system across Eurasia.[39] Because China will be confronted with a much more hostile and polycentric environment, the country might, after all, not be the winner in postpandemic Eurasia.

Notes

1. See Jacopo Pepe, *Beyond Energy-Trade and Transport in a Reconnecting Eurasia* (Berlin: Springer Verlag, 2018); and Kent Calder, *The New Continentalism, Energy and Twenty-First-Century Eurasian Geopolitics* (Yale University Press, 2012).

2. Pomeranz, Kenneth, *The Great Divergence: China, Europe, and the Making of the Modern World Economy* (Princeton University Press, 2000).

3. Kent Calder, *Supercontinent: The Logic of Eurasian Integration* (Stanford University Press, 2019).

4. Jacopo Pepe, "Continental Drift: Germany and China's Inroads in the German–Central Eastern European Manufacturing Core—Geopolitical Risks and Chances," Edwin O. Reischauer Center, Emerging Issues in Eurasia Research, 2017.

5. Pepe, *Beyond Energy-Trade*, 282–305.

6. European Commission, "Countries and Regions: China," http://ec.europa.eu/trade/policy/countries-and-regions/countries/china/.

7. Richard Pomfret, *China's Belt and Road Initiative, the Eurasian Landbridge, and the New Mega-Regionalism* (Singapore: World Scientific, 2020), 18.

8. Pepe, "Continental Drift."

9. Calder, *Supercontinent*; Pepe, "Continental Drift."

10. Data retrieved from International Monetary Fund, Directorate of Trade Statistics.

11. Global Energy Interconnection Development and Cooperation Organization, "About Global Energy Interconnection," https://en.geidco.org/aboutgei/.

12. Bobo Lo, *Axis of Convenience: Moscow, Beijing, and the New Geopolitics* (Brookings, 2008).

13. Bloomberg, "China's Economy Plows On as World's Only Major Growth Engine," October 18, 2020, https://www.bloomberg.com/news/articles/2020-10-18/china-s-rebound-helps-to-sta"bilize-a-shattered-world-economy.

14. Organization for Economic Cooperation and Development, "Building Confidence Amid an Uncertain Recovery: OECD Interim Report," September 2020, http://www.oecd.org/economic-outlook/.

15. See, e.g., Alexander Gabuev, "The Pandemic Could Tighten China's Grip on Eurasia," *Foreign Policy*, April 23, 2020, https://foreignpolicy.com/2020/04/23/coronavirus-pandemic-china-eurasia-russia-influence/.

16. Thomas S. Eder and Jacob Mandell, "Powering the Belt and Road: China Supports Its Energy Companies' Global Expansion and Prepares the Ground for Potential New Supply Chains," June 27, 2019, https://merics.org/en/analysis/powering-belt-and-road.

17. "China's Coal Projects Outside Its Borders," *Belt & Road News*, July 5, 2020, https://www.beltandroad.news/2020/07/04/chinas-coal-projects-outside-its-borders/.

18. Christoph Nedopil Wang, "Investments in the Chinese Belt and Road Initiative (BRI) in the First Half of 2020 during the COVID-19 Pandemic," Green BRI Center, International Institute of Green Finance, Beijing, July 2020.

19. Alexander Chipman Koty, "What Is the China Standards 2035 Plan and How Will It Impact Emerging Industries?" https://www.china-briefing.com/news/what-is-china-standards-2035-plan-how-will-it-impact-emerging-technologies-what-is-link-made-in-china-2025-goals/.

20. See, e.g., "Guide to China's Dual Circulation Economy," October 25, 2020, https://news.cgtn.com/news/2020-10-25/Guide-to-China-s-dual-circulation-economy-US8jtau4h2/index.html.

21. Based on data from the American Enterprise Institute's China Investment Tracker, https://www.aei.org/china-global-investment-tracker/.

22. Marina Kaneti, "ASEAN Must Make the Best of Its New Centrality in China's Diplomacy," *Diplomat*, June 2020, https://thediplomat.com/2020/06/asean-must-make-the-best-of-its-new-centrality-in-chinas-diplomacy/.

23. Bloomberg, "Japan to Fund Firms to Shift Production Out of China," April 8, 2020, https://www.bloomberg.com/news/articles/2020-04-08/japan-to-fund-firms-to-shift-production-out-of-china.

24. "South Korean Government to Promote Reshoring," *Business Korea*, June 6, 2020, http://www.businesskorea.co.kr/news/articleView.html?idxno=46788.

25. European Commission, "EU-Vietnam Trade Agreement Enters into Force," July 30, 2020, https://ec.europa.eu/commission/presscorner/detail/en/ip_20_1412.

26. European External Action Service, "Strengthening EU–ASEAN Partnership, an Urgent Necessity; Statement by Joseph Borrell," September 20, 2020, https://eeas.europa.eu/headquarters/headquarters-homepage/85434/strengthening-eu-asean-partnership-urgent-necessity_en.

27. Public and confidential discussions both at national and European levels have been ongoing for the past few years, culminating in the French–German Industrial Policy Manifesto of early 2019, in which both countries pledged a strong European industrial policy to foster innovation in new key sectors like health, energy, climate, security, and digital technology. See, e.g., https://www.bmwi.de/Redaktion/DE/Downloads/F/franco-german-manifesto-for-a-european-industrial-policy.pdf?__blob=publicationFile&v=2.

28. See https://ec.europa.eu/info/sites/info/files/communication-eu-industrial-strategy-march-2020_en.pdf.

29. See https://www.consilium.europa.eu/media/43384/roadmap-for-recovery-final-21-04-2020.pdf.

30. "EU-Japan Tryst Is a Sign of Shifting Geopolitical Times," *Financial Times*, May 25, 2020, https://www.ft.com/content/cc9ba993-3da1-481a-947f-8e691e0f0f98.

31. Alice Ekman, Sinikukka Saari, and Stanislav Secrieru, "Stand by Me! The Sino-Russian Normative Partnership in Action," European Union Institute for Security Studies, August 6, 2020, https://www.iss.europa.eu/sites/default/files/EUISSFiles/Brief%2018%20China%20Russia_0.pdf.

32. Лавров допустил возможность прекращения диалога между Россией и (Lavrov considers the possibility of stopping the dialogue between Russia and the EU), October 13, 2020, https://www.rbc.ru/politics/13/10/2020/5f85bae79a7947948934fddb.

33. Alexander Gabuev, "Huawei's Courtship of Moscow Leaves West in the Cold," *Financial Times*, June 21, 2020, https://www.ft.com/content/f36a558f-4e4d-4c00-8252-d8c4be45bde4.

34. Russian Foreign Ministry, "Statement for the Press after the BRI-Forum," June 18, 2020, https://www.mid.ru/ru/foreign_policy/news/-/asset_publisher/UdAzvXr89FbD/content/id/4169112.

35. "Decree of the President of the Russian Federation on the Principles of the State Politics in the Sphere of Nuclear Arms," June 2, 2020, http://publication.pravo.gov.ru/Document/View/0001202006020040?index=0&rangeSize=1.

36. "Beijing Suffers Light Casualties in China–India Border Skirmish but Keeps Quiet to Avoid Conflict Escalation," *South China Morning Post*, June 24, 2020, https://www.scmp.com/news/china/military/article/3090454/beijing-suffers-light-casualties-china-india-border-skirmish.

37. Dimitry Trenin, "How Russia Can Maintain Equilibrium in the Post-Pandemic Bipolar World," Carnegie Moscow Center, May 1, 2020, https://carnegie.ru/commentary/81702.

38. Please note that this argument is based on the assumptions that the United States will continue to pursue technological decoupling from China and the current geopolitical struggle between the two countries will persist. Although the outcome of the November 2024 presidential elections will be crucial for determining the foreign policy of the United States and its strategic approach to Europe for the next four years, the United States will continue to promote a national agenda based on geoeconomic and geopolitical competition after 2021. Neither a second Trump administration nor a new Biden administration will fundamentally change the isolationist attitude that the country currently holds toward China. Also, either administration would keep decoupling from Europe – at least in the short term. In the case of a Biden administration, however, a rapprochement with Europe is more probable. Still, US conflicts with China could result in a limited pragmatic-tactical rapprochement rather than the renewal of the transatlantic alliance in order to promote a global agenda centered on the enforcement of Western values and technological standards.

39. Economist Intelligence Unit, "The Great Unwinding, COVID-19 and the Regionalisation of Global Supply Chains," May 2020, http://www.eiu.com/Handlers/WhitepaperHandler.ashx?fi=covid19-and-the-regionalisation-of-global-supply-chains.pdf&mode=wp&campaignid=BusinessesandC19.

Six

The Possibilities for "Effective Multilateralism" in the Coming Global Order

ALAN S. ALEXANDROFF, *GLOBAL SUMMITRY PROJECT,*
MUNK SCHOOL OF GLOBAL AFFAIRS & PUBLIC POLICY,
UNIVERSITY OF TORONTO

Multilateralism through the Decades of the Global Order

The concept "multilateralism" is described by international relations and its many experts, analysts, and researchers as though it were either an evident known international arrangement or, in contrast, an "empty vessel" that they then proceed to fill with a variety of actors with different aims and goals.[1] The confusion over the meaning of multilateralism and its conduct is evident. Yet the variety of forms describing multilateralism is at least somewhat explicable. The international relations system has evolved dramatically since 1945. Multilateralism looks rather different dependent on the particular era and shape of the liberal or global order.[2] The structures, the actors, and their behaviors influenced by governing principles differ in the changing global order. Today's global order differs significantly from the Cold War decades, or the years after the "Unipolar Moment" and the era of global governance.[3] Now the global order is again being reshaped with the reemergence of geopolitical challenges, particularly the rising United States–China tensions. How multilateralism may look and operate in this new global order context is what this chapter is about. Traditional multilateralism that international relations scholars have described and redescribed through the decades is examined closely but, in the end, we are intent to understand contemporary multilateralism. How does multilateralism look like with the growing geopolitical tensions of the current era, the consequences of the global COVID-19 pandemic, and pointedly with the Biden administration at the helm in the United States? The question we end with here, then, and attempt to answer, is the possibilities for what we describe as "effective multilateralism." What is it, and how does it, or could it, operate in the contemporary global order?

The Definition

There is a broad definition of multilateralism that has served, possibly poorly, but more often than not, as the traditional meaning for multilateralism in the international relations literature. Below I identify this, but I also note that many of these definitions of multilateralism occur on the heels of the demise of the Cold War. Traditional multilateralism both reflects the decades of the Cold War as well as the rise of the "Unipolar Moment." Structurally, the liberal international order was jolted by the collapse of the Soviet Union and the rise of the United States as the sole superpower. We should keep this in mind: traditional multilateralism is conditioned by the structure, meaning the shape of the global order, the range of actors and their arrangements, and, of course, their behaviors.

A number of the best-known international relations scholars of the contemporary period tackled the definition and function of "multilateralism" at the end of the bipolar period. Robert Keohane concluded that multilateralism was "the practice of co-ordinating national policies in groups of three or more states."[4] He was followed relatively shortly thereafter by the international relations scholar John Ruggie.[5] For Ruggie, the key understanding of multilateralism was less determined by the minimum number of actors as opposed to the normative basis of the arrangement. As Ruggie wrote, "multilateralism is an institutional form which coordinates relations among three or more states on the basis of 'generalized' principles of conduct—that is, principles which specify appropriate conduct for a class of actions, without regard to the particularistic interests of the parties or the strategic exigencies that may exist in any specific occurrence."[6] This capture of the normative basis of multilateralism is a key because it suggests that multilateralism may not be governed solely by the power equation of the principal actors—states. This becomes important after decades of US leadership of the liberal order. As John Ikenberry, the contemporary chronicler of the liberal international order, has written very recently, "This is what John Ruggie calls 'multilateralism,' an 'architectural form' of international organization that coordinates relations among a group of states 'on the basis of generalized principles of conduct.'"[7] The rules, and the principles they embody, have some impartiality and independent standing. They are not merely the exhortations of a powerful state but also norms of conduct to which a group of states adheres, regardless of their specific power or circumstance.

So, we start with a negative proposition—multilateralism can be distinguished in part by the reality that it is not bilateralism—it cannot be established by just two actors. It must be something greater than just two states. And as Ruggie points out, even two may not constitute bilateralism, if the arrangement is built on a discriminatory basis.[8] So, presumably, is the case of multilateralism. Ruggie underscores the focus of multilateralism on the norms and the arrangements in geoeconomic as well as geopolitical arrangements. As Ruggie describes, "When we speak here of multilateralism in international trade, we know immediately that it refers to trade organized on the basis of certain principles of state conduct-above all, nondiscrimination. Similarly, when we speak here of multilateralism in security relations, we know that it refers to some expression or other of collective security or collective self-defense. In sum, what is distinctive about multilateralism is not merely that it coordinates national policies in groups of three or more states, which is something that other organizational forms also do, but that it does so on the basis of certain principles of ordering relations among those states."[9]

Miles Kahler, again in the same post–Cold War period, adds another layer of meaning to traditional multilateralism.[10] Kahler examines in part the multilateralism of the Bretton Woods period that saw the emergence of formal international institutions at the end of World War II—the International Monetary Fund, the World Bank, the General Agreement on Tariffs and Trade, and others. These Bretton Woods institutions, along with the United Nations, are notable for their universal or near-universal character. As Kahler notes, "Closely linked to multilateralism's aspiration to universality and welcoming of large numbers of participants was a strong leveling impulse."[11] These multilateral institutions admitted a large range of states from great powers to more recently decolonized newly independent states.

But as Kahler points out, significant decision-making arrangements other than the universal operated with these institutions—some evident, but many more disguised. First, below this presumed universalism or near universalism of the formal institutions, other arrangements often actually governed. One such organizational concept, "minilateralism," functioned over many decades. As pointed out by Moses Naim, the need for collaboration in international relations soared, but multilateralism was unable to deliver.[12] Minilateralism, however, consisted of small subsets of actors, and the arrangement was frequently used to solve particular global governance issues. As Kahler identifies: "The collective action problems posed by multilateral governance were

addressed for much of the postwar era by minilateral great power collaboration disguised by multilateral institutions and by derogations from multilateral principles in the form of persistent bilateralism and regionalism."[13]
American leadership, combined with other "leading states," frequently provided
the governing means to address policy problems and reform. And the institutional forms were subsets or clubs of states.

Additionally, regional institutional arrangements emerged, and bilateralism
continued to play a significant governance role as well. These regional institutions were often founded because of discontent by developing countries with the
global institutions that were viewed as dominated by the established powers. The
institutional setting was far more varied than was often recognized at the time,
driven in part by the failure to achieve solutions in the context of Bretton Woods
multilateralism. As Kahler would acknowledge today, the term "minilateralism"
has given way to the contemporary term "plurilateralism." These arrangements
are particularly apparent in various trade arrangements throughout the international system.[14] The decision-making rule remained "both minilateral 'great
power' collaboration within multilateral institutions (to reduce the barriers to
cooperation raised by large numbers) and bilateral and regional derogations
from multilateralism (as the great powers exerted their bargaining power) were
commonplace. What multilateralism consisted of through the Cold War decades
and beyond was formalistically near universalism but, in reality, frequently
minilateralism or today's plurilateralism, organized and led frequently by the
United States."[15]

Formal Institutional versus Informal Institutional Forms

The decision rules, as noted above, were far more varied than appeared in the
decades of the dominance of the Bretton Woods institutions and the Cold
War. At the same time, however, new institutional forms were appearing in
the global order that again altered the forms of multilateralism. The slow fading
of formal institutions does not appear to have inhibited multilateralism—in
fact, it actually may have enhanced it. In this contextualized narrative of multilateralism, we start with the emergence of different classes of international
institutions. In what Miles Kahler has dubbed recently the "Bretton Woods
Moment," a set of formal international institutions, including both the economic and international security institutions, were established after World
War II, as I noted above.[16] But institutional development was not limited to such
formal institutions. Newer institutional forms emerge that took their place
alongside the formal institutions. In the 1970s, in fact, a new institutional form—
the "Informals"—emerged. In what Alexandroff and Brean have referred to

since as the "Rise of the Informals," the Informals emerge, in part, with the Nixon administration's closing of the "gold window," collapsing the fixed exchange rate system of Bretton Woods.[17]

These Informals, a classic case being today's Group of Seven (G7), are what Vabulas and Snidal refer to as informal intergovernmental organizations (IIGOs), which differ significantly from their counterparts—the formal institutions, which these same authors call formal intergovernmental organizations (FIGOs).[18] In contrast to the FIGOs, these IIGOs are established without a binding treaty or other legal foundation, and have no headquarters and no secretariats, though the members appear to meet on a relatively regular schedule and in some instances transfer leadership organizing the summits by a fixed order of hosting. There were, of course, a number of informal institutions before the 1970s. For instance, in 1962, the Group of Ten emerges. But the rather more unique form that emerges in the 1970s, with the G7 being a classic case, are the set of Informals whose attending participants are the heads of government and in some instances heads of state.[19] These institutions are the contemporary organization of what becomes modern global summitry.[20] The first of these institutions was the Group of Six in 1975, and it was followed almost immediately by the G7 in 1976, and then, in what Cooper and English refer to as the "apex of global summitry," the Group of Twenty (G20).[21] The G20 emerges as a leaders' summit at the time of the global financial crisis after existing as a forum for finance ministers and central bankers for a decade.[22]

These GX leader-organized Informals form the foundation of today's global summitry system.[23] These leaders' gatherings are just the tip of informal summits, with additionally a large array of ministerial and working party meetings occurring throughout the year as well as what are referred to as "engagement groups," civil society organizations.[24] But they represent another multilateral forum of a significant subset of states. It is also these global summits that form a contemporary setting, possibly, for effective multilateralism, as I discuss below. Moreover, the emergence of the Informal G20 Leaders' Summit promised an equality of the G20 states, including established powers, rising and large emerging market powers, traditional middle powers, and a few developing states as well. The G20 offered promise of what Stewart Patrick and others suggested would be a "shifting coalition of consensus":[25] "As the G20 matures and expands its agenda, it has the potential to shake up the geopolitical order, introducing greater flexibility into global diplomacy and transcending the stultifying bloc politics that have too often hamstrung cooperation in formal, treaty based institutions (including the United Nations)." These arrangements provide shifting coalitions instead of blocs that emerged frequently in formal institutions and settings generated by the structure and politics of the period. With these arrangements, new "shifting coalitions of consensus" could emerge in this post bipolar world, and the coalitions could well vary depending on the issue in these new global governance settings. These shifting coalitions of consensus were seen as particularly likely to support American efforts to promote collaboration and advance policymaking at the global governance level.

As Patrick suggested: "The very size and diversity of the G20—while not without drawbacks—may inject new dynamism into global governance by facilitating the formation of shifting coalitions of interests. As such, the G20 presents particular strategic advantages for the United States, which will likely remain the indispensable partner for most winning coalitions within the new "America First" policy, a nationalist approach advanced by the Trump administration that spurned multilateralism and operated largely by transactional and bilateral policymaking. And of course, that is exactly what has affected contemporary multilateralism and is reshaping the global order, even in the context of the subsequent Biden administration.

IIGOs expanded rapidly in the 1980s and 1990s, favored, it would seem, for their flexibility and lack of binding obligations.[26] As economic interdependence grew, regulatory clashes became more frequent. New actors were drawn into the emerging global governance era. As Kahler has recently pointed out: "Transgovernmental networks became a seemingly favored means for national bureaucracies to negotiate and coordinate in shared domains."[27] And these transgovernmental networks highlight the fact that contemporary multilateral forms have been extended beyond just the traditional actors: states. This transformation from a purely state system has been under way for some time, but analysts have been alert, certainly since the new century, to the enhanced role of actors beyond the state.[28] As Kahler describes it: "Just as the turn of the current century marked a shift toward the new regionalism and new movements calling into question the benefits of global governance, the first decade of the century was also marked by a significant increase in innovative forms of governance that included nonstate actors as well as subnational governments."[29] So, in facing global governance challenges such as climate change, global health pandemics, and so on, states' IGOs and IIGOs were now joined by substate actors, regions, provinces and states, large urban conurbations, and nonstate actors such NGOs, firms, foundations, and individuals. The form extends, of course, to "bad actors" as well: criminal gangs, cybercriminals, terrorist organizations, and so on. The range of actors in multilateralism has significantly expanded. As Avant and colleagues have suggested: "They are active agents who want new structures and rules (or different rules) to solve problems, change outcomes, and transform international life."[30] While their authority and influence remain in question, it would be a mistake to not see their involvement in global governance and in contemporary multilateralism. The result of this additional evolution of multilateralism leaves a number of questions that we also try and tackle in the next section.

The Questions Arising from the Evolution of Multilateralism

Following the elaboration of the classic definition of multilateralism, we have seen new forms of multilateralism that have arisen in the changing global order. This necessitates an inquiry into the leadership, form and generalized principles that today appear in contemporary multilateralism. There are three aspects that we are going to examine in some detail to help clarify what contemporary multilateralism looks like and what may be possible in the contexts of the current global order. The first two contexts are (the third is given below):

1. Are there certain actors required for contemporary multilateralism to operate successfully in today's global order? More pointedly, will contemporary multilateralism likely only work if organized or accepted by the leading powers—the United States or say possibly the United States and China. A further but related question is whether hegemony is required to enable multilateralism and whether power provides the organizing glue for multilateralism. Can multilateralism develop without all, or at least some the leading powers?

2. What actors can be active participants in multilateralism and in particular what do analysts' mean when they reference, as they often do, "middle powers" in multilateralism?

Multilateralism certainly does take place with great powers. Particularly in the decades of the Cold War, but also in the period after the "Unipolar Moment," the United States is seen as critical to the construction and the maintenance—and possibly the demise—of the liberal order and its attending multilateral arrangements. For instance, Robert Kagan of Brookings has pressed the point that contemporary international governance requires US leadership, or chaos is likely to ensue in the global order.[31] Others have suggested that without the leading states—namely, the United States and now China—multilateralism will "sputter and fail." Without the resources and the commitment of the leading powers, contemporary multilateralism will fail. Multilateralism to function requires the inclusion of the leading powers. Such an assertion is not surprising in the face of decades of the United States' multilateral and alliance action.

Power and Multilateralism

Certainly, historically, multilateralism does not seem to rely only on the hierarchy that generally accompanies hegemony. Ruggie makes the point that the instances of hegemony differ. As Ruggie reflects: "Thus, all hegemonies are not alike. The most that can be said about a hegemonic power is that it will seek to construct an international order in some form, presumably along lines that are compatible with its own international objectives and domestic structures. But, in the end, that really is not saying much."[32]

There are those, of course, who are committed to the notion that without a hegemon, and more directly, the United States, for example, multilateralism is hollow. This perspective, I believe, is built on structural factors, most notably global order relations, that rely on power and rely on the United States willingness to bear the costs of collective action. There is, however, a fair history that suggest multilateralism and the "generalized principles of conduct" can be effective without a hegemon. The "Bretton Woods Moment," the creation of near universal membership, seems to provide a mix between governing principles and power. And this is not totally surprising, given that the institutions were constructed in part on the basis of universal global order that failed to materialize.

The hegemonic, or at least the "leading powers," thesis seems to me to be constructed, in part, on traditional international relations notions of structural power as the driver of international relations behavior. You can see this debate over power and leadership emerge in the earliest instances of global order, the European Concert of the post-Napoleonic period in Europe. There was a long-running debate—mainly among diplomatic historians—as to whether the underlying dynamic of the Concert in the nineteenth century was a balance of power or not.[33] For those urging power and a balance of power, the rules and norms of the Concert, the generalized principles of conduct, were minimized or barely acknowledged. Power advocates relied on the balance of power dynamic in this generally acknowledged first global order mechanism constructed some two hundred years ago. But there was a strand of analysis that expressed the view that in fact collective action by a select group of powers exercised through norms of great power restraint and a determination to resolve differences through negotiation at collective gatherings operated more or less effectively for decades in this early "global order" system.

So, from this latter perspective, it was less power and more generalized principles, rules, and norms. The collaborative mechanism appears to have secured international stability through a good part of the nineteenth century.

As suggested recently by the historian Margaret McMillan, "The Congress of Vienna, on the heels of the Napoleonic Wars, created a settlement that provided Europe with an unprecedented several decades of peace."[34] It did, and according to Ruggie, the concert was constructed by the great powers of the time in the post-Napoleonic period but operating on a set of principles that had been constructed by these states and agreed to at the Treaty of Paris in 1814–15. As Ruggie points out with respect to the then-emerging concert diplomacy, relying on Charles and Clifford Kupchan, "the concert version is characterized by the dominance of the great powers, decisions taken by informal negotiations and consensus, and no explicit specification of the mechanisms for implementing collective action."[35] Leading powers, yes, but also generalized principles of conduct.

This historical examination seems to suggest that generalized principles of collective action and restraint governed, but it leaves open whether the Concert worked because the major European powers were in Concert even though the balance of power was not the means to secure collaboration and international stability.

What Are the Middle Powers?

For many analysts, the essential actors in building multilateralism, if not limited to the leading powers, then require the committed efforts of what many describe as middle powers. Robert Keohane, decades ago reviewing several books on "small powers," pointed to these powers and their interest in multilateralism: "Middle power is a state whose leaders consider that it cannot act alone effectively but may be able to have a systematic impact in a small group or through an international institution."[36]

Unfortunately, suggesting that multilateralism is built on middle powers raises more questions than the term might otherwise resolve. The category "middle power" creates confusion. What are the middle powers? What are the middle powers in contemporary multilateralism and the emerging global order? South Korea perhaps is one, and there are frequent references to the same. Traditionally identified so-called middle powers such as Canada and Australia might also qualify as middle powers. But, then, what of Japan, France, the United Kingdom, Germany, or Turkey? And what about the large emerging market states, such as Indonesia, Brazil, and India? All have been identified at one time or another as middle powers in various examinations of contemporary multilateralism. The middle power label is, unfortunately, in the end not particularly helpful. It seems that a middle power in today's international relations literature is just about anything that is not a leading power, or is not using the traditional notion of a great power. Nevertheless, the impact of "small group" action of a set of actors seems to identify what analysts are looking at, at least in contemporary global governance in the global order. And, it would appear that these actors need not include the great or leading powers.

What may be helpful, in fact, is a designation recently proposed by the current French foreign minister, Jean-Yves Le Drain, along with the German foreign minister, Heiko Maas. In 2019, these foreign ministers launched the new "Alliance for Multilateralism," tied to the United Nations.[37] The leaders and the participants in this alliance are not referred to as middle powers, but the host and cohost countries and the participants are all designated as "goodwill powers." This designation emphasizes the collective action purpose of this contemporary multilateralism. There is no reference to "middle powers," or powers generally, which, as I have just pointed out, is rather misleading in any case. Thus, "goodwill powers" may be a useful term. We will come back to the idea of goodwill powers as we explore "effective multilateralism" in the final section.

As an added feature, the Alliance for Multilateralism details its conception of multilateralism: "In the field of foreign policy, multilateralism means that states cooperate with each other in order to promote common objectives and balance and regulate competing interests. They do this because they know that, ultimately, all states reap the greatest gains if they work together and agree on rules. Such cooperation relies on certain principles and values being shared by all parties. In the age of globalisation, almost all countries on Earth are interconnected. Conflicts raging thousands of miles away may have a direct impact on people's lives in Europe. Phenomena such as climate change cause problems that do not stop at any borders, which is why multilateral cooperation is more important than ever today."

The above inquiry suggests that that multilateralism may be constructed on governing principles of conduct with a variety of actors, including, it seems, in the contemporary global order even actors beyond states. What remains unclear is whether multilateralism can operate effectively without the leading powers. While leading powers—the United States and China—have organizing power for global governance analysts, as noted above, suggest that these "middle powers" do not alone have lasting organizing ability. And so we turn to that question in the final section.

Pointing to the Possibility of "Effective Multilateralism"

Can it follow, then, that multilateralism can be anchored on principles of governance that are not tied to power and may be constructed in some circumstances without the leading powers? This form of multilateralism we have referred to as "effective multilateralism." This is the last but critical question of our examination of multilateralism. Raising this form of multilateralism seemed to us to be particularly relevant as we saw the foreign policy actions of the Trump administration. But it still may be highly apposite with the current Biden administration and its foreign policy course. In other words, in meeting global governance challenges, is it possible that we can marshal collective action without the leading powers—for example, the United States or Xi Jinping's China. Such collective action would constitute, in our view, the notion of "effective multilateralism" (the third context):

3. What is the possible meaning for "effectiveness" in our effort to describe "effective multilateralism," and does it include, in fact, multilateralism without the leading powers? How would such effective multilateralism look like, and how would it function in the contemporary global order?

The Vision20 Principals, who followed the "trail of G20 summits" early on, hypothesized the possibility of just such a form of contemporary multilateralism.[38] Indeed, these Principals have pressed the case for "effective multilateralism," at least in the context of the G20 Leaders' Summit. The Principals have argued that effective multilateralism in the context of the contemporary global order Informal could be seen as: "We assess that 'effective multilateralism' today resides in those fora and coalitions that are prepared to move forward on policy and act on a collective action basis whether they include all, or not. Formal or informal institutions are not the limiting concern."[39] Nor do we suggest that effective multilateralism operates only at the state level. In what is referred to as "complex governance" by Kahler, the Vision20 Principals have suggested that effective multilateralism operates beyond the state level, capturing the wide array of actors in global governance today: "including foundations and other private and public corporations. These actors engage substate actors such as cities, regions, and provinces."[40] Collectively, this variety of communities increases the number of actors with enhanced resources, and in some instances intense commitment to a collective outcome, and enables "these actors press for more collective and effective action." For us, effective multilateralism is all about advancing collective global governance policy.

We start, however, with the disappointing multilateral response to the COVID-19 pandemic. As Stewart Patrick points out: "The dismal multilateral response to the pandemic reflects, in part, the decisions of specific leaders, especially Chinese President Xi Jinping and US President Donald Trump. Their behavior helps explain in part why the WHO struggled in the initial stages of the outbreak and why forums for multilateral coordination, such as the G7, the G20, and the UN Security Council, failed to rise to the occasion."[41] The failure of the leaders' summits in the face of this global pandemic is reveal- ing. The G20's inaction is in sharp contrast to the 2008 global financial crisis. It would seem to reflect the antipathy of the Trump administration, and the presi- dent himself, to multilateral action. "America First" hardly comprehended col- lective action. And the growing tensions between the United States and China under Xi Jinping have seemingly curtailed major G20 multilateral action.[42] And so it has also been reflected in G7 actions. The G7 Leaders' Summit, as described by George Parker and Jasmine Cameron-Chileshe, was hosted by the United Kingdom's Boris Johnson and did commit to the provision of 1 bil- lion vaccines to poorer countries.[43] This G7 effort, however, was seen as an initiative to compete with efforts by China and Russia to provide vaccines, not to encourage a collective global governance effort. So, looking to recent actions by the G20 and the G7 and other international institutions reflects appar- ently failed collective efforts. Geopolitics appears to have undermined the col- lective effort. It reinforces the position of some analysts that contemporary multilateralism is unattainable when the leading powers fail to support global governance initiatives. But this is not the complete story of contemporary multilateralism, and we briefly chronicle instances that point to the exercise of effective multilateralism.

Germany has periodically pressed effective multilateralism. The most evident instance has been Chancellor Angela Merkel's insistence, when she hosted the G20 Leaders' Summit in Hamburg in 2017, that even without US support for the Paris Climate Change Agreement, the Leaders' Declaration would include support for the Paris Agreement by all the G20 members except the United States. This insistence by Merkel was pointed. Before the Hamburg G20 Leaders' Summit, there was seemingly a hard-and-fast rule of consensus with the G20 Leaders' declarations. If a consensus was unattainable, the matter was dropped from the Leaders' G20 statement or declaration.

In another instance—surprisingly, perhaps, given past leadership roles— Japan under Prime Minister Shinzo Abe's leadership promoted effective multi- lateralism as well. As we saw in a brief examination of Japan by Alexandroff, Abe chose to pick up the pieces of the Trans-Pacific Partnership (TPP) after the Trump administration's decision to withdraw from the agreement.[44] Abe orchestrated continuing negotiations for this significant plurilateral agree- ment and successfully concluded what became the Comprehensive and Progressive Trans-Pacific Partnership. Let me highlight Japan's unexpected action with an insight from the *Financial Times*' Gideon Rachman: "The way in which Japan moved to save the TPP, after Mr. Trump withdrew the US from it in 2017, demonstrated that medium-sized powers like Japan have a clear interest in preserving international rules—at a time when both the US and China are challenging the multilateral order. Post-Brexit Britain will share that interest and should work with other midsized G20 powers that share its global outlook, including Australia, Canada and South Korea."[45] The question is whether this break with earlier leadership behavior and the leadership action by the Abe government is limited to this prime minister, now retired and deceased, or may we see such effective multilateralism behavior again under new Japanese leadership?

Let us return for a moment to the Alliance for Multilateralism. It appears as yet to be another instance of effective multilateral effort in the contemporary global order. As pointed out above, this initiative was launched by the foreign ministers of France and Germany. Its initial meeting was on April 2, 2019, in New York during the German UN Security Council Presidency. It was followed by a meeting on September 26, held during the High-Level Week at the UN General Assembly. The meeting was called by Germany and France and was cohosted by Canada, Mexico, Chile, Singapore, and Ghana. Forty-eight countries participated in this September gathering.

At its heart, the Alliance for Multilateralism seeks support for a rules-based order. Here is how the Alliance describes "multilateralism": "In the field of foreign policy, multilateralism means that states cooperate with each other in order to promote common objectives and balance and regulate competing interests. They do this because they know that, ultimately, all states reap the greatest gains if they work together and agree on rules. Such cooperation relies on certain principles and values being shared by all parties. In the age of globalisation, tight interdependence is the nature of many relationships. The Alliance underscores the tight interdependence that still underlines the global order today."

The Alliance for Multilateralism sees its multilateral structure operating in this way: "The Alliance is not a formal institution, but a network allowing for the constitution of flexible issue-based coalitions formed around specific projects and policy outcomes. Engagement in a specific initiative does not entail automatic participation in other initiatives pursued in the framework of the Alliance. Participation in the Alliance remains open to all who share its vision." It is a network and encourages but does not insist on states committing to all issues. It is a loose network of nonleading powers—the so-called goodwill powers. The initiative is organized around three goals according to the Alliance hosts. The Alliance aims to: renew the global commitment to stabilize the rules-based international order, uphold its principles, and adapt it where required. The goals, as declared by the Alliance, are

—to protect and preserve international norms, agreements and institutions that are under pressure or in peril;

—to pursue a more proactive agenda in policy areas that lack effective governance and where new challenges require collective action; and

—to advance reforms, without compromising on key principles and values, in order to make multilateral institutions and the global political and economic order more inclusive and effective in delivering tangible results to citizens around the world.

The Alliance also makes a point of identifying its outreach to nonstate actors as stakeholders and partners for the challenges the Alliance faces. The Alliance has held four meetings since its creation. These gatherings sought to promote, among other things,

—improved governance for the digital world. The Alliance bolstered support for the Paris Call for Trust and Security in Cyberspace;

—implementation of international humanitarian law to protect the work of humanitarian workers and space for humanitarian action and support for the fight against impunity, at the opening of the session of the Human Rights Council in Geneva on February 24, 2020; and

—support for the central role of the World Health Organization in the management of COVID-19.

These actions are supportive, but the question remains, beyond the evident declarative support expressed by the Alliance: Will participants, the goodwill powers, be willing to take concrete collective action to advance the goals that it supports?

These initiatives are noteworthy, but the question remains about the level of collective commitment to advancing concrete policy actions and solutions in these areas with support from states and nonstate actors. We have seen the G20 host countries advance collective efforts. South Korea, for instance, has shown the capability to further global governance policy initiatives. One of the most successful G20 Leaders' Summits, the 2010 Seoul Summit, underlined Korean leadership. Korea was the first government to be a non-G7 host. Korea showed that it has global governance organizing means and commitment.[46] Japan, as pointed out above, recently offered another instance of successful hosting in a far less collaborative environment. But the case for effective multilateralism remains to be fully proven.

Part of the issue, I believe, may well be the painful but necessary desocialization by states from earlier global order behavior. States in the G20 and beyond have been conditioned to expect and accept that the leading states, and most particularly the United States, will step up to organize collective security and global governance action. It is clear from the past Trump presidency years, and now potentially, with the Biden administration's focus on a democracy-versus-autocracy approach, that that path to multilateral action relying on US leadership cannot be assumed or assured. It may also be that the global commons challenges—including climate change, global health, protection of the high seas and other looming threats—may encourage effective multilateralism.[47] If not them, then who? Collective action will have to be organized by the goodwill powers if the leading powers are unable to collaborate, and may in fact seek to compete. It appears to be a lesson still being learned.

And while the Trump administration did much to undermine the alliances and partnerships of the liberal order, it would seem that the American public is not inclined to see the global order in the same way. As pointed out by Stewart Patrick, the American public seems to support the relationships built in the liberal order over seventy years: "Fortunately, we now have better insight into public attitudes, thanks to three surveys recently released by the Pew Research Center, the Chicago Council on Global Affairs, and the Better World Campaign, an advocacy arm of the UN Foundation. They show robust global and US support for international cooperation and the United Nations. At the same time, they reveal stark partisan differences in public attitudes in the US, where Democrats and Republicans seem to be living on different planets."[48]

We leave with two strands of optimism. First, American public attitudes may yet encourage the Biden administration to encourage greater support for global governance collaboration. It might well lead the administration to go beyond just US alliance efforts and to recommit to multilateral efforts on climate change and collaborative efforts to head off future pandemics. The Biden administration may also find itself more accepting of effective multilateral actions that are "birthed" by others, permitting so-called shifting coalitions of consensus to be reinterpreted to advance effective multilateralism in the evolving global order.

Notes

1. The author would like to thank colleagues who reviewed and commented on earlier drafts of this chapter, including Lim Wonhyuk, Colin Bradford, Homi Kharas, and Susan Thornton. Improvements are gratefully acknowledged, and the errors remain with the author.

2. This is not the place to tackle the distinction between the global and liberal order. The liberal order follows, I believe, from the work of G. John Ikenberry. Over several volumes—the most recent of which is by G. John Ikenberry, *A World Safe for*

Democracy: Liberal Internationalism and the Crises of Global Order (Yale University Press, 2020)—it becomes clearer what he calls the liberal international order is inclusive of the rule of law, open markets and an element of liberal democracy. It may also include American leadership. Thus, the liberal international order fades with the end of the Cold War and the incorporation of illiberal and even authoritarian states. Here, then, is the global order that develops following the end of the Cold War.

3. The term was coined by Charles Krauthammer: "The Unipolar Moment," *Washington Post*, July 20, 1990, https://www.washingtonpost.com/archive/opinions/1990/07/20/the-unipolar-moment/62867add-2fe9-493f-a0c9-4bfba1ec23bd/. Highly insightful, this conservative writer captured the transition from bipolarity to a period led by the sole superpower, the United States. It is worth reflecting back on the period with Krauthammer: "The Unipolar Moment Revisited," *National Interest*, December 1, 2002, https://nationalinterest.org/article/the-unipolar-moment-revisited-391.

4. Robert O. Keohane, "Multilateralism: An Agenda for Research," *International Journal* 45, no. 4 (1990): 731–64, at 731.

5. John Gerard Ruggie, "The Anatomy of an Institution," *International Organization* 46, no. 3 (1992): 561–98.

6. Ruggie, 571.

7. Ikenberry, *World Safe for Democracy*, 35.

8. Ruggie, "Anatomy," 569.

9. Ruggie, 566.

10. Miles Kahler, "Multilateralism with Small and Large Numbers," *International Organization* 46, no. 3 (1992): 681–708.

11. Kahler, 681.

12. Moses Naim, "Minilateralism: The Magic Number to Get Real International Action," *Foreign Policy*, June 21, 2009, https://foreignpolicy.com/2009/06/21/minilateralism/.

13. Kahler, "Multilateralism," 707.

14. This comes from a personal conversation and a video interview I organized on September 1, 2020, with Miles Kahler for my graduate course, "Governing with and without the State," at the Munk School of Global Affairs & Public Policy, University of Toronto.

15. Kahler, "Multilateralism," 682.

16. Miles Kahler, "Global Governance in the 21st Century: End of the Bretton Woods Moment?" unpublished report, 2020.

17. Alan S. Alexandroff and Donald Brean, "Global Summitry: Its Meaning and Scope: Part One," *Global Summitry* 1, no. 1 (2015): 1–26.

18. Felicity Vabulas and Duncan Snidal, "Organization without Delegation: Informal Intergovernmental Organizations (IIGOs) and the Spectrum of Intergovernmental Arrangements," *Review of International Organization* 8 (2013): 193–220.

19. The G10 was made up of finance ministers and central bankers who agreed to participate in the General Arrangements to Borrow, an agreement to provide the International Monetary Fund with additional funds to increase its lending ability. The ministers and central bankers would meet annually and included these members:

Belgium, Canada, France, Germany, Italy, Japan, the Netherlands, the United Kingdom, Switzerland, Sweden, and the United States.

20. This first Leaders' Summit, the G6 Leaders' Summit met in 1975 hosted by France at Rambouillet. Leaders included heads of government and a head of state from France, West Germany, Italy, Japan, the UK, and the US. The following year in Puerto Rico, Canada was invited to join and the G6 became the G7.

21. Andrew F. Cooper and John English, "Introduction: Reforming the International System from the Top: A Leaders' 20 Summit," in *Reforming from the Top: A Leaders' 20 Summit* (United Nations University Press, 2005).

22. The first G20 occurred in late 1999 as a meeting of finance ministers and central bankers. It included nineteen governments plus the EU. Members included: Argentina, Australia, Brazil, Canada, China, Germany, France, India, Indonesia, Italy, Japan, Mexico, Russia, Saudi Arabia, South Africa, South Korea, Turkey, the UK, and the United States.

23. Alan Alexandroff, "Between the Old and the New: Can Japan Help Lead the Way to a New Liberal Order?" In *Japan's Leadership in the Liberal International Order: Impact and Policy Opportunities for Partners*, July 15, 2020.

24. A definition of "engagement groups" is provided by Scheler and Dobson: "It is now institutionalized in the form of "engagement groups," defined as "independent collectives that are led by organizations from the host country [and which] work with other organizations from G20 countries to develop policy recommendations that are formally submitted to G20 leaders for consideration (G20 n.d.)"; Ronja Scheler and Hugo Dobson, "Policy Brief: Joining Forces: Reviving Multilateralism through Multi-Stakeholder Cooperation," *Task Force 5: The Future of Multilateralism and Global Governance*, 2020, 4.

25. Stewart Patrick, "The G20: Shifting Coalitions of Consensus Rather Than Blocs," in *The Consolidation of the G20: From Crisis Committee to Global Steering Committee*, edited by Colin Bradford and Lim Wonhyuk (Seoul: Korea Development Institute; and Washington: Brookings, 2010), 358–70, at 358). For a further elaboration of the concept of "shifting coalitions of consensus," see the video segment by Colin Bradford, YouTube, 2013, https://www.youtube.com/watch?v=ZTRGmgPgW4U.

26. Charles Roger, *The Origins of Informality: Why the Legal Foundations of Global Governance Are Shifting, and Why It Matters* (Oxford University Press. 2020).

27. Kahler, "Global Governance," 12.

28. Certainly, a number of analysts signalled the change. Especially noteworthy was the edited volume by Deborah Avant, Martha Finnemore and Susan Sell, eds. (2010), *Who Governs the Globe*. Also, noteworthy is *Global Governance: Why? What? Whither?* by Thomas Weiss et al. (Hoboken, NJ: John Wiley & Sons, 2013). For Weiss and his coauthors, it is evident that enlargement of the types of actors is linked to emergence of global governance challenges in the international system.

29. Miles Kahler, "'Global Governance': Three Futures," *International Studies Review* 20 (2018): 239–46, at 242.

30. Deborah Avant, Martha Finnemore, and Susan K. Sell, eds., *Who Governs the Globe?* Cambridge Studies in International Relations (Cambridge University Press, 2010), 1.

31. Robert Kagan, *The Jungle Grows Back: America and Our Imperiled World* (New York: Alfred A. Knopf, 2018).

32. Ruggie, "Anatomy," 585–86.

33. The debate is intense. Just a few of the "contestants" are Richard B. Elrod, "The Concert of Europe: A Fresh Look at an International System," *World Politics* 28, no. 2 (1976): 159–74; Robert Jervis, "From Balance to Concert: A Study of International Security Cooperation," *World Politics* 38, no. 1 (1985): 58–79; Kyle M. Lascurettes, *Orders of Exclusion: Great Powers and the Strategic Sources of Foundational Rules in International Relations* (Oxford University Press, 2020); Paul W. Schroeder, *The Transformation of European Politics, 1763–1848* (Oxford: Clarendon Press, 1994); and Paul W. Schroeder, "The Cold War and Its Ending in 'Long-Duration' International History," in *Peace, Prosperity, and Politics*, edited by John Mueller (Boulder, CO: Westview Press, 2000). Both Elrod and Schroeder are historians who suggest that norms and rules supplied the foundations principally for multilateral arrangements— in this instance, concert diplomacy. Jervis and very recently Lascurettes, among others, see the concert as built on power, balance of power, and great power hierarchy.

34. Margaret McMillan, *War: How Conflict Shaped Us* (New York: Random House, 2020).

35. Ruggie is referring to Charles Kupchan and Clifford Kupchan, "Concerts, Collective Security, and the Future of Europe," *International Security* 16, no. 1 (1991): 114–61, https://www.jstor.org/stable/2539053. Ruggie, "Anatomy," 578.

36. Robert Keohane, "Lilliputians' Dilemmas: Small States in International Politics," *International Organization* 23, no. 2 (1969): 291–310, at 269. Keohane here quotes Robert L. Rothstein. *Alliances and Small Powers* (Columbia University Press, 1968).

37. For an examination of this new Alliance for Multilateralism, see Stewart M. Patrick, "Can an 'Alliance for Multilateralism' Succeed in a New Era of Nationalism?" *World Politics Review*, September 9, 2019, https://www.worldpoliticsreview.com/articles/28174/can-an-alliance-for-multilateralism-succeed-in-a-new-era-of-nationalism. Also see the Alliance for Multilateralism website, https://multilateralism.org/the-alliance/.

38. The Vision20 principals—Colin Bradford, senior nonresident fellow at Brookings; Yves Tiberghien, professor of political science at the University of British Columbia; and the author, the director of the Global Summitry Project and teaching at the Munk School of Global Affairs & Public Policy at the University of Toronto—began to use the concept in examining the G20 Leaders' Summit several years ago; Vision20, "Effective Multilateralism: 2019 Vision20–Brookings Blue Report," April 2019, https://14c9fea5-3892-4633-ad46-2c6aa4f930ea.filesusr.com/ugd/1bfab0_1141546a09a74a5085b7b2ae2cf9cde0.pdf. The Principals in one way or another have followed, analyzed, and written about G20 leaders' summits since even before the Leaders' Summit was created.

39. Vision20, "Effective Multilateralism 3."

40. Kahler, "Global Governance."

41. Stewart Patrick, "When the System Fails: COVID-19 and the Costs of Global Dysfunction," *Foreign Affairs*, July–August 2020, https://www.foreignaffairs.com/articles/world/2020-06-09/when-system-fails.

42. There has been the Debt Service Suspension Initiative, but the limited credit provision stands in sharp contrast to the major coordination of efforts by the G20 in 2008.

43. George Parker and Jasmine Cameron-Chileshe, "G7 Leaders to Pledge 1 Bn COVID-19 Vaccine Doses for Poorer Countries," *Financial Times*, June 10, 2021, https://www.ft.com/content/000e6968-8ae4-4f00-9cb5-324b98aa779b.

44. Alexandroff, "Between the Old and the New."

45. Gideon Rachman, "Boris Johnson's Chance to Forge a New Role for Britain," *Financial Times*, December 13, 2019, https://www.ft.com/content/db8d1e24-1d9b-11ea-97df-cc63de1d73f4?emailId=5df4aa8f019ef7000497a47b&segmentId=2f40f9e8-c8d5-af4c-ecdd-78ad0b93926b.

46. Bradford and Wonhyuk, *Consolidation of the G20.*

47. This point was made in personal communications with my Brookings colleague Homi Kharas.

48. Stewart Patrick, "Gauging Public Support for Multilateralism—Around the World, and in the US," *World Politics Review*, September 28, 2020, https://www.worldpoliticsreview.com/articles/29089/gauging-public-support-for-multilateralism-around-the-world-and-in-the-u-s.

Seven
Technology, Growth, and Inequality
CHANGING DYNAMICS IN THE DIGITAL ERA

ZIA QURESHI, *GLOBAL ECONOMY AND DEVELOPMENT AT BROOKINGS*

Digital transformation is a defining feature of our time. The COVID-19 pandemic is accelerating this transformation. The new technologies hold considerable promise. But they also pose new challenges. Digital technologies have dazzled for sure, but they have not so far delivered the expected dividend in higher aggregate productivity growth. And inequality has been rising. As digitalization and new advances in artificial intelligence transform markets, policies must rise to the challenges of change. The digital economy must be broadened to disseminate new technologies and productive opportunities among smaller firms and wider segments of the labor force. Policies must play their part to better harness the potential of innovation in our digital era and turn it into a driver of stronger and more inclusive growth in economic prosperity.

The Era of Brilliant New Technologies

Ours is an era of dazzling new technologies. It is often referred to in epochal terms—as a time of technological renaissance powered by brilliant new technologies, a second machine age, and a new industrial revolution.[1] Some scenarios see the world approaching a technological singularity of accelerating technological change—and a consequent economic singularity of a takeoff in productivity and economic growth.[2]

Such exuberance is understandable. While some characterizations of technological change may be overly grand and visionary, the pace and scope of the advances being made are surely impressive. Technology has been booming in recent decades, led by an array of digital innovations. Ranging from increasingly sophisticated computer systems, software, and mobile telephony to digital platforms and robotics, these innovations have been reshaping markets and the worlds of business and work. New advances in artificial intelligence, machine learning, cyber-physical systems, and the internet of things are driving digital transformation further. This latest wave of innovations can take the digital revolution to a whole new level.[3]

The COVID-19 Digital Accelerator: The Future Is Arriving Faster

The pace of technological change will accelerate as a consequence of the COVID-19 pandemic.[4] The crisis may be remembered as the Great Digital Accelerator, marking an inflection point in the advance of digital transformation.

The pandemic is reinforcing firms' incentives to automate production processes. Trade and commerce are going digital at a faster clip. Digital platforms are expanding their economic sway. Teleworking has increased sharply. Education and training have rapidly shifted online. The use of automated and online processes is speeding up across most sectors of the economy. The digitalization of economic activity in general has intensified.

This trajectory of further technological change was expected, but the pandemic is making it happen sooner. The future is arriving faster than expected. Even as economies recover from the pandemic, some of its effects will be long lasting. Before the pandemic, a paradigm shift toward digitalization was already well under way. The pandemic has accelerated the shift.

Booming Technology but Slowing Productivity and Rising Inequality

Technology drives productivity, and productivity drives economic growth. But as digital technologies have boomed, productivity growth has slowed rather than accelerated. This is a great paradox of our time.[5] The new technologies have dazzled but so far have not delivered the expected dividend in higher aggregate productivity growth. Economic growth, with its main engine slowing, has trended lower.

Productivity growth has slowed significantly in advanced economies since the 1980s. The slowdown extends across economies that are members of the Organization for Economic Cooperation and Development (OECD). It is broad-based, affecting more than two-thirds of the sectors.[6] For the past decade or so, productivity growth has slowed in many emerging economies as well. Over the five-year period 2013–17, productivity growth was lower than the long-term average in about 65 percent of all countries.[7]

Concurrent with the slowdown of productivity growth, income inequality within countries has been rising. Inequality has risen in all major advanced economies since the 1980s, and quite appreciably in several of them. In many cases, there has been a particularly sharp increase in income concentration at the top end of the distribution. Wealth concentration at the top end of the distribution is still more acute—on average, roughly twice as high as income concentration. Trends in income distribution are more mixed across emerging economies, but many of them have also experienced rising inequality over the same period.

While income inequality has been rising within many countries in recent decades, inequality between countries has been falling, thanks to the rise of faster-growing emerging economies that are narrowing the income gap with advanced economies. Technological change poses new challenges for this economic convergence. Manufacturing-led growth in emerging economies has been propelled by their comparative advantage in labor-intensive manufacturing based on large pools of low-skilled, low-wage workers. This source of comparative advantage increasingly will matter less as automation of low-skilled work progresses, disrupting traditional pathways to development.[8] The COVID-19 pandemic could add to the challenges emerging economies face in recalibrating their growth models by disrupting global supply chains and triggering stronger moves to reshore production in advanced economies.

The US economy vividly illustrates the concurrent trends of slowing productivity growth and rising within-country inequality. The United States has been the global leader in the digital revolution. Yet productivity growth has slowed considerably since the early 2000s (figure 7-1). Over the last ten years, labor productivity growth has averaged less than half the growth rate of the decade before the slowdown. Total factor productivity growth shows a similar trend. Productivity growth picked up in the latter half of the 1990s, partly spurred by increased initial investment in the adoption of digital technologies. But this surge proved short-lived. Even as these technologies continued their advance in the subsequent two decades, and automation of production deepened and became more sophisticated, productivity growth slowed, settling into a longer-term trend of persistent weakness.

Meanwhile, income inequality in the United States has been rising—and more sharply than in other major advanced economies (figure 7-1). Since the early 1980s, the share of the top 10 percent in national income has risen from

Figure 7-1. Falling US Productivity Growth and Rising Inequality, 1985–2019

% annual change   % share

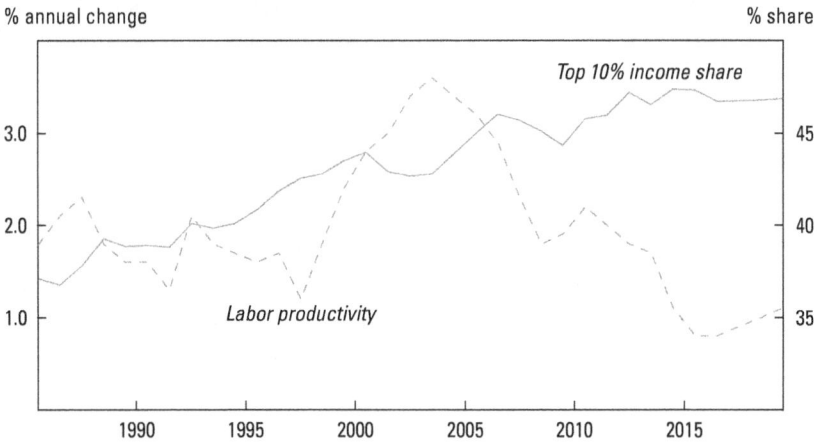

Sources: Bureau of Labor Statistics (nonfarm business output per hour worked) and World Inequality Database (pretax national income shares).
Note: The productivity series given in this figure shows five-year moving averages to smooth year-to-year fluctuations.

35 percent to 47 percent. The income share of the top 1 percent has roughly doubled, from 11 percent to 21 percent. The share of the top 1 percent in wealth has risen from 23 percent to about 40 percent. Those with middle-class incomes have been squeezed. For the median worker, real wages have been largely stagnant over long periods. Real median wage growth has been weighed down not only by slower productivity growth but also by wages lagging productivity growth and rising wage inequality. Job insecurity has increased, with mounting fears of a "robocalypse"—large job losses from automation.[9] As income inequality has risen, intergenerational economic mobility has declined.[10]

Across economies, rising inequality and related disparities and anxieties have stoked social discontent. They are a major fault line underlying the increased popular disaffection and political polarization that are so evident today.

Recent economic history, in short, presents a striking contrast between the promise of brilliant new technologies and the actual economic and social outcomes. The national economic pie has been growing more slowly and more unequally. The benefits of technological transformation have been shared highly unevenly. This should not, however, lead to a Luddite backlash against technology. Technology itself is not the problem. On the contrary, the new technologies hold considerable potential to boost productivity and economic growth, create new and better jobs to replace old ones, and raise human welfare. The challenge for policymakers is to better harness this potential and turn innovation in our digital era into a driver of stronger and more inclusive growth in economic prosperity.

Technology: Changing Growth and Distributional Dynamics but Lagging Policies

Technological change is inherently disruptive and entails difficult transitions. Inevitably, it creates winners and losers. Policies have a crucial role to play, to improve the enabling environment for firms and workers—to broaden access to the new opportunities that come from technological change and to enhance capabilities to adjust to the new challenges.

Unfortunately, policies and institutions have been slow to rise to the challenges of technological change, as it has shifted dynamics across product and labor markets. Slowing productivity growth and rising inequality are closely linked to the way new technologies have interacted with the prevailing policy and institutional environment. As discussed below, there is a strong, common nexus connecting technology, policies, and the productivity and distributional outcomes.[11]

Transformations Affecting Firms

Digital technologies are altering business models and reshaping market structures. How technology diffuses within the economy matters greatly for both productivity growth and income distribution. But so far, the benefits of digital innovations have not been diffusing widely across firms. They have been captured mostly by a relatively small number of large firms. There is a pronounced gap between the digital "haves" and "have-mores." Even the economy at the digital frontier—the United States—may be reaching only about a fifth of its digital potential.[12]

At its root, the slowdown in productivity reflects a growing inequality in productivity performance between firms. Productivity growth has been relatively strong in leading firms at the technological frontier. However, it has slowed considerably in the vast majority of other firms, pulling aggregate productivity growth lower. Over a fifteen-year period starting in 2000, labor productivity among frontier firms in OECD economies rose by around 45 percent; among nonfrontier firms, the increase was well below 10 percent.[13] Productivity divergence between firms is wider in more digitally intensive industries.[14]

A weakening of competition is one important reason for this outcome. Barriers to competition and related market frictions are preventing a broader diffusion of new technologies and causing a persistent rise in productivity and profitability gaps between firms. Evidence for OECD economies shows that in industries less exposed to competition, technological innovation and diffusion are weaker, interfirm productivity divergence is wider, and aggregate productivity growth is slower. It links the weakness in productivity to diminished competitive intensity in markets.[15]

The erosion of competition is reflected in a variety of indicators: rise in market concentration in industries, higher markups showing increased market power of dominant firms, these firms' supernormal profits (rents) that account for a rising share of total corporate profits, low churning among high-return firms, and corporate ossification with declining business dynamism as measured by new firm formation.[16] The decline in business dynamism and the rise in market concentration are greater in industries that are more intensive users of digital technologies.

These trends are observable broadly across advanced economies but have been particularly pronounced in the United States. The share of top four US companies in total sales has risen since the 1980s in all major sectors of the economy—and more sharply in digitally intensive sectors.[17] Markups over marginal cost for US publicly traded firms are estimated to have nearly tripled between 1980 and 2016, with the increase concentrated in high-markup firms gaining market share, indicating a strong rise in their market power.[18] Over roughly the same period, rents (profits in excess of those under competitive market conditions) are estimated to have risen from a negligible share of national income to about one-fifth.[19] The distribution of returns on capital has become more unequal, with a relatively small number of firms reaping supernormal profits.[20] The share of young firms (five years old or less) in the total number of US firms has declined from about one-half to one-third.[21] American markets, a model of competition for the world, have been shifting toward more monopolistic structures.[22]

The new technologies are contributing to increased market concentration by altering competition in ways that produce winner-takes-all outcomes. They offer first-mover advantages, strong economies of scale and network effects, and the leverage of big data that encourage the rise of "superstar firms."[23] The rise of "the intangible economy"—where assets such as data, software, and other intellectual property matter more for economic success— has been associated with a stronger tendency toward the emergence of dominant firms.[24] The winner-takes-all dynamics are most marked in the high-tech sectors, as reflected in the rise of tech giants such as Apple, Facebook, and Google. But they are increasingly affecting economies more broadly, as digitalization penetrates business processes in other sectors, such as transportation, communications, finance, and commerce. In retail trade, for example, the big box stores, which previously had replaced mom and pop outlets, are now losing market share to online megastores such as Amazon.

Failures in competition policy have reinforced these technology-driven forces, producing higher market concentration. Competition policy has lagged behind the digital economy as it shifts market structures and poses new challenges to keep markets competitive, notably those related to data. Antitrust enforcement has been weak in the face of rising monopoly power and takeover activity. Facebook alone, for example, has acquired more than seventy companies over roughly fifteen years, including potential competitors like Instagram and WhatsApp. Increased overlapping ownership of companies that compete, by large institutional investors, also has affected competition. Regulatory policies have not been consistently supportive of competition, with elements of both overregulation that restricts competition and deregulation without adequate safeguards to protect competition.

Flaws in patent systems have acted as barriers to new or follow-on innovation and wider diffusion of knowledge embodied in new technologies. These systems, which typically were designed many decades ago, have been slow to adapt to the knowledge dynamics of the digital era. In the United States, the ownership of patents has become more concentrated in the hands of firms with the largest stock since the 1980s—mirroring broader patterns of market concentration—coupled with more strategic use of patents by market leaders to limit knowledge diffusion.[25]

Transformations Affecting Workers

As in product markets, technology has been the big story in labor markets. It has been transforming the nature and future of work. A similar interplay between rapid, technology-driven change and lagging policies to that seen in product markets has been at work in labor markets, limiting productivity gains from new technologies and exacerbating inequality. While product markets have seen rising inequality between firms, labor markets have seen rising inequality between workers.

Automation and digital advances have shifted labor demand toward higher-level skills. In advanced economies, globalization has exerted pressure in the same direction. Demand has shifted, in particular, away from routine, middle-level skills that are more vulnerable to automation, as in jobs like clerical work and repetitive production. Job markets have seen an increasing polarization, with the employment share of middle-skill jobs falling and that of higher-skill jobs, such as technical professionals and managers, rising. The employment share of low-skill jobs has also increased but mainly in nonroutine manual jobs in services such as personal care that are hard to automate. Over the two decades since the mid-1990s, the share of middle-skill jobs in total employment fell by about 9.5 percentage points in OECD economies on average, while the shares of high-skill and low-skill jobs rose by about 7.5 and 2 percentage points, respectively.[26]

As artificial intelligence advances, displacement risks will affect some higher-level skills as well, in contrast to previous waves of automation. However, the displacement risk at higher-level skills is likely to apply more at the task level than at the level of entire jobs or occupations, as has been the case with low- to middle-level skills.[27]

While demand for skills has been shifting, adjustment on the supply side to equip workers with skills that complement the new technologies and support their transition to new tasks and jobs has lagged. Education and training have been losing the race with technology.[28] Even in an advanced economy such as the United States, almost two-thirds of workers do not have a college degree. Growth in the years of education completed slowed considerably in the United States around the 1980s. So just when demand for higher-level skills picked up as the digital revolution gathered steam, the attainment of those skills slowed. While precollege education gaps by family income level have narrowed, gaps in college and higher-level education have widened. The slowing of improvement in educational attainment is observable more broadly across economies—both advanced and emerging economies—around this period.[29] Moreover, the capacity of systems for continuing education has been far exceeded by the fast-growing need for worker upskilling and reskilling. Access to retraining is typically more difficult for lower-skilled workers.

Shortages of new and higher-level cognitive, technical, and managerial skills demanded by the digital economy have hampered technology diffusion across firms and broader productivity gains. Across industries, skills mismatches have increased: in OECD countries, on average around one-quarter of workers report a mismatch between their skills and those required by the job.[30] Workers with skills complementary to the new technologies have increasingly clustered in dominant firms at the technological frontier.

The shifting balance between skills demand and supply has increased the premium on higher-level skills and widened wage differentials, exacerbating higher labor income inequality and diminished job prospects for less skilled workers. The skill premium has been rising since the 1980s and has more recently risen particularly sharply at the higher end of educational attainment—graduate and professional education. Skill-biased technological change has been a factor in the "convexification" of returns to education and training.[31]

Interfirm wage inequality has increased as well. Across OECD economies, increased inequality in firm productivity and profitability is mirrored by increased inequality in labor incomes. [32] As profitability gaps have widened between firms, so have wage gaps. Rent sharing also has contributed to wider wage differences between firms. Better-performing firms have reaped a higher share of total profits and shared part of their supernormal profits with their workers. Between-firm wage inequality has risen more in industries that invest more intensively in digital technologies.

While workers in firms at the technological frontier are earning more than those in other firms, gains from higher productivity at these firms have been shared unevenly, with wage growth lagging productivity growth. Wages have risen in the better-performing firms but by less than the rise in productivity. For most other firms, limited wage growth has reflected limited productivity growth, although even at these firms, wage growth has tended to fall short of the meager gains in productivity. In the United States, between the mid-1970s and the mid-2010s, labor productivity rose by about 75 percent and average worker compensation in real terms rose by about 50 percent—with the productivity and compensation growth divergence increasing in the most recent decades. Over the same period, real compensation for the median worker rose by less than 15 percent, reflecting rising wage inequality.[33]

The decoupling of wages from productivity has contributed to a shift in income distribution from labor to capital. In the past couple of decades, most major economies have experienced both increasing inequality of labor earnings and declining shares of labor in total income.[34] In the United States, for example, the percentage share of labor in nonfarm business income dropped from the mid-60s in about 2000 to the mid-50s in about 2015.

Increased market concentration in product markets also has played a role in the shifting of income from labor to capital as it has reallocated labor within industries to dominant firms with supernormal profits and lower labor income shares.[35] Dominant firms are not only acquiring more monopoly power in product markets to increase markups and extract higher rents but also monopsony power to dictate wages in the labor market.[36] While employer market power has strengthened, worker bargaining power has weakened with a decline in unionization and an erosion of minimum wage laws.

These labor and product market developments have reinforced the effect of the labor-substituting nature of many of the new technologies on the distribution of income between labor and capital. Production is shifting toward firms and processes using more capital (tangible and intangible) and less labor. The largest US firm in 2017 (Apple) had a market capitalization forty times as high as that of the largest US firm in 1962 (AT&T), but its total employment was only one-fifth that of the latter.[37] The shift of income from labor to capital has increased overall income inequality, as capital ownership is highly uneven.[38]

In advanced economies, international trade and offshoring also have contributed to the shift in income toward capital by putting downward pressure on wages, especially of lower-skilled workers in tradable sectors. The expanding digital trade—the new phase of globalization—can add to these pressures. With a growing range of digitally deliverable services, workers further up the skill spectrum also will face more competition from across borders.[39] Overall, globalization has played a significant role in the decline of the labor income share in advanced economies. However, its role has been much smaller than that of technology—about half or less.[40]

COVID-19: Reinforcing New Market Dynamics

The COVID-19 pandemic reinforced the technology-driven shifts in product and labor market dynamics as it accelerated the digitalization of production, commerce, and work. As economies recovered from the immediate crisis, the further advances in digital transformation spurred productivity and boosted economic growth. But they also reinforced the market dynamics that have in recent years inhibited productivity growth and increased economic inequality.

In product markets, the pandemic may fortify the trend toward more concentrated market structures.[41] The big shift in demand toward online modes of business is adding to the preexisting advantages of technologically advanced, well-positioned large firms. The pandemic is likely to disproportionately cull the ranks of smaller, less automation-intensive firms—also because smaller firms lack the liquidity and access to credit needed to survive in a crisis. While smaller firms struggle, tech giants are further increasing market shares. This is already evident in some industries, such as in retail trade, where an unfolding wave of bankruptcies is pushing more business toward big tech retail giants. Market dynamism and competition will face added challenges, with more firm exits and fewer new entrants, and increased takeover opportunities. The reinforcement of the dominant positions of large firms associated with more demand shifting online will not be limited to the period of COVID-19 shutdowns but will extend into the future.

In labor markets, increased automation and telework triggered by the pandemic can further tilt the balance against less-skilled, low-wage workers.[42] Forced by closures and social distancing requirements, firms are automating even more, discovering new ways to harness emerging technologies to accomplish tasks with less labor. This is happening more in industries with business models heavily reliant on human contact and a less-skilled workforce. The further consolidation of economic activity in large firms in product markets will reinforce recent trends toward higher wage inequality and lower labor income share.

The pandemic spurred an overnight revolution in telework. The beneficiaries of telework are primarily higher-educated workers. Not only do low-skilled workers have fewer options to telework and are thus less shielded from the immediate impact of the crisis, they face longer-term job losses as telework reduces demand for a range of personal and business services that employ them in large numbers, such as office space maintenance, transportation, and hospitality. Much of the shift toward telework is likely to endure. In the post-pandemic period, the share of working days delivered through telework by full-time employees is expected to be at least three times higher than before.[43]

Policies Must Catch Up with Technological Change

The rise of the digital economy is a defining feature of our time. The latest advances in artificial intelligence and machine learning are expanding the digital frontier. The COVID-19 pandemic accelerated this technological transformation. But technological change is not delivering its full potential to boost productivity and economic growth. And it is pushing income inequality higher, with the distribution of both capital and labor income becoming more unequal and income shifting from labor to capital.

However, these outcomes are not inevitable. With more responsive policies, better outcomes are possible. Digital technologies can be the source of as much as two-thirds—or perhaps even more—of potential productivity growth over the next decade.[44] How to realize the potential of these technologies to deliver stronger and more inclusive economic growth lies at the core of the public policy agenda. Today's innovation economy must be broadened from its narrow confines to disseminate new technologies and productive opportunities among smaller firms and wider segments of the labor force. Innovation must be "democratized."[45]

There is much concern today about rising inequality and its adverse economic, social, and political consequences. Policies to reduce inequality are often seen narrowly in terms of redistribution tax-and-transfer policies. This is, of course, an important element, especially given the erosion of the state's redistributive role in recent decades as tax progressivity has declined and social programs have felt the pressure of tighter fiscal constraints. In particular, systems for taxing income and wealth should be bolstered in light of the new distributional dynamics. But there is a much broader policy agenda of "predistribution" that can make the growth process itself more inclusive.[46]

Much of the reform agenda to achieve more inclusive outcomes from technological change is also an agenda to achieve stronger growth outcomes, given the linked dynamics between the recent rise in inequality and the slowdown in productivity. Specific policy needs and priorities, of course, differ across groups of economies, especially between advanced and emerging economies. Broadly, five areas need more focused attention from national policymakers.

First, competition policy should be revamped for the digital age to ensure that markets continue to provide an open and level playing field for firms. Antitrust enforcement should be strengthened, supported by updated laws and guidelines on mergers and acquisitions (M&As)—covering not only horizontal M&As but also nonhorizontal ones. Recent filings of antitrust lawsuits in the United States against Facebook and Google and congressional antitrust hearings, together with related actions in the European Union, suggest that momentum may be building for reform of the antitrust legal framework and stronger enforcement.

New regulatory challenges posed by the digital economy must be addressed. These include regulatory responses to proprietary agglomeration of data, competition issues relating to digital platforms that have emerged as gatekeepers in the digital world, and market concentration resulting from tech giants that resemble natural or quasi-natural monopolies. An overarching issue is the regulation of data, the lifeblood of the digital economy. Issues relating to how data are handled—use, access, portability, openness while protecting privacy and security—matter increasingly for competition. There has been more action on these issues in Europe than in the United States, an example being the General Data Protection Regulation introduced in Europe.

To address the competition policy challenges of the digital economy, some countries—such as Australia, France, Germany, and the United Kingdom—are now establishing or contemplating new regulatory bodies focused on digital markets.[47] These bodies would be tasked to develop procompetition standards, rules, and codes of conduct for digital markets (including new competition issues that may arise as artificial intelligence and machine learning algorithms advance), and could also serve as focal points for international coordination on regulation of digital markets. There are also emerging proposals for similar reform in the United States.[48]

Second, in an increasingly knowledge-driven economy, the innovation ecosystem should be improved so that it spurs new knowledge and technological advances but also fosters their wide diffusion. Patent systems should be reformed with an eye to changing excessively broad and stringent protections, addressing the problems of patent thickets and trolling, aligning rules with today's realities, and giving freer rein to competition that, ultimately, is the primary driver of technological innovation and diffusion.[49] One possible reform is to replace the one-size-fits-all approach enshrined in current systems with a differentiated approach. While long patent terms may continue to be appropriate for some innovations, such as in pharmaceuticals that involve protracted and expensive testing, the case is less clear for digital technologies that have much shorter gestation periods and typically build on previous innovations in an incremental fashion.[50]

Government investment in research and development (R&D), which has been falling in many countries, should be revitalized, as it supplies the important public good of basic research that produces broad knowledge spillovers and complements the focus of private R&D on narrower, applied research.[51] Public R&D support programs can improve access to innovation financing for small and medium-sized enterprises.[52] Also, a robust public R&D program—including direct investment and tax incentives and subsidies—can influence the direction of technological change toward innovation that serves broader economic and social goals rather than the interests of narrow groups of investors. It can, for example, address the concern that the current private technological paradigm is geared toward "excessive automation," producing technologies that displace labor without much gain in total factor productivity.[53] Correcting biases in the tax system favoring capital relative to labor would also help.[54]

Many breakthrough innovations developed commercially by private firms originate from government-supported research. Examples include Google's basic search algorithm, key features of Apple smartphones, and even the internet itself.[55] Governments should explore ways of better recouping some of their investment in research, not least to replenish their research budgets—producing a better balance in sharing risks and rewards of public research investment compared with the current paradigm, where risks are socialized but rewards are privatized. Ensuring that companies do not take advantage of loopholes in the tax system and pay adequate taxes on their profits is the obvious way. Other possibilities include requiring companies to repay research grants if their products succeed financially or acquiring equity stakes in the commercialization of successful technologies directly supported by public research funds.[56]

Third, digital infrastructure must be strengthened to expand access to new opportunities. This requires increased public investment as well as frameworks to encourage more private investment to improve digital access. Broadband is becoming as much of a necessity in this century as electricity was in the twentieth century. But the digital divide remains wide within economies, a fact brought into starker relief by the COVID-19 crisis. Most sectors of the US economy are less than 15 percent as digitalized as the leading sectors, and there are large gaps in access between major urban/industrial centers and other areas.[57]

The digital divide is even wider in developing economies. A stronger foundation of digital infrastructure will be crucial for these economies as technology forces a shift toward growth models less reliant on low-skill, low-wage manufacturing. It is essential to capturing the new growth opportunities that technology offers, such as the expanding trade in digitally deliverable services. Success in using mobile telephony to connect large populations to the formal economy, including financial markets, in many countries illustrates the new leapfrogging possibilities in development.

Fourth, education and training programs must be revamped to emphasize the acquisition of skills that complement the new technologies. This will require innovation in the content, delivery, and financing of these programs, including new models of public–private partnerships. With the fast-changing demand for skills and the growing need for upskilling, reskilling, and lifelong learning, the availability and quality of continuing education should be greatly scaled up.[58] The effort should span both the general education system and the institutions for vocational education. It should include expanded partnerships with employers, including exploring a larger role for apprenticeship arrangements.

To improve workers' access to retraining, one approach is through Lifelong Learning Accounts in which workers accumulate rights to training that are portable across jobs.[59] Such accounts have recently been introduced at the national level in some countries, such as France and Singapore. More flexibility can be built into government student aid programs (grants, loans, and tax incentives) so that they benefit not just first-time college entrants but also returning older adults. The potential of technology-enabled solutions must be harnessed, supported by a stronger foundation of digital literacy. The COVID-19 pandemic has dramatically demonstrated the scope for scaling up the use of online learning tools.

Persistent inequalities in access to education and (re)training must be addressed. While gaps in basic capabilities across income groups have narrowed, those in higher-level capabilities that will drive success in the twenty-first century are widening.[60]

Fifth, social protection systems should be strengthened, indeed overhauled, to realign them with the changing economy and nature of work. The pandemic exposed weaknesses in these systems. Unemployment insurance schemes should better support workers in adjusting to change, retraining, and transitioning to new jobs. They should be designed to provide adequate coverage and encourage reemployment. Worker benefits systems, covering benefits such as pensions and health care, which traditionally have been based on formal, long-term employer–employee relationships, will need to adjust to a job market with more frequent job transitions and more diverse work arrangements. This means greater portability and adaptability to address the needs of more people working independently. The gig economy is expanding.[61] The increased use of teleworking stemming from the pandemic will spur it further.

The dominant part of the policy agenda to make technology work better for all lies at the national level, especially in the key areas outlined above. But there is a complementary agenda at the international level. The rise of nationalist populism has increased protectionist sentiment. The pandemic can further stoke the backlash against globalization. Concerns about the security of critical supplies can spur more reshoring of supply chains. International cooperation will need to ensure that past gains in establishing a rules-based global trading system are shielded from these headwinds. At the same time, new rules and cooperative arrangements must be devised to underpin the new phase of globalization led by digital flows to ensure open access and fair competition.[62] This includes adequate disciplines for digital trade, cross-border data flows, and fast-growing digitally deliverable services. With more knowledge-intensive globalization, appropriate frameworks governing intellectual property take on added significance. International cooperation on tax matters becomes even more important in view of the new tax challenges of the digital economy.

Conclusion

Ours is a time of exciting technological change. The era of smart machines holds the promise of a more prosperous future for all. But it also demands smarter policies to realize this promise. To capture potential gains in productivity and economic growth and to address rising inequality, policies will need to be more responsive to change as technology reshapes markets. And change will only intensify as artificial intelligence and other new advances drive digital transformation further—and at an accelerated pace, in the aftermath of the COVID-19 pandemic.

As technology shifts market dynamics, policies must ensure that markets remain inclusive and support broad access to the new opportunities for firms and workers. New thinking and policy adaptations are needed in areas such as competition policy, the innovation ecosystem, digital infrastructure development, upskilling and reskilling of workers, and social protection programs. Fostering a wider diffusion of new technologies among firms and building complementary capabilities in the workforce can deliver both stronger and more inclusive economic growth.

Major economic reform, inevitably, is politically complex. Today's deeper political divisions add to the challenges. But political support appears to be building in some key areas of reform, such as addressing the market dominance of tech giants and putting in place an adequate regulatory framework governing data. Crises can shift the political setting for reform. The fault lines exposed by the COVID-19 pandemic can catalyze action to address mounting economic disparities. All too often, reform is paralyzed by trite debates about conflicts between boosting economic growth and reducing inequality. Encouragingly, however, policy is increasingly being informed by research findings that show this to be a false dichotomy. In realizing the promise of brilliant new technologies, the growth and inclusion agendas are one and the same.

Notes

1. See, e.g., Erik Brynjolfsson and Andrew McAfee, *The Second Machine Age: Work, Progress, and Prosperity in a Time of Brilliant Technologies* (New York: W. W. Norton, 2014); and Klaus Schwab. *The Fourth Industrial Revolution* (Geneva: World Economic Forum, 2016).

2. William Nordhaus, *Are We Approaching an Economic Singularity? Information Technology and the Future of Economic Growth*, NBER Working Paper 21547 (Cambridge, MA: National Bureau of Economic Research, 2015).

3. Darrell West and John Allen, *Turning Point: Policymaking in the Era of Artificial Intelligence* (Brookings, 2020).

4. Alex Chernoff and Casey Warman, *COVID-19 and Implications for Automation*, NBER Working Paper 27249 (Cambridge, MA: National Bureau of Economic Research, 2020).

5. Current statistical methods may not be fully capturing the new value created in the digital space. But research finds that, even allowing for such underestimation, the productivity slowdown is real, not illusory. See Kemal Derviş and Zia Qureshi, "The Productivity Slump: Fact or Fiction? The Measurement Debate," Research Brief,

Brookings, 2016. For the debate among "techno-pessimists" and "techno-optimists" on the productivity growth potential of digital technologies, See also "The Productivity Outlook: Pessimists versus Optimists," by Zia Qureshi, Research Brief, Brookings, 2016.

6. McKinsey Global Institute, *Solving the Productivity Puzzle: The Role of Demand and the Promise of Digitization* (New York: McKinsey & Company, 2018).

7. World Bank, *Global Economic Prospects: Broad-Based Upturn, but for How Long?* (Washington: World Bank, 2018). See also World Bank, *Global Productivity: Trends, Drivers, and Policies*, edited by Alistair Dieppe (Washington: World Bank, 2020).

8. Brahima Coulibaly and Karim Foda, "The Future of Global Manufacturing," in *Growth in a Time of Change: Global and Country Perspectives on a New Agenda*, edited by Hyeon-Wook Kim and Zia Qureshi (Brookings, 2020).

9. David Autor and Anna Salomons, "Robocalypse Now: Does Productivity Growth Threaten Employment?" in *Proceedings of the ECB Forum on Central Banking: Investment and Growth in Advanced Economies* (Frankfurt: European Central Bank, 2017).

10. Raj Chetty, David Grusky, Maximilian Hell, Nathaniel Hendren, Robert Manduca, and Jimmy Narang, "The Fading American Dream: Trends in Absolute Income Mobility since 1940," *Science* 356, no. 6336 (2017): 398–406.

11. On these linked dynamics, see also Brookings and Chumir Foundation, *Productive Equity: The Twin Challenges of Reviving Productivity and Reducing Inequality* (Brookings and Chumir Foundation, 2019); and Jason Furman and Peter Orszag, *Slower Productivity and Higher Inequality: Are They Related?* Working Paper 18-4 (Washington: Peterson Institute for International Economics, 2018).

12. McKinsey Global Institute, *Digital America: A Tale of the Haves and Have-Mores* (New York: McKinsey & Company, 2015).

13. Dan Andrews, Chiara Criscuolo, and Peter Gal, *The Best Versus the Rest: The Global Productivity Slowdown, Divergence across Firms and the Role of Public Policy*, OECD Productivity Working Paper 5 (Paris: OECD Publishing, 2016); and Orbis data. In this estimate, frontier firms are defined as the top 5 percent of firms with the highest labor productivity within each two-digit industry. Nonfrontier firms include all other firms.

14. Giuseppe Berlingieri, Sara Calligaris, Chiara Criscuolo, and Rudy Verlhac, *Laggard Firms, Technology Diffusion, and Its Structural and Policy Determinants*, OECD Science, Technology, and Industry Policy Paper 86 (Paris: OECD Publishing, 2020).

15. See, e.g., Andrews, Criscuolo, and Gal, *Best Versus the Rest*; Gilbert Cette, Jimmy Lopez, and Jacques Mairesse, "Market Regulations, Prices, and Productivity," *American Economic Review* 106, no. 5 (2016): 104–8; and Balázs Égert, "Regulation, Institutions and Productivity: New Macroeconomic Evidence from OECD Countries," *American Economic Review* 106, no. 5 (2016): 109–13. These studies use panel data for a broad range of OECD economies and industries. For a recent review of research on the productivity slowdown, see Ian Goldin, Pantelis Koutroumpis, François Lafond, and Julian Winkler, "Why Is Productivity Slowing Down?" OMPTEC Working Paper 2020-1, Oxford Martin School, 2020.

16. Zia Qureshi, "The Rise of Corporate Market Power," *Up Front*, Brookings, May 21, 2019.

17. David Autor, David Dorn, Lawrence Katz, Christina Patterson, and John Van Reenen, "The Fall of the Labor Share and the Rise of Superstar Firms," *Quarterly Journal of Economics* 135, no. 2 (2020): 645–709.

18. Jan de Loecker, Jan Eeckhout, and Gabriel Unger, "The Rise of Market Power and the Macroeconomic Implications," *Quarterly Journal of Economics* 135, no. 2 (2020): 561–644.

19. Gauti Eggertsson, Jacob Robbins, and Ella Getz Wold, *Kaldor and Piketty's Facts: The Rise of Monopoly Power in the United States*, NBER Working Paper 24287 (Cambridge, MA: National Bureau of Economic Research, 2018). Mordechai Kurz— "On the Formation of Capital and Wealth: IT, Monopoly Power and Rising Inequality," Working Paper 17-016, Institute of Economic Policy Research, Stanford University, 2018—estimates that, between 1985 and 2015, as monopoly profits boosted the market value of corporate stocks and produced outsize capital gains, the share of total US stock market value reflecting monopoly power (what he terms "monopoly wealth") rose from negligible levels to about 80 percent.

20. Jason Furman and Peter Orszag, "A Firm-Level Perspective on the Role of Rents in the Rise in Inequality," in *Toward a Just Society: Joseph Stiglitz and Twenty-First-Century Economics*, edited by M. Guzman (Columbia University Press, 2018).

21. Ryan Decker, John Haltiwanger, Ron Jarmin, and Javier Miranda, "Declining Business Dynamism, Allocative Efficiency, and the Productivity Slowdown," *American Economic Review* 107, no. 5 (2017): 322–26.

22. Thomas Philippon, *The Great Reversal: How America Gave Up on Free Markets* (Harvard University Press, 2019); Jonathan Tepper, *The Myth of Capitalism: Monopolies and the Death of Competition* (Hoboken, NJ: John Wiley & Sons, 2019).

23. Autor et al., "Fall of the Labor Share."

24. Jonathan Haskel and Stian Westlake, *Capitalism without Capital: The Rise of the Intangible Economy* (Princeton University Press, 2017).

25. Ufuk Akcigit and Sina Ates, *What Happened to US Business Dynamism?* NBER Working Paper 25756 (Cambridge, MA: National Bureau of Economic Research, 2019).

26. OECD Employment Database. See also World Bank, *World Development Report 2019: The Changing Nature of Work* (Washington: World Bank, 2019).

27. David Autor, David Mindell, and Elisabeth Reynolds, *The Work of the Future: Shaping Technology and Institutions*, MIT Task Force on the Work of the Future (Massachusetts Institute of Technology, 2019); Michael Webb, "The Impact of Artificial Intelligence on the Labor Market," Economics Department paper, Stanford University, 2020.

28. David Autor, Claudia Goldin, and Lawrence Katz, *Extending the Race between Education and Technology*, NBER Working Paper 26705 (Cambridge, MA: National Bureau of Economic Research, 2020); Claudia Goldin and Lawrence Katz, *The Race between Education and Technology* (Harvard University Press, 2008).

29. Robert Barro and Jong-Wha Lee, "A New Data Set of Educational Attainment in the World, 1950–2010," *Journal of Development Economics* 104 (2013): 184–98;

Christian Morrisson and Fabrice Murtin, "The Kuznets Curve of Human Capital Inequality: 1870–2010," *Journal of Economic Inequality* 11 no. 3 (2013): 283–301.

30. Muge Adalet McGowan and Dan Andrews, "Labor Market Mismatch and Labor Productivity: Evidence from PIAAC Data," *Research in Labor Economics* 45 (2017): 199–241.

31. Autor, Goldin, and Katz, *Extending the Race.*

32. Chiara Criscuolo, Alexander Hijzen, et al., *Workforce Composition, Productivity, and Pay: The Role of Firms in Wage Inequality*, OECD Social, Employment, and Migration Working Paper 241 (Paris: OECD Publishing, 2020); Jae Song, David Price, Faith Guvenen, Nicholas Bloom, and Till von Wachter, "Firming Up Inequality," *Quarterly Journal of Economics* 134, no. 1 (2019): 1–50; Giuseppe Berlingieri, Patrick Blanchenay, and Chiara Criscuolo, *The Great Divergences*, OECD Science, Technology, and Industry Policy Paper 39 (Paris: OECD Publishing, 2017).

33. Anna Stansbury and Lawrence Summers, *Productivity and Pay: Is the Link Broken?* Working Paper 18-5 (Washington: Peterson Institute for International Economics, 2018).

34. Organization for Economic Cooperation and Development, *OECD Economic Outlook,* vol. 2018, issue 2, chapter 2, "Decoupling of Wages from Productivity: What Implications for Public Policies?" (Paris: OECD Publishing, 2018); Cyrille Schwellnus, Mathilde Pak, Pierre-Alain Pionnier, and Elena Crivellaro, *Labor Share Developments over the Past Two Decades: The Role of Technological Progress, Globalization and "Winner-Takes-Most" Dynamics*, Economics Department Working Paper 1503 (Paris: OECD Publishing, 2018).

35. Autor et al., "Fall of the Labor Share."

36. José Azar, Ioana Marinescu, and Marshall Steinbaum, *Labor Market Concentration*, NBER Working Paper 24147 (Cambridge, MA: National Bureau of Economic Research, 2017).

37. Darrell West, *The Future of Work: Robots. AI, and Automation* (Brookings, 2018).

38. The role of uneven capital ownership and returns on capital as sources of inequality has been particularly emphasized by Thomas Piketty in his bestseller *Capital in the Twenty-First Century* (Harvard University Press, 2014).

39. Richard Baldwin, *The Globotics Upheaval: Globalization, Robotics, and the Future of Work* (Oxford University Press, 2019).

40. International Monetary Fund, *World Economic Outlook,* April 2017, chapter 3, "Understanding the Downward Trend in Labor Income Shares" (Washington: International Monetary Fund, 2017). The study finds that, in advanced economies, technology accounts for about half the decline in the labor income share, global integration accounts for about a quarter, and policies and institutions and other factors such as measurement issues account for the remainder.

41. Nancy Rose, "Will Competition Be Another COVID-19 Casualty?" Hamilton Project, Brookings, 2020.

42. David Autor and Elisabeth Reynolds, "The Nature of Work After the COVID Crisis: Too Few Low-Wage Jobs." Hamilton Project, Brookings, 2020.

43. David Altig, Jose Maria Barrero, Nick Bloom, Steven Davis, Brent Meyer, Emil Mihaylov, and Nick Parker, "Firms Expect Working from Home to Triple." Macroblog, Federal Reserve Bank of Atlanta, Atlanta, 2020.

44. McKinsey Global Institute, *Solving the Productivity Puzzle*.

45. Zia Qureshi, "Democratizing Innovation: Putting Technology to Work for Inclusive Growth," Brookings, 2020; Dani Rodrik, "Democratizing Innovation," Project Syndicate, August 11, 2020.

46. Jacob Hacker, "The Institutional Foundations of Middle Class Democracy," Policy Network, May 6, 2011.

47. For the United Kingdom, e.g., see Digital Competition Expert Panel, *Unlocking Digital Competition: Report of the Digital Competition Expert Panel* (London: Digital Competition Expert Panel, 2019).

48. See Tom Wheeler, Phil Verveer, and Gene Kimmelman, *New Digital Realities; New Oversight Solutions in the US—The Case for a Digital Platform Agency and a New Approach to Regulatory Oversight* (Harvard Kennedy School, 2020); Stigler Committee on Digital Platforms, *Final Report* (University of Chicago, Booth School of Business, 2019).

49. "The copyright and patent laws we have today look more like intellectual monopoly than intellectual property"; Brink Lindsey and Steven Teles, *The Captured Economy: How the Powerful Enrich Themselves, Slow Down Growth, and Increase Inequality* (Oxford University Press, 2017).

50. Benjamin Roin, "The Case for Tailoring Patents Based on Time-to-Market," *UCLA Law Review* 61 (2014): 672–759; Zia Qureshi, "Intellectual Property, Not Intellectual Monopoly," Project Syndicate, July 11, 2018. On differentiating patent policy by firm size, see also Alberto Galasso and Schankerman, *Patent Rights and Innovation by Small and Large Firms*, NBER Working Paper 21769 (Cambridge, MA: National Bureau of Economic Research, 2015). In tailoring patents to different types of innovation and innovators, care must be taken not to excessively complicate the patent system. More research on possible approaches is needed.

51. In the United States, e.g., public R&D spending has fallen from 1.2 percent of GDP in the early 1980s to half that level in recent years, with its share in total R&D spending declining from 45 percent to less than a quarter; Jay Shambaugh, Ryan Nunn, and Becca Portman, "Eleven Facts about Innovation and Patents," Hamilton Project, Brookings, 2017.

52. In the United States, venture capital plays a disproportionate role in financing start ups. The industry is highly concentrated, with the top 5 percent of investors accounting for 50 percent of the capital raised; Josh Lerner and Ramana Nanda, "Venture Capital's Role in Financing Innovation: What We Know and How Much We Still Need to Learn," *Journal of Economic Perspectives* 34, no. 3 (2020): 237–61.

53. Daron Acemoglu and Pascual Restrepo, *The Wrong Kind of AI? Artificial Intelligence and the Future of Labor Demand*, NBER Working Paper 25682 (Cambridge, MA: National Bureau of Economic Research, 2019). The authors refer to these technologies as "so-so technologies."

54. Daron Acemoglu, Andrea Manera, and Pascual Restrepo, "Does the US Tax Code Favor Automation?" *Brookings Papers on Economic Activity*, Spring 2020. The authors find that, in the United States, labor is taxed much more heavily than capital and that this difference has increased in recent years. They estimate that the US effective tax rate in the 2010s was 25.5 to 33.5 percent for labor and 5 to 10 percent for capital.

55. Mariana Mazzucato, *The Entrepreneurial State: Debunking Public vs. Private Sector Myths* (London: Anthem Press, 2015).

56. Mazzucato, *Entrepreneurial State*; Dani Rodrik, "From Welfare State to Innovation State," Project Syndicate, January 14, 2015. Ideas such as government acquiring equity stakes are not without controversy. Government stakes could be "passive" and temporary, with the research investments focused in priority areas that entail high risks that private investors would not take on their own, and managed by independent entities shielded from day-to-day political pressures.

57. McKinsey Global Institute, *Digital America*.

58. The need to scale up continuing education is reinforced by the aging of the workforce in many countries.

59. Alastair Fitzpayne and Ethan Pollack, *"Lifelong Learning and Training Accounts: Helping Workers Adapt and Succeed in a Changing Economy* (Washington: Aspen Institute, 2018).

60. United Nations, *Human Development Report 2019: Beyond Income, Beyond Averages, Beyond Today—Inequalities in Human Development in the 21st Century* (New York: United Nations, 2019).

61. Erik Brynjolfsson and Andrew McAfee, *Machine, Platform, Crowd: Harnessing Our Digital Future* (New York: W. W. Norton, 2017); Arun Sundarajan, *The Sharing Economy: The End of Employment and the Rise of Crowd-Based Capitalism* (MIT Press, 2016).

62. Klaus Schwab, "Globalization 4.0: A New Architecture for the Fourth Industrial Revolution," *Foreign Affairs,* January 2019; World Economic Forum, *Globalization 4.0: Shaping a New Global Architecture in the Age of the Fourth Industrial Revolution*, White Paper (Geneva: World Economic Forum, 2019).

Eight

The Future of Democracy

Norman J. Ornstein, *American Enterprise Institute*

As I write this, the COVID-19 pandemic is in the midst of a new wave that will likely last at least through the winter, and possibly longer, with hope on the horizon both through vaccine development and potential broad dissemination, and the hopeful arrival of rapid, accurate, and inexpensive in-home saliva testing. But there are signs that even with those achievements, COVID will continue to be a factor for a longer time, as many people in a range of countries will continue to resist the clear preventive measures of masks and social distancing, and will refuse to take the vaccine when available.

In the United States—unlike countries like Australia, Canada, South Korea, Taiwan, and many European democracies—the failure to implement early safety measures for COVID-19 meant a surge in cases that has not abated; by December 2020, the United States neared 14 million cases, with up to 200,000 more per day, and were approaching 300,000 reported deaths, with the actual number likely at least a third higher. The worst problems, on a per capita basis, were coming in states like South Dakota, where governors or state legislatures had refused to implement mask mandates or temporary closures of businesses and other entities where the risk of congregating in large numbers in close quarters was great. The US response was driven by a president who downplayed the virus in its early stages, even though he was well aware of the dangers, as he made clear in his interviews with Bob Woodward and continued to ignore science and his scientific experts and ridiculed masks, while refusing to counter conspiracy theories suggesting the virus was a hoax and simultaneously blaming China for its creation and dissemination and vowing retaliation.

As the weather changed in the late fall, meaning more indoor gatherings and more travel for holidays, the problem worsened. Even in countries with textbook responses leading to few cases and deaths, there have been new outbreaks, but few large countries, other than perhaps Brazil, have had explosions of cases and strains on the health care system to rival those in the United States. The reverberations will be there for a long time, in social cohesion, economic growth and equity, the medical system's ability to respond, and stresses on the political system. And globally, even as advances are made in vaccines and testing and the pandemic's threat recedes, the challenges to democracies will also resonate.

When the Berlin Wall fell thirty-one years ago, it signaled the demise of the Soviet Union and a new era of democracy flowering around the world. Within a month, the Ceausescu regime was toppled in Romania. Before long, we saw a dramatic move away from autocracy and toward democracy in a series of former Soviet satellites, in places like Czechoslovakia, which soon became the Czech Republic and Slovak Republic; and in Hungary, Poland, Ukraine, and other countries in Central and Eastern and Europe. Before long, the political scientist Francis Fukuyama had proclaimed "the end of history."

The sense of the near inexorability of the march to democracy accelerated two decades later, with the Arab Spring, a popular uprising that started in Tunisia and quickly spread to countries like Libya, Egypt, and Syria. But Tunisia proved the exception, as the other Arab states faced grimmer futures—near anarchy, a more brutal dictatorship, or a violent and ongoing civil war with multiple proxies—including an aggressive and resurgent Russia. Other Arab countries, like Saudi Arabia, saw their dictatorships become even more rigid and cruel.

But as the decade of the 2010s proceeded, the democracies in Hungary, the Czech Republic and Slovak Republic, and Poland, among others, slid back toward autocracy, undermining many categories critical to democracies, including an independent judiciary and a free press. The same pattern emerged in Turkey, under Recep Tayyip Erdoğan, and in more distant places like the Philippines under Rodrigo Duterte. In countries like India, Myanmar, and Malaysia, leaders undercut other elements of democracy, including promoting ethnic division and warfare. In China, predictions that economic liberalization would lead to a more open political system proved disastrously wrong—from the move of a million or more Uighurs into concentration camps to the brutal crackdown on Hong Kong. And in the Western Hemisphere, we saw countries like Venezuela move further into autocracy when Maduro succeeded Chávez, and Brazil with the election of Bolsonaro.

In short, the obstacles to governance and democracy were sharp and growing well before COVID-19 swept the globe. Some of these challenges were driven by broad demographic and economic trends. In this chapter, I first reflect on the challenges, with a particular focus on my home country, the United States, while noting that many of the trends are being replicated in other countries and regions. I then turn to what the impact of the pandemic has been on the future of democratic rule and norms.

The first trend is *political tribalism.* In the United States, the trend began with political polarization, starting decades ago as our political parties altered regional dominance, and once-broad ideological coalitions moved toward parliamentary-style homogeneous and ideologically consistent groupings. American political parties could operate with cross-party cooperation, even with polarization. But in the 1980s and 1990s, political actors like Newt Gingrich, combined with the rise of talk radio, moved the process to a more difficult place—via deliberate efforts to define the opposition not as good people with different views, but as enemies trying to destroy our way of life. There were some notable exceptions, such as when John McCain defended Barack Obama in October 2008 as "a decent family man, citizen, that I just happen to have disagreements with on fundamental issues."[1] But the criticism McCain took for his graciousness made any further gestures to reduce the vitriol less likely. And, of course, the delegitimization of Obama fit the electoral strategy of Republicans.

The process of tribalism began in Washington but metastasized to state governments and to the public as a whole. It became more insidious when social media emerged, amplifying the tribal messages coming from mass media and from political actors. In a presidential, as opposed to a parliamentary, system, where different parties can control different levers of power, cross-party cooperation is a necessity more often than not—and tribalism has made this far more challenging to achieve. And the inability to build a broad leadership consensus across party lines, which meant the inability to act fruitfully to solve major societal problems, undermined trust in the political system and in political institutions and actors.

Of course, tribalism is not confined to nonparliamentary systems. In recent decades, we have seen the growth of nativist and extremist right-wing parties across Europe, promoting division, challenging the concept of the common good and the establishment, often inciting violence, and gaining traction, to varying degrees, in countries from Norway to France to Belgium, the Netherlands, and Germany.

Another global phenomenon has come with the changing media landscape. The explosion of information sources, and technologies like the remote control and the cell phone, moved people in America from being passive receptors of information from a few key places, like the three television networks, to being able easily to seek out and get information from places that reinforced their sentiments and views. The common core of information that was the norm in the 1950s, 1960s, and 1970s disappeared—now people could get their own "facts" and interpretations, often with no basis in reality, so the ability to purvey misinformation and disinformation exploded. The explosion of social media, encouraged by the regulatory climate and rules, was a major accelerant.

The challenge for governance here is palpable; if decision-makers do not share a common set of facts, or an understanding of the nature of policy problems, it becomes more difficult to make decisions and build a consensus; a good example is climate change policy. Other established democracies may not have had Newt Gingrich equivalents, and, if in parliamentary systems, do not have the same challenge of gridlock, but it is clear that the technological and information system revolutions of the past few decades have also had their impact, including creating a greater gulf on shared information and loosening the control of governments on information sources like state-run television. And the availability of new sources of social media have made it easier for extremist groups and hostile powers to undermine confidence in governments by recruiting more people into their networks and bringing isolated followers into more organized groups.

A related trend is the spread of *populism*. The global financial collapse in 2008–9 brought with it a wave of populist reaction; in the United States, it occurred on the right with the Tea Party movement, and on the left with the Occupy Wall Street movement. While other countries did not have movements with names like that, they also had a rise in populism. Populism, driven by economic unease and dislocation, brings with it a distrust of political leaders and elites in other realms, and often a rise in nativism, racism, and protectionism.

Populism is not a new phenomenon, globally or in the United States. But the current populism is distinct in an important way. Usually, when we have seen American populism—for example, in the late 1980s and early 1990s, with Pat Buchanan on the right, Ralph Nader on the left, and H. Ross Perot in the center—it emerges during economic turmoil and recedes when the economy improves. This latest wave did not recede during the decade after the economic collapse, even when we moved to rapid growth and low unemployment—before COVID-19 blew up that economy. That has meant the distrust of leaders and elites, including a distrust across many categories of science and scientists,

Figure 8-1. The Gaps in Income Between Upper-Income and Middle- and Lower-Income Households Are Rising, and the Share Held by Middle-Income Households Is Falling

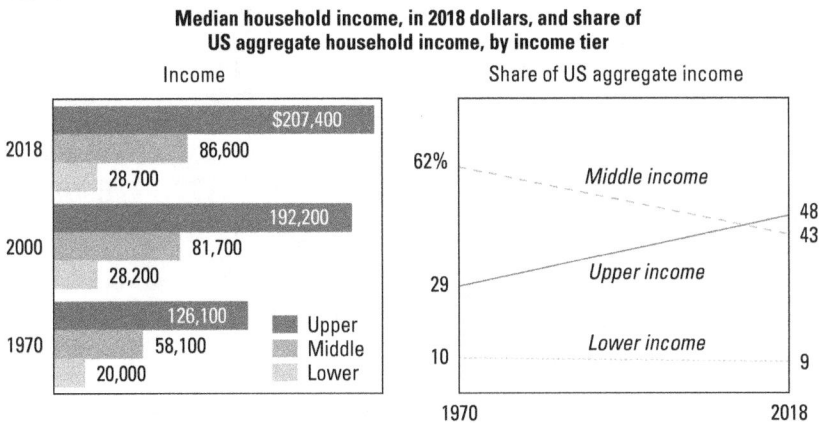

Median household income, in 2018 dollars, and share of US aggregate household income, by income tier

Source: Juliana Menasce Horowitz, Ruth Igielnik, and Rakesh Kochhar, "Most Americans Say There Is Too Much Economic Inequality in the US, but Fewer Than Half Call It a Top Priority," Pew Research Center, used by permission; https://www.pewresearch.org/social-trends/2020/01/09/most-americans-say-there-is-too-much-economic-inequality-in-the-u-s-but-fewer-than-half-call-it-a-top-priority/.

and of expertise, which in turn has added to the challenge of governance. Why is this wave different? Because this populism had its roots more in status anxiety, especially among working-class whites, particularly men, than in economic dislocation.

The next trend has been the *rise in economic inequality*. This is true both in incomes and wealth. To pick one indicator of income inequality, in 1965, American CEOs made on average 20 times the compensation of average workers; in 1989, it was 58 times. In 2019, CEO pay was a staggering 278 times that of the average worker! Put another way, CEO compensation grew over 1,000 percent in the forty years from 1978 to 2018—while the average worker's pay grew 11.9 percent.[2] Beyond the top business executives, the gap has been growing between upper-income households and others—and middle-income households are falling further behind (figure 8-1).

The United States is not alone in its problem of income inequality, but it is worse than other nations (figure 8-2). But all have this same set of issues. And all have had the problem exacerbated by the pandemic.

Then there is wealth inequality. Here, while there is a huge gap between the top 20 percent of the American population and the bottom 80 percent, the gap is much greater when it comes to the top 1 percent. In 1989, the top 1 percent

Figure 8-2. Rising Income Inequality in the United States, and in the Group of Seven Countries

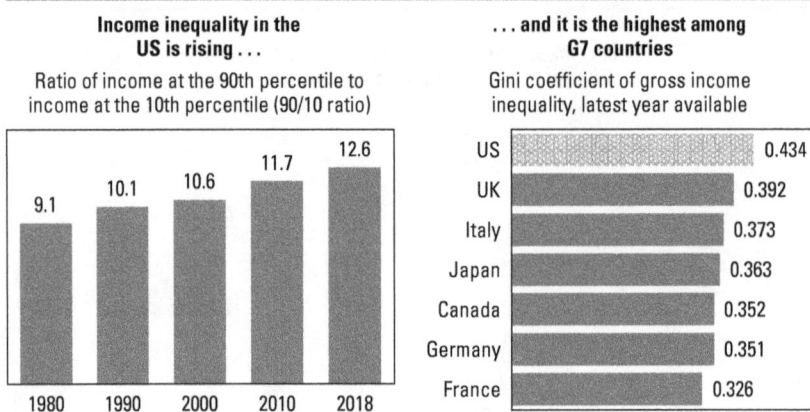

Income inequality in the US is rising ...	... and it is the highest among G7 countries
Ratio of income at the 90th percentile to income at the 10th percentile (90/10 ratio)	Gini coefficient of gross income inequality, latest year available

Year	90/10 ratio
1980	9.1
1990	10.1
2000	10.6
2010	11.7
2018	12.6

Country	Gini coefficient
US	0.434
UK	0.392
Italy	0.373
Japan	0.363
Canada	0.352
Germany	0.351
France	0.326

Source: Juliana Menasce Horowitz, Ruth Igielnik, and Rakesh Kochhar, "Most Americans Say There Is Too Much Economic Inequality in the US, but Fewer Than Half Call It a Top Priority," Pew Research Center, used by permission; https://www.pewresearch.org/social-trends/2020/01/09/most-americans-say-there-is-too-much-economic-inequality-in-the-u-s-but-fewer-than-half-call-it-a-top-priority/.

had 23.5 percent of the nation's wealth—and the bottom 50 percent had only 3.7 percent. A decade later, in 1999, the share of the top 1 percent had grown to 28.1 percent—while that of the bottom 50 percent shrunk to 3.5 percent. In 2009, after the enormous hit that came from the financial collapse, the share of the top 1 percent was stable—while the bottom 50 percent saw its share shrink dramatically, to only 0.6 percent. The fundamental cause was the collapse of the housing market, since most Americans had their wealth in their homes, not in financial assets. In 2019, after some years of economic growth and low unemployment, the richest 1 percent saw their share grow to 31.2 percent. And while the share of the bottom 50 percent had improved, it was still only at 1.6 percent of the total wealth in the country.[3]

The wealth gap is even more striking when we look at the top 1/10th of 1 percent. Data gathered by Emmanuel Saez and Gabriel Zucman point out that they hold as much wealth as the bottom 80 percent of the entire population. And in 2018, they note, the 400 richest families paid a lower effective tax rate than the bottom 50 percent![4]

The inequality across quartiles or deciles of populations is not uniform for all demographic groups; there are growing divisions across education, gender, region, race, and ethnicity, inequities that existed before but have been sharply amplified by the nature of the global economy and by the jolt and dislocations of the global financial collapse of 2008, which continues to reverberate more than a decade later. And COVID has made these disparities starker and more challenging. More people with lower incomes are in jobs deemed essential, like orderlies in hospitals, making them more vulnerable to the virus. And we know that racial minorities, because of low incomes and a lack of health insurance or care, are more likely to be killed or seriously damaged by COVID, adding to the cycle of racial disparities in income, health, and wealth.

The income gap has another characteristic: *regional disparity.* In a global economy in an advanced information age driven by technology, economic performance, growth, and response will be most robust in areas with a combination of a more highly educated population, top education institutions and infrastructure, a high-speed internet, and easy transportation for workers. These characteristics have combined to enable suppleness, flexibility, and innovation, with jobs that fit demand. And they occur in major metropolitan areas.

At the same time, outer ring suburbs, exurbs, smaller towns, and rural areas, with lesser education and infrastructure and few ways to replace jobs in obsolete industries, have fallen further behind, as their jobs have disappeared, with fewer opportunities or initiatives for retraining or innovation, and a subsequent decline in social cohesiveness and an increase in resentment against elites—fertile ground for antielite populist appeals.

This divide—bigger cities versus smaller towns and rural areas—is sharpest in the United States but also occurs in many other countries around the globe. In the United States, it is increasingly defining our politics. In a tribal political universe, America has many firmly red, or Republican, states, and many firmly blue, or Democratic-dominated states, with a smaller number of purple, or competitive, ones. But within the states, the metropolitan areas are generally more Democratic, and Republican support grows as one moves out to smaller cities and towns and to rural areas—and is correlated, at least for white voters, as well with income and education.

Another factor, a backlash against globalization, is the collapse of the longstanding trade architecture and model that prizes free trade and multilateral trade agreements. The Trans-Pacific Partnership, a model for broad-based multilateral trade, was under siege in the United States even during the 2016 presidential campaign, when Hillary Clinton pledged to oppose it as written. With the collapse of the Trans-Pacific Partnership, another anchor of global stability and a sense of interconnection was undermined. While we have seen some bilateral and even multilateral trade agreements since then, the dominant theme of trade during the Trump years was trade warfare and tariffs. If the global trade architecture has not collapsed, it has not been particularly robust or resilient. And this has meant disruption across many areas, including agriculture, steel, and manufacturing more broadly.

A further factor, with many consequences, has been demographic change. In the United States, this change is reflected in the inexorable move toward a society where people of color will, within a decade or so, make up a majority of the country, creating dislocation and a sense of loss of prestige and power by many white people, especially working-class ones otherwise suffering from economic dislocation. In many European countries, it is a result both of long-standing trends in immigration—Muslims from many countries in, for example, Belgium, the Netherlands, and France, going back many years—and the more recent stresses caused by refugee movements.

The former trend has long brought deep societal strains to societies that viewed themselves as liberal welfare states. The tendency of immigrant groups not to assimilate in any fashion, and to take advantage of societal benefits while many do not work, created a serious backlash, which was exacerbated by violent incidents like the murder of Theo Van Gogh in Amsterdam and the brutal murder of several journalists at Charlie Hebdo in Paris. This has led to the rise in visibility, traction, and power of anti-immigrant, right-wing populist parties and movements.

The latter trend has been exacerbated by two dynamics. One is the turmoil in the Middle East, especially in Syria, which has led to millions of refugees fleeing to Europe, straining resources and leading again to a backlash giving traction to right-wing movements. The second is climate change. Droughts in Northern Africa took areas that had thrived with small farmers providing the backbone to the economies and turned them into wastelands. This in turn provided opportunities for extremist groups like Boko Haram to infiltrate and bring disruption and violence, leading many to flee across the sea to Italy and Greece, further straining countries' resources.

In the United States, there was another set of issues. The economic inequality and wage stagnation after the financial collapse of 2008, combined with demographic change, led to a sharp nativist reaction. And that was not all. Problems of weak governments in Central America that left a vacuum for violent gangs pushed many to leave their countries and move across Mexico to seek asylum in the United States—joining with many from Mexico seeking better jobs and, in some cases, fleeing drug cartels. The Obama administration struggled with the surge of asylum seekers even before the more extreme reaction of Trump's administration. Trump's 2016 campaign mantra of building a wall across the Southern border and making Mexico pay for it was a core part of his appeal. However, there was little wall construction and no role for

Mexico in paying for what little there was—but Trump followed through with a vengeance in going after asylum seekers, separating families and treating all with extreme malice.

Beyond those trends was another, disturbing one mentioned at the beginning of this chapter: the reversion of countries, in Central and Eastern Europe and elsewhere, from democracy to autocracy. Perhaps the poster child for this trend was Hungary, where Viktor Orban, over successive elections and periods of governing, using tropes like anti-Semitic attacks on George Soros, has chipped away at every protection of civil society. Attacks on newspapers and other media—including through economic means, the destruction of an independent judiciary, the expulsion of the Central European University, and undermining civic leaders and other political parties, all straight out of the playbook of authoritarians—have turned Hungary into a nascent autocracy. While the European Union has taken some steps to sanction Hungary for its actions, they have had little impact.

The same dynamic has occurred in Poland, and many other countries, from the Slovak Republic to the Czech Republic, have also slid away from thriving, multiparty democracies. And of course, we have seen some of the sharpest moves to autocracy in Turkey, where Recip Erdoğan has cracked down viciously on civil society and tightened his grip on power, while enabling his family and cronies to enrich themselves in Putin-esque style.

The move away from democracy, and from democracy as a model of governance, is a global phenomenon, including the Philippines, Malaysia, Myanmar, and many others. With the help of Vladimir Putin, the efforts to undermine democracy in Ukraine and to support thuggery in Belarus have added to instability and the advance of autocratic regimes. And, of course, we have also seen China crackdown on and erase democracy in Hong Kong and tighten its control in Beijing, while putting a million Uighurs in concentration camps.

The factors noted above have jibed directly with elections and election outcomes, at least in the United States. Donald Trump was able to win election in 2016 because he held on to Republicans in affluent suburbs in metropolitan areas, and was able to garner substantial support from white voters in the outer suburbs, exurbs, small towns, and rural areas. Why? Because Trump directly spoke to people in these areas who have felt disrespected and condescended to by elites, and have been told that their jobs—like, for example, coal miners in Pennsylvania—are obsolete and that they will have to retrain or move, that they are going to lose any favored status they have had in society. Trump told them that he would be on their side, and that their jobs would be safe. Even though Trump—a clear, card-carrying member of the elites they despise—was at best an imperfect vessel for their dissatisfactions, he brilliantly exploited the anger and these discontents with the phrase "Drain the Swamp!"

Much research has shown that values and race mattered more in these people's votes than economic self-interest—and despite the fact that their jobs have not come back, that the economy with COVID has dealt them another blow, they voted again disproportionately for Trump in 2020. Why then did Trump lose in 2020? For one thing, 2016 was an open presidential contest, and not a referendum on the sitting president; it was a choice between two major candidates who were both viewed unfavorably by a majority of voters; and some votes were drained from Hillary Clinton by support for Green Party candidate Jill Stein, who was in turn helped by a sophisticated social media campaign run by Russia. And in a contest defined as the lesser of two evils, the candidate of change has an edge.

In 2020, running as an incumbent, Donald Trump faced serious headwinds from his botched response to the pandemic—but he also faced a backlash from many college-educated white suburban voters, including Republicans and independents, who first showed their displeasure with his personal behavior and divisiveness in the midterm elections in 2018, which resulted in major gains for Democrats, and this was repeated in their presidential votes in 2020. And Trump faced an opponent who was not viewed unfavorably by those voters, or among core Democrats.

The great irony is that if Trump had responded to the pandemic the way his conservative counterpart in Australia, Prime Minister Scott Morrison, did—by relying on scientists and infectious disease specialists for guidance, using mask mandates, practicing social distancing, having early shutdowns, expediting provision of personal protective equipment for hospital workers, along with carrying out massive testing and early economic stimulus—he would likely have waltzed to reelection. Before the pandemic, Morrison was not well regarded by Australians—he had 37 percent approval. Late in 2020, his approval was 66 percent.[5]

Because Trump took a completely different course, he lost—and the consequences, very much related to the pandemic, were significant. Biden, of course, handled the pandemic in a dramatically different fashion from Trump—but that does not mean we saw a quick reversal in its course. In our tribal environment, a substantial share of Americans now believe that scientists are part of a broader conspiracy, that wearing masks is an affront to freedom, and that gathering with large crowds indoors will stick it to liberals. That attitude is joined by one of fundamentalist religious leaders in ultra-Orthodox Judaism and evangelical Protestantism; their behaviors created more super spreader events and created an additional surge in COVID cases, even after vaccines were available.

And vaccines alone did not eliminate the spread of the virus. In the United States and around the world, an antivaxx movement, accelerated through social media, created a broader resistance to the COVID vaccines, and created outbreaks of other dangerous diseases like measles.

Joe Biden has reversed course on many of Trump's foreign policies, including rebuilding international alliances via the Paris Accords and the World Health Organization, along with NATO. He has taken a tougher stance with China and Saudi Arabia, among others, on human rights. He has altered relationships with Russia and Iran. He has eliminated tariffs. He has been less accommodating to dictators like Erdoğan, Sisi, Orban, Duterte, and Bolsonaro. And he has tried to reestablish America's role as a serious factor in the world.

All these changes, and the decline in bombast, have helped create a reset—and have put dictators and autocrats on the defensive, without the moral protection given by Trump as president of the United States. But there are many, many challenges to a move in a positive direction. First, the pandemic took a world that was moving, if slowly, toward an extended period of economic prosperity after the long deterioration from the 2008 financial collapse, and set it back into a period of economic stagnation or worse.

The costs of economic dislocation strained government budgets, adding to debt, which may be manageable for a time with low interest rates but will be a major challenge if and when rates increase. In many countries, businesses that were forced to shut down or cut back, from restaurants to retail shops, will not be able to come back. In countries where the pandemic meant that in-person shopping was replaced by turning to e-commerce, the trend away from retail stores will accelerate, which will have implications not just for jobs directly lost but also for the vibrancy of downtown neighborhoods and shopping malls. It is no wonder that the biggest winner from the pandemic is Jeff Bezos of Amazon. As more and more people have grown used to working from home, law firms, accounting firms, and other businesses have rethought the need for a massive presence in office buildings, which has created a major strain on commercial real estate—which represents a significant share of global pension funds.

The pandemic put a tremendous strain on many health systems. It appears that the long term health challenges created by exposure to the virus—organ failure, chronic diseases, loss of memory—will linger for a long time, adding to the strain. Governments facing large deficits, and the likely need to add more of a stimulus to help economies jump-start, may feel compelled to cut back on health budgets at an inopportune time. And this is complicated by a further likely consequence of COVID-19, the rise in mental illness, from increased depression and anxiety to suicidal ideation and suicide, to the increase in serious mental illnesses like schizophrenia that seem to follow pandemics.

Add one other frightening consequence, pointed out in a UN report: "Member States and researchers have warned that extreme right-wing terrorists are using COVID-19-related conspiracy theories and disinformation to radicalize, recruit and fundraise, as well as seeking to inspire plots and attacks."[6]

The pandemic has led to significant increases in social isolation, making people more vulnerable to these appeals. And if they lead to a rise in right-wing terrorism, this type of violence can add to pressures for antidemocratic crackdowns, and increase the appeals of strongmen promising an end to the violence and disorder.

Of course, there are broader global challenges, well described by Fareed Zakaria: "The health crisis has accelerated a number of forces that were already gathering steam. Most fundamentally, it is blindingly clear that human development as it is happening now is creating ever-greater risks. The backlash from nature is all around us, from wildfires to hurricanes to pandemics, of which COVID-19 may simply be the first in a series. The pandemic has intensified other trends, too. For demographic and other reasons, countries will likely see more sluggish economic growth. Inequality will get worse, as the big get bigger in every sphere. Machine learning is moving so fast that, for the first time in history, human beings might lose control over their own creations. Nations are becoming more parochial, their domestic politics more isolationist. The United States and China are headed toward a bitter and prolonged confrontation."[7]

Zakaria, at the same time, has a hopeful message—while these problems could lead down a dangerous path, they can also promote a broader urgency for countries to look outward rather than inward, to foster greater international cooperation, to bring China and the United States, the two superpowers, to a broader understanding instead of a destructive confrontation. This future is of course possible, but it is far from likely. The conflicts in the South China Sea, the differences on fundamental human rights, the trade frictions, the desire for China to expand its regional hegemony and for the United States to counter it, mean deep frictions. And global economic unease, combined with related domestic turmoil, might itself bring pressures to turn inward.

As dictators have gained control over levers of power like the judiciary and levers of communication like newspapers and television, with the ability to shut down destructive social media and exploit these tools of communication for their own purposes, dislodging them, or moving them toward more freedom, will become harder, not easier. As turmoil in regions like the Middle East and the Horn of Africa intensifies the flow of refugees, the nativist and racist impulses that feed ultranationalist and populist parties will also intensify. The ability of pernicious regimes like Russia and China to exploit these divisions and interfere in elections through the use of social media and cyberterror will grow. Job insecurity created by the nature of global competition will make it harder to build multinational trade pacts and alliances. The pandemic was not responsible for these conditions, but it made countering them more difficult.

History is full of surprises, and making linear projections is rarely fruitful, while at the same time change tends to be cyclical. The world has seen challenges as great or greater as those we now face, in health, internal and external conflict, the rise of authoritarianism, and economic disaster. It is entirely possible that Zakaria's optimistic future will prevail. But the work to get there is formidable.

In the short and medium terms, waves of immigration and refugees will expand, not contract, placing economic and social pressures on many countries, and giving more traction to nativist, racist, and authoritarian parties and factions. Even after vaccines for COVID-19 emerged, leading to its removal as a global disruptor, other deadly viruses still lurk, and could at some point lead us back into dark times. Global leadership and the reinforcement of alliances can and should make a difference, and have been helped by the leadership of the Biden administration, but it will take bold action on climate, trade, and immigration to ease the pressures that will otherwise be there. And continued dysfunction in key countries like the United States and the United Kingdom, along with the continued pernicious activity of Russia and China and with the temptations of autocracy bringing order to disorder, add to our challenges.

Notes

1. Danny Clemens, "'He's a Decent Family Man': Watch the Moment John McCain Defended Barack Obama on 2008 Campaign Trail," WLS-TV, Chicago, August 26, 2018, https://abc7chicago.com/mccain-defends-obama-arab-2008-campaign-john/4058948/.

2. Jeff Cox, "CEOs See Pay Grow 1,000% in the Last 40 Years, Now Make 278 Times the Average Worker," CNN, August 16, 2019, https://www.cnbc.com/2019/08/16/ceos-see-pay-grow-1000percent-and-now-make-278-times-the-average-worker.html.

3. Federal Reserve, "Distribution of Household Wealth in the US since 1989," https://www.federalreserve.gov/releases/z1/dataviz/dfa/distribute/table/#quarter:123;series:Net%20worth;demographic:networth;population:all;units:shares.

4. Christopher Ingraham, "For the First Time in US History, Billionaires Paid a Lower Tax Rate Than the Working Class Last Year," *Washington Post*, October 8, 2019, https://www.washingtonpost.com/business/2019/10/08/first-time-history-us-billionaires-paid-lower-tax-rate-than-working-class-last-year/.

5. Soraya Lennie, "Scott Morrison Is Now Very Popular in Australia; He Hasn't Earned That," *Washington Post*, May 6, 2020, https://www.washingtonpost.com/opinions/2020/05/05/scott-morrison-is-now-very-popular-australia-he-hasnt-earned-that/.

6. United Nations, "Member States Concerned with the Growing and Increasingly Transnational Threat of Extreme Right-Wing Terrorism," July 2020, https://www.un.org/sc/ctc/wp-content/uploads/2020/07/CTED_Trends_Alert_Extreme_Right-Wing_Terrorism_JULY.pdf.

7. Fareed Zakaria, "The Pandemic Upended the Past; but It's Given Us a Change to Learn Lessons," *Washington Post*, October 6, 2020, https://www.washingtonpost.com/opinions/2020/10/06/fareed-zakaria-lessons-postpandemic-world/?arc404=true.

Nine

The Global Response to High-Impact Pandemics Requires New Approaches

JENNIFER B. NUZZO, *JOHNS HOPKINS BLOOMBERG SCHOOL OF PUBLIC HEALTH; JOHNS HOPKINS CENTER FOR HEALTH SECURITY; COUNCIL ON FOREIGN RELATIONS*

The scale and protracted nature of pandemics necessitate different approaches to preparedness than other health security threats. The fundamental requirement for pandemic preparedness is to, first, ensure that individual countries are equipped to rapidly detect and respond to infectious disease events in order to contain them before they spill across borders; and, second, if containment of outbreaks at the source of their emergence fails, to ensure the availability of global resources to support countries in their own responses. But inadequate progress at bolstering countries' capacities to adequately respond to infectious disease threats, global governance structures that are unable to remove disincentives for global cooperation, limited global tools to support nationally led response efforts, and a failure to address even more challenging pandemic scenarios, such as deliberate releases and engineered pathogens, limit support to countries to aid in their response. New global solutions are needed to ensure there are (1) adequate governance of global efforts to detect and respond to pandemics; (2) global agreements to facilitate the development of and access to medical countermeasures; and (3) participation in preparedness by nonhealth actors, including nongovernmental organizations.

Why High-Impact Pathogen Pandemics Are Different from Other Health Security Threats

The ongoing COVID-19 pandemic has been called a "once-in-a-century health crisis, the effects of which will be felt for decades to come." This title likely stems from comparisons of COVID-19 with "the Great Influenza" pandemic of 1918–19, which is estimated to have sickened about a third of the world's population and killed at least 50 million people.[1] Like the 1918 pandemic, the combined health, social, and economic toll of COVID-19 has eclipsed all other infectious disease emergencies that have occurred within the past century. Ten months into the pandemic, 191 countries have reported tens of millions of cases and close to 2 million deaths. International travel has been restricted by countries. But the pandemic is likely not the last major health security that will occur within the next century, and may not even be the worst.

The COVID-19 pandemic has exposed a world that is unprepared for significant infectious disease events. Lacking sufficient capacity to conduct targeted public health interventions to stop the spread of the virus, countries were left with few options but to implement broad societal restrictions, such as shutdowns and stay-at-home orders. The measures worked well enough to slow the growth in cases in the late spring of 2020. But facing political and economic pressures, governments began to relax these restrictions, and transmission of the virus began to steadily increase once again. In early November, more than 500,000 new cases were reported globally each day—representing an all-time high.

The pandemic has had severe effects on society at large. Global gross domestic product (GDP) in 2020 was expected to contract by 4.9 percent.[2] In the United States, it was estimated that the pandemic would cause $16 trillion in lost GDP, premature deaths, and health impairment.[3] The pandemic interrupted education for more than a billion children around the world, which was expected to exacerbate inequality and erode progress in expanding educational opportunities.[4] The World Bank warned that the pandemic could increase by 150 million the number of individuals living under extreme poverty.[5] The World Health Organization (WHO) warned that the effects of the pandemic will be felt for decades.[6]

Global Conditions Favor the Emergence and Pandemic Spreading of Deadly Pathogens

The emergence and global spread COVID-19 are not surprising, and we must assume more of such events will occur. Respiratory viruses—like the novel coronavirus, SARS-CoV-2, that is causing the COVID-19 pandemic—can have features that facilitate widespread transmission. First, the ability of an infected person to sicken several others helps the virus spread exponentially until public health control measures are put in place and/or behaviors change. Second, these viruses tend to have short periods between exposure and contagiousness, which leaves only a narrow window of time to intervene to stop subsequent cases from occurring. Third, these viruses often cause symptoms that can look like a number of other more common diseases—or, sometimes, cause no symptoms at all—making it difficult, without a diagnostic test, to identify who is infected and who is not. All these traits mean that when a new respiratory virus emerges, it may be difficult to act quickly enough and with enough precision to contain these pathogens at the source of their emergence. Finally, respiratory pathogens, like coronaviruses, have demonstrated their potential to cause serious illness and death in a sizable percentage of cases. The coronaviruses that caused the 2003 Severe Acute Respiratory Syndrome (SARS) epidemic and outbreaks of Middle East Respiratory Syndrome (MERS), are, respectively, estimated to have killed up to 10 and 35 percent of cases.

Once a pathogen with these features emerges and begins to transmit locally, if it is not contained quickly at the source, global conditions are ripe to help it spread to become a pandemic. Though there is no single definition of what constitutes a "pandemic," epidemiologists use this word to describe an infectious disease event that involves wide, geographic spread, generally across multiple parts of the globe. International travel, mass displacement, migration, and urbanization enable pathogens to reach new, susceptible populations. The high global burden of chronic diseases and obesity increases the vulnerability of populations to develop severe illness and death once infected. All these conditions serve to exacerbate the tolls of a pandemic. In 2009 a pandemic influenza emerged, and within two months it was circulating within most countries. It has been estimated that within the first twelve months, the virus likely killed between 150,000 and 575,000 people.[7]

The last decade has witnessed a series of infectious disease emergencies: pandemic spread of a new H1N1 influenza virus, the emergence of the deadly coronavirus that causes MERS, the two biggest Ebola epidemics on record in West Africa and the Democratic Republic of Congo, and the global spread of the previously obscure Zika virus. We should expect more. Even when we account for increasing surveillance, the number of new, emerging infectious diseases has steadily increased since 1940.[8] The majority of these new pathogens originated in wildlife and jumped to humans—a phenomenon called "spillover." Global socioeconomic and environmental changes are thought to be drivers of spillover events.

While we should expect to see the continued emergence of new, worrisome pathogens, whether these pathogens go to cause a global pandemic depends in part on the response of individual countries and international global health security organizations. Former smallpox eradicator Dr. Larry Brilliant has noted that "outbreaks are inevitable. Epidemics are optional."[9] While global conditions may favor the continued emergence of new pathogens that can cause fast-growing outbreaks in humans, measures can be taken to stop outbreaks from spreading to become epidemics and to prevent epidemics from growing to become pandemics. Whether we can interrupt this progression of events depends both on the readiness of countries where outbreaks are occurring to act and the ability and willingness of the global community to support national efforts.

Twenty-First-Century Disease Threats

As challenging as COVID-19 has proven to be, worse pandemic scenarios could occur. The same scientific advances that are necessary to ensure the development of new therapies and vaccines also raise the possibility of the deliberate or accidental release of deadly pathogens found in nature or that have been engineered or recreated in laboratories. These twenty-first-century disease threats could cause even greater harms that eclipse the worst yet seen. The deliberate release of a deadly pathogen can result in a pandemic with an epidemiology never before seen. If the released organism is engineered, disease severity may be greater than known diseases and existing diagnostic and therapeutic approaches may not work. Though the probability of such an event occurring is unknown, these scenarios warrant greater attention in ongoing preparedness efforts due to the severity of the harm they can cause. Governments should work to prevent deliberate biological events by continuing to support the Convention on the Prohibition of the Development, Production and Stockpiling of Bacteriological (Biological) and Toxin Weapons and on Their Destruction, commonly known as the Biological Weapons Convention. Additionally, the bolstering of domestic preparedness capacities has the potential to mitigate the effects of a deliberate biological event, which can deter state and nonstate actors from using these weapons.[10]

The Inadequacy of International Governance for Pandemics

The International Health Regulations (IHR) are the primary governance framework for preventing and responding to transnational health security threats. This legally binding agreement outlines WHO's and states parties' responsibilities in preparing for and responding to infectious disease emergencies. After the global SARS epidemic in 2003, the IHRs were fundamentally revised. The 2005 IHR recognized that emerging public health events pose a significant risk to the global community, and so it created a process that requires state parties to develop the capacity to detect, assess, notify, and respond to events that have the potential to become a Public Health Emergency of International Concern (PHEIC). The IHR empowers the Office of the WHO Director-General to convene an Emergency Committee (EC) of international experts to review and provide advice as to whether an ongoing health event may constitute a PHEIC and what recommendations should be given to member states to bolster the response and control the outbreak. The WHO director-general has sole authority to declare a PHEIC and make recommendations for member states.

Arguably, the IHR's greatest strength lies in its requirements for early disease detection and outbreak control. The IHR establishes the expectation that countries will develop the public health capacities necessary to detect and report potential PHEICs, with the goal of providing early warning of outbreaks that could spread beyond borders and threaten others. If national surveillance and response systems can quickly detect and notify WHO of significant outbreaks, the international community may be able to act to limit the spread of the disease, with the hope of preventing an outbreak from becoming an epidemic or pandemic.

Despite its value, the IHR faces challenges in its implementation and content. Countries have inadequately addressed the IHR's requirement to develop the capacities needed to detect, assess, notify, and respond to potential public health emergencies. To ensure compliance with this requirement, member states passed a resolution at the Sixty-First World Health Assembly held in 2008 that countries should report annually on the status of their implementation of their IHR requirements. By 2012, these self-assessments indicated that less than a quarter of all WHO member states had met their IHR core capacity requirements. Two years later, just over a third of member states reported full compliance with core capacity requirements.

The West African Ebola epidemic highlighted the consequences of countries' lack of progress toward IHR implementation. Delays in detecting an outbreak in Guinea allowed Ebola to spread internationally, sickening close to 30,000 people and killing more than 11,000 in Liberia, Guinea, Sierra Leone, and Nigeria. The UN Security Council unanimously passed a resolution urging UN member states to provide resources to combat the epidemic, which it deemed a threat to peace and security. National governments and organizations around the world sent response personnel and other resources to help contain the epidemic.

Several independent commissions convened in response to the epidemic in West Africa recommended that countries' compliance with the IHR core capacity requirements be assessed through rigorous, external review, rather than by self-assessment.[11] In response, WHO developed a framework for external evaluation of countries' capacities. WHO's Joint External Evaluation (JEE) process relies on international teams of outside experts to identify for countries that choose to participate critical gaps and challenges in national preparedness capacities and mechanisms. To date, more than a hundred countries have completed JEEs; however, there are important geographic holes in participation. Russia, China, and India have not participated, along with many countries in Western Europe and much of Latin America.[12]

While the JEE process represents an improvement over self-assessments in measuring countries' compliance toward IHR implementation, ultimately, the lack of resources to address gaps in countries' capacities is what undermines the power of the IHRs to address pandemic threats. The JEEs that have been completed indicate that there are significant gaps in countries' development of the IHR core capacities. Few countries, even wealthy ones, show evidence of having taken steps to begin to address gaps identified by their assessment.

WHO's implementation of its IHR authorities has also come under scrutiny. A key point of contention has been how WHO makes decisions about whether an infectious disease event should be declared a PHEIC. Global commissions strongly criticized the organization for waiting four months after the international spread of Ebola in West Africa (2014–16) before convening an EC, which ultimately declared the epidemic a PHEIC.[13] WHO received criticisms again during the 2018–20 Ebola epidemic in the Democratic Republic of Congo (DRC), when it waited eleven months to declare an outbreak. Though WHO was quick to convene an EC to review the DRC epidemic, comments made by the director-general suggested that concerns that other countries to implement travel and trade restrictions in response to a PHEIC delayed its declaration. WHO's judgment in reviewing the COVID-19 outbreak was also questioned. Though it was convened early, the EC initially delayed its recommendation due to having insufficient data from China. At a second EC meeting at the end of January, the director-general declared a PHEIC but noted that the IHR should be reformed to allow intermediate levels for declaring an emergency, rather than an all-or-nothing standard.

The strength of the IHR has been limited by its lack of provisions to penalize countries for not adhering to its legal requirements. The IHR aims to prevent the unnecessary restriction of global trade and travel in response to infectious disease emergencies and grant WHO the power to make recommendations of what evidence-based actions countries should take. But countries often do not conform to these recommendations. During the West African Ebola outbreak, more than a third of states parties to the IHRs implemented restrictions on travel that exceeded recommendations made by WHO. There is no evidence that these measures prevented the exportation of Ebola cases from West Africa, but they did hinder efforts to contain the epidemic by making it harder for health care personnel and supplies to move to and from the affected countries. Similar actions occurred during the 2009 H1N1 influenza pandemic. Though WHO issued strong warnings against the use of travel or trade restrictions, the United States and Mexico, which were the first to report H1N1 cases, were the target of punitive travel and trade measures. Countries quarantined planes from North America and announced bans on US pork imports, which did little to slow the movement of the virus, but likely exacerbated the social and economic tolls of the pandemic.

Though member states have criticized WHO for not recommending travel restrictions in response to COVID-19, larger considerations were at stake. When member states implement travel and trade restrictions, it may hinder countries' willingness to report significant disease outbreaks. This, in turn, can make the world less safe from pandemics by undermining the IHRs' greatest strength: early detection of infectious disease outbreaks. Learning late about significant infectious disease outbreaks limits the abilities of countries to prepare and respond and increases the likelihood that these events can be contained and increases their potential to become epidemics and pandemics.

The COVID-19 pandemic has exposed the limits of IHR in preventing pandemics and in enabling a global response to mitigate their pandemics. These shortcomings have yet again surfaced calls to revise the IHR. WHO director-general Tedros Ghebreyesus has called COVID-19 "an acid test" for the IHRs, and in August 2020 he announced the creation of an independent expert committee to review the functioning of the IHR during the COVID-19 pandemic and to advise on the need to revise the IHR. Though the IHR review committee may identify areas where the IHRs may be strengthened, it would be up to WHO member states to adopt changes. Renegotiating the IHR is not an easy prospect. The last major overhaul in 2003 occurred after the shock of the SARS epidemic and at least ten prior years' worth of lobbying for reform by some member states, including the United States. The US decision to leave WHO could change the politics of future reform efforts.

New Global Solutions: Governance, Research and Development, Multisectoral Preparedness, and Response Efforts

Given the inadequacy of current arrangements, new global solutions require adequate governance of efforts to detect and respond to pandemics, agreements to facilitate the research and development (R&D) and dissemination of medical countermeasures, and multisectoral participation in preparedness and response efforts, where nonhealth actors, including nongovernmental organizations, work together with health professionals to fight the pandemic. International cooperation and peer learning should help to bolster preparedness and response efforts.

Governance

These staggering tolls show the inadequacy of the existing global health security architecture to protect us from pandemics. This architecture was built and trained on outbreaks and epidemics, but pandemics require different approaches. While there have been challenges in responses to infectious disease outbreaks and epidemics, there at least exists the theoretical possibility that unaffected nations may be able to contribute funds, personnel, and other resources to assist in these efforts. However, this model is largely not applicable during a pandemic, in which many, if not all, countries may be affected at once. This means that whatever resources that exist within WHO, the World Bank, and other international organizations that typically help countries respond to significant outbreaks and epidemics, will have to be spread out among a greater number of countries. With the prospect of need exceeding the availability of global resources, countries will have to rely on domestic resources to stop a pandemic spread.

The issue of scarcity of resources, coupled with high demand, needs to be considered ahead of time. COVID-19 has demonstrated both the fragility of international supply chains and the consequences of national governments competing for access to the same limited supplies. Shortages in personal protective equipment, testing reagents and related supplies, essential medical resources, food products, and other goods have been reported around the globe. Countries have differed in their abilities to procure these supplies in the midst of this global competition, as well as their abilities to produce needed materials domestically.

COVID-19 has shined a light on the need to reexamine existing frameworks for global governance of pandemic threats. Already under way are efforts to reform WHO's powers to detect and designate as an global emergency potential pandemic threats. In addition to needing a stronger mandate to press countries for more information about suspected disease emergencies, WHO also needs enhanced resources to enforce IHR requirements and to provide incentives to countries to comply.

Research and Development

The availability of safe and effective medical countermeasures (MCMs) will greatly enhance global abilities to respond to a pandemic. The availability of

MCMs (i.e., vaccines, therapeutics, diagnostics, and other medical supplies, such as personal protective equipment) represent our best opportunities to limit morbidity, mortality, and disease transmission. Vaccination is the single most effective pharmaceutical intervention and would likely be the preferred MCM in a high-impact pandemic because it can typically prevent infection in individuals and limit transmission in populations. Antivirals and other therapeutics like monoclonal antibodies, if available to treat the ill, might be of great clinical value; and, in some cases, if there were sufficient supplies of these products (seemingly unlikely in most places under current conditions), they could serve as prophylactic agents. Personal protective equipment, including masks and respirators, would also play a critical role in infection prevention and control, particularly if no vaccine or therapeutics are immediately available.

Global debates over development and access to COVID-19 vaccines has demonstrated the potential for countries to prioritize national needs ahead of global interests when it comes to MCM development and access. Though global recovery from the pandemic would be enhanced by ensuring that all countries have access to vaccines in a pandemic, a global agreement that ensures that all countries will have access to vaccines during a pandemic does not exist. Some potential models do exist, but more work is needed to ensure full global participation that would ensure equity in vaccine allocation. The COVID-19 Vaccines Global Access (COVAX) Facility is a promising model developed by WHO, GAVI, and the Coalition for Epidemic Preparedness Innovations that aims to expedite vaccine development and ensure that all countries have access to vaccines for their highest-risk populations. To date, more than 170 countries have opted to participate in COVAX, but the notable absence of the United States from the agreement has raised concerns about further global participation and has stoked worries about the nationalization of vaccine supplies.[14]

There is the possibility that individual countries will broker bilateral agreements or donate excess stocks of vaccines, but experience during a previous pandemic suggests that these efforts may be inadequate in size and too late to meaningfully protect the population of countries that do not have their own vaccine stocks. During the 2009 H1N1 influenza pandemic, some countries initially announced their support of efforts to donate a portion of their pandemic influenza vaccine stocks to countries without access and declared they would share a percentage of their vaccine with low- and middle-income countries. However, the number of vaccines ultimately committed was considerably lower than the original pledged amounts. In December 2009, countries had pledged to donate 200 million doses; but in the end, less than 125 million doses (enough to cover only 10 percent of the population of countries eligible to receive donated vaccine) were committed.[15] This drives home the concern that in a pandemic scenario, a country's national capacity will be even more important as international support, particularly from other affected countries, will be limited and quickly exhausted.

Multisector Involvement in Preparedness

Preparedness for pandemics requires the involvement and coordination of multiple sectors. As COVID-19 has demonstrated, the wide geographic spread of a high-impact pathogen can cause harm that extends beyond the health sector, so it is crucial that other major sectors be involved in both preparedness planning and response efforts. Government human health agencies alone also do not possess sufficient resources or capabilities to detect and respond to the deliberate release of a novel respiratory pathogen.

Increased participation in pandemic preparedness efforts by animal and environmental health sectors is essential. However, many reviews have underscored the continued lack of integration among the human, animal, plant, and environmental health sectors. One example of the consequence of a lack of such integration is the delayed ability of the human health sector to recognize Ebola as the cause of an outbreak in West Africa in 2014, which was in part due to the human health community's belief that the virus was not present in the region—a finding that had been previously predicted by animal health experts who were not consulted in public health assessments of the event.[16] Current debates over the origin and possible intermediate host of the SARS-CoV-2 virus that causes COVID-19 also underscores the need for strengthening collaborations between human, animal and environmental health sectors.

The potential for deliberate release of a pathogen with pandemic potential provides a clear case of an instance when engagement with the security sector is required. However, the need to involve security in disease outbreak preparedness is not limited to deliberate events. The ongoing outbreak of Ebola in the DRC also underscores the importance of having robust partnerships between health and security. Generally, a national or international security sector will include military, law enforcement, and intelligence agencies.

Militaries may have a mandate and well-defined protocols for disaster relief operations, but their experience in disease preparedness and response may be limited. National militaries may have experience in medical countermeasure research and development, transportation elements, military health or other surveillance programs, and other initiatives that may prove relevant to outbreak preparedness and response.

There has also been acknowledgment in recent years of the need to engage private sector organizations in the work of pandemic preparedness. COVID-19 has shown that a severe pandemic can devastate economic growth. Therefore, both out of self-preservation and for reasons of corporate social responsibility, the private sector needs to play a greater role in planning for and responding to such events. Increasingly, public–private partnerships are being proposed as a model to expand the availability of financial resources for preparedness. The Coalition for Epidemic Preparedness Innovations—an international partnership of public, private, philanthropic, and civil society organizations—receives financial contributions from governments and private philanthropists to accelerate vaccine development for priority pathogens identified in the WHO R&D Blueprint, as well as investments in platform technologies to accelerate the development of vaccines for previously unrecognized diseases.[17]

Governments have historically viewed the private sector as a potential source of support for public sector–led operations, including in-kind donations and purchases of equipment, supplies, or medical countermeasures. But the private sector has additional capabilities and expertise that can be tapped to support preparedness efforts. The unique expertise and services of several industries deserve special attention.[18] The first is the pharmaceutical and medical supply industry, which plays a key role in the research, development, and manufacture of medical countermeasures, diagnostics, personal protective equipment, and other essential medical supplies. The second are the airlines, transportation, and logistics/shipping industries, which can ensure the transfer of medical personnel and equipment for scaling up operations. The third is the medical supply industry, which would also be of high global importance in a pandemic. And fourth is the global communications sector—both those who provide the hardware and software around communications, as well as those who are global leaders in delivering content and helping to serve public information needs, including contact tracing and case investigation and monitoring. Industries that may have a large economic stake, such as travel and tourism, should also be involved in government preparedness efforts.[19]

Despite its potential, private sector involvement to date has been haphazard and mostly limited to the response phase of a disease outbreak. A key challenge is the lack of advance communication and coordination between public and private actors, which is needed to clarify the appropriate roles, responsibilities, and expectations of each during a pandemic. The Private Sector Roundtable and a variety of efforts at the World Economic Forum vis-à-vis private sector engagement in preparedness and response are notable exceptions in which global business has been leading or participating in the development of new partnerships and potential solutions with WHO and governments.

The partnership between government and the private sector will be most effective if defined and agreed on well in advance of an event. The ad hoc inclusion of private sector services into a health response could conceivably hinder a response in that it could risk public suspicion of private sector involvement for monetary or financial gain. Prenegotiated partnerships and/or memoranda of understanding that transparently define the nature and extent of private sector involvement are needed.

Private sector organizations can also meaningfully contribute to preparedness by preparing continuity plans to ensure their continued operations in the event of a potential pandemic. Many communities rely on such organizations to provide essential services. Therefore, these organizations can also serve as extensions of government health response by educating their employees, families, and surrounding communities about recommended protective actions and planning to provide support for employees who become ill.

Recommendations

Both national and global efforts are needed to address the threats of new infectious diseases that can quickly spread around the world. At the national level, priority should be given to preparedness, not only to detect the outbreak of infectious diseases but also to take effective early countermeasures—for example, by having a stockpile of masks and personal protective equipment and addressing frailties of the health care system. Globally, new partnerships should be established to improve surveillance, facilitate R&D and access to medical countermeasures, increase financing for pandemic preparedness, and set rules and standards for deliberate pathogen releases.

National Governments Must Prioritize Preparedness

Ultimately, the responsibility for pandemic preparedness falls to sovereign nations. But efforts to motivate national leaders to take action to bolster their capacities to prevent and respond to pandemics have been largely unsuccessful. Though COVID-19 may have caught political leaders by surprise, health experts had issued prior warnings that the occurrence of serious global pandemic was a matter of "'when, not 'if'" and had been urging governments to take action. Perhaps one of the highest-profile warnings came from the independent Global Preparedness Monitoring Board (GPMB), chaired by Gro Harlem Brundtland, who formerly served as the prime minister of Norway and WHO director-general, and Elhadj As Sy, former secretary-general of the International Federation of the Red Cross and Red Crescent Societies.[20] Months before COVID-19, the GPMB issued a report that warned of the "very real threat" that a rapidly moving, highly lethal pandemic could kill millions and cause significant social and economic harm. They urged political leaders to prioritize and strengthen preparedness.

Despite these warnings, governments were slow to take action to stop the spread of COVID-19, which allowed the virus to spread widely. Though most countries closed their borders or implemented restrictions on travel from China and other initially affected countries, many were slow to take domestic action to control the spread of the virus. Though countries learned in January that the novel coronavirus, SARS-CoV-2 was readily transmissible and more deadly than the influenza pandemic of 2009, many governments did not begin to adopt domestic control measures until mid-March or later. The consequence of this lack of action is evidenced that by the tens of millions of cases of COVID-19 that were reported by more than 190 countries.

Though WHO was early to warn countries about the need to prepare for the spread of the virus within their borders, its reluctance to call the health emergency a "pandemic" may have downplayed risks posed to countries by the virus and undermined its own efforts to motivate governments to act. WHO first used this word to describe the spread of COVID-19 at a press conference on March 11, 2020. By that point, more than a hundred thousand cases and more than 4,000 deaths had been reported by 114 countries. WHO's use of the word did not carry official significance, as there is no formal way or legal mechanism by which WHO or any other body can declare a pandemic. So its delay in using the word to describe the spread of a virus that was detected in more than half of its member states was puzzling. Director-General Ghebreyesus explained WHO's hesitation as due to concerns that misuse of the word "pandemic" could result in "unreasonable fear, or unjustified acceptance that the fight is over, leading to unnecessary suffering and death."[21] In hesitating to use the term, WHO missed an opportunity to educate the public that "pandemic" is an indication of geographic spread in multiple areas of the world, and not an indication of disease severity. By failing to illustrate for countries that had yet to detect cases or were not yet hard hit how ably the virus was spreading, WHO may have failed to properly motivate national leaders to take preemptive action to prevent the virus from spreading widely within their borders.[22] Countries' delayed response in failure to implement domestic control efforts may have reflected a lack of understanding about the transmission potential of the virus or the urgency for bolstering domestic capacities to combat the virus.

Efforts to Improve Health Security Must Address Health System Frailties

The ongoing pandemic has also exposed the inadequacy of countries' health systems. Government efforts to flatten the curve, such as shutdowns and other restrictions, have been aimed, in large part, at preventing hospitals and health clinics from becoming overwhelmed by a surge of seriously ill patients. In the United States, images of overrun intensive care units in Italy spurred political leaders to take action out of fear that the US epidemic was only a few weeks behind. Observations that the United States lacked adequate supplies of personal protective equipment to keep health care workers safe increased the urgency of concern about the resilience of the countries' health facilities.

The worry that health facilities would not be able to cope was reasonable. The 2019 Global Health Security Index, published in 2019, found countries' health systems are often the weakest in readiness for an epidemic or pandemic.[23] Among the 195 countries included in the index, the average score for the category on health systems was 26.4 out of a maximum of 100 points—the lowest average among all categories. Even high-income countries lost the most points in this category.[24]

Though health facilities play a central role in mitigating or amplifying the toll of infectious disease emergencies, they have not been central to national efforts to develop core capacities to detect and respond to infectious disease emergencies. While WHO's JEE provides for countries a well-defined list to assess the availability of core capacities needed for infectious disease emergencies, this tool does not include capacities that health facilities would be expected to need to cope with serious infectious disease outbreaks and other public health emergencies. These include the capacity to manage continuity of critical government functions, despite widespread illness and absenteeism, and the capacity to rapidly acquire medicines and equipment when other countries are concurrently seeking the same countermeasures and materials (e.g., masks).

The availability of essential medical supplies and equipment must also be included in global planning efforts. COVID-19 revealed both the fragility of global supply chains and the effects of a severe maldistribution of medical supplies between countries and health systems around the world. Dedicated efforts are needed to determine how countries, especially low- and middle-income ones, can maintain access to critical supplies (e.g., masks, respirators, gloves, gowns, intraveous fluid bags, and medical gases).

The Global Community Must Improve Surveillance to Detect and Respond to Pandemic Threats

COVID-19 has also revealed the inadequacies of the existing global health security architecture's ability to conduct surveillance for pandemic threats. The absence of a single, official source to track the spread of COVID-19 in real time sent public health researchers scrambling to fill the void of data needed to support response to the pandemic. The Johns Hopkins COVID-19 Dashboard emerged as one of the first places to reliably see up-to-date global case numbers and remains one of the most cited resources for tracking the pandemic.[25]

Global utilization of the Johns Hopkins COVID-19 Dashboard resource reflects gaps in official international surveillance efforts. Though international disease surveillance systems exist for individual routine infections, such as seasonal influenza, dedicated efforts to provide real-time surveillance for pandemic threats has not been established. Ideally, WHO would lead efforts to collect, analyze, and disseminate data from each country to help track the pace and progress of potential pandemic threats. But national sovereignty concerns often hinder countries' willingness to share needed data. Moreover, delays and gaps in global surveillance result from a lack of interoperability and standardization between national governments' surveillance efforts.[26]

Global surveillance efforts' reliance on official reports from countries about the occurrence and extent of significant outbreaks has also limited pandemic preparedness efforts. Though some may argue that the emergence of a novel coronavirus with demonstrated capacity for sustained human to human transmission should have motivated countries to bolster their domestic preparedness, China's delay in sharing information about its COVID-19 cases and likelihood that the virus was spreading between people, initially hindered global understanding of the pandemic potential of the new pathogen.[27] The Council on Foreign Relations Independent Task Force's 2020 report "Improving Pandemic Preparedness: Lessons from COVID-19" concludes that relying on individual governments to report emerging information in a timely, complete fashion has not proved to be an effective method for global data collection.[28] Noting the important contributions of efforts—such as the Seattle Flu Study, which was the first to detect community transmission of SARS-CoV-2—the task force recommends expanding surveillance from nongovernmental sources. As an example of what can be done to bolster surveillance to support the early detection of outbreaks, it calls for the creation of an international sentinel surveillance network of health care facilities that regularly reports hospitalization data to identify unusual trends.

International agreements for sample and benefit sharing are also needed to improve the development of medical countermeasures. Clinical specimens, as opposed to genetic sequencing data, are needed to test vaccines, medicines, and diagnostics. Though researchers from China shared early sequence data from the SARS-CoV-2 virus, challenges in obtaining virus samples were reported. In previous years, international disagreements over whether and how to share avian influenza samples, hindered global surveillance efforts for the virus, which was feared could cause a global pandemic. These disagreements were ultimately addressed through the negotiation and adoption of the Pandemic Influenza Preparedness framework, which created an agreement among countries for ensuring access to viral samples and ensuring that the vaccines, medicines, and diagnostics derived from this information are more equitably distributed among WHO member states. While this framework represents important progress toward improving the sharing of specimens and their derived benefits, sample and benefit sharing agreements need to be developed that apply to pathogens beyond influenza.

New Global Partnerships Are Needed to Improve Medical Countermeasure Development and Access

The Global Health Security Architecture must also support the development of and ensure the widespread availability of medicines, vaccines, therapeutics, and diagnostics. In a global pandemic, these tools represent our best opportunity to limit the spread of disease and prevent harms to health and society. However, COVID-19 has demonstrated the need for global approaches to expedite the development and to ensure equitable access to these resources. The pace of development of medicines and vaccines has been limited by underpowered investigator- or country-led clinical trials. Larger, international research and development efforts, such as the global Solidarity trial, have yielded more robust data than smaller trials into the lack of effectiveness of certain therapeutics (e.g., remdesivir) being used in some countries to treat COVID-19.[29]

Enhanced global approaches are needed to ensure global access to all needed medical countermeasures. Existing frameworks, such as the Pandemic Influenza Preparedness framework and COVAX, are promising models, but neither fully ensure that countries will share medical countermeasures in future pandemics. Full participation by all WHO member states is needed to normalize global approaches to medical countermeasure development and allocation.

New Approaches Are Needed to Ensure There Is Adequate Funding for Pandemic Preparedness

The absence of funding for preparedness has consistently been identified as a challenge for improving readiness for pandemics. Estimates by the World Bank suggest that the cost of developing the core public health capacities needed to prepare for public health emergencies is well below the cost of responding to such events, but governments continue not to make such investments in advance of an emergency. There are similar funding shortfalls for advancing preparedness on the global level. While multiple existing mechanisms provide emergency funds for global response operations—such as WHO's Contingency Fund for Emergencies, the UN Central Emergency Response Fund, and the Pandemic Emergency Financing Facility—these funds generally are not available to support preparedness activities.

While national governments should continue to be encouraged to increase and sustain their investments in preparedness, there is also a need to explore the availability of financing from nongovernment sources. New models and sources of financing are needed to increase the availability of resources for preparedness. Historically, funding allocated to health security threats have gone to support response to epidemics and other public health emergencies. Comparatively little investment has been made in preparedness for such events.[30] The global economic tolls of the COVID-19 pandemic may reduce the availability of resources to address future disease threats, as was the case following the global economic downturn of 2008.

New financing mechanisms to fill pandemic preparedness gaps are urgently needed to address the gaps in national core capacities and to bolster global surveillance and response efforts. One option is to expand the availability of the World Bank's International Development Association concessional allocations to allow for preparedness financing. Another idea that has been floated is to create new multilateral financing mechanisms, such as a global health security challenge fund, to expand governmental and nongovernmental resources to fund preparedness and to incentivize countries to prioritize preparedness in national funding decisions.[31] It is envisioned that the fund would, like GAVI and the World Bank's International Development Association funding, provide financing to countries, while encouraging countries to commit additional domestic resources to improve preparedness.

Clarifying Roles and Responsibilities for Deliberate Pathogen Releases

If an epidemic or pandemic that was thought to possibly be deliberate in origin were to occur, it would necessitate central involvement of the security sector.

The activation of national and international security and intelligence apparatuses may limit transparency and information sharing about the nature of the pathogen and its impact. This, in turn, could compromise countries' abilities to conduct risk assessments and develop evidence-based response plans.

An international tabletop exercise conducted in 2019 at the Munich Security Conference revealed the insufficiency of existing international response mechanisms to respond to deliberate release scenarios, particularly when the origin of the pathogen is unknown.[32] While WHO's mandate includes leading the global response to responding to outbreaks, epidemics, and pandemics of natural origin, the UN Secretary-General's Mechanism is authorized to lead an investigation of an alleged deliberate biological attack by a state actor. It is unclear, however, what organization would lead an investigation of an event that is not clearly natural in origin or caused by a state actor.

Notes

1. Centers for Disease Control and Prevention, "1918 Pandemic (H1N1 Virus): Pandemic Influenza (Flu)," June 16, 2020, https://www.cdc.gov/flu/pandemic-resources/1918-pandemic-h1n1.html.

2. "World Economic Outlook Update, June 2020: A Crisis Like No Other, An Uncertain Recovery," International Monetary Fund, https://www.imf.org/en/Publications/WEO/Issues/2020/06/24/WEOUpdateJune2020.

3. "The COVID-19 Pandemic and the $16 Trillion Virus: Infectious Diseases," *JAMA*, https://jamanetwork.com/journals/jama/fullarticle/2771764.

4. "Education and COVID-19," UNICEF data, https://data.unicef.org/topic/education/covid-19/.

5. "COVID-19 to Add as Many as 150 Million Extreme Poor by 2021," World Bank, https://www.worldbank.org/en/news/press-release/2020/10/07/covid-19-to-add-as-many-as-150-million-extreme-poor-by-2021.

6. "COVID-19 Emergency Committee Highlights Need for Response Efforts Over Long Term," World Health Organization, https://www.who.int/news/item/01-08-2020-covid-19-emergency-committee-highlights-need-for-response-efforts-over-long-term.

7. "Estimated Global Mortality Associated with the First 12 Months of 2009 Pandemic Influenza A H1N1 Virus Circulation: A Modelling Study," *Lancet Infectious Diseases*, https://www.thelancet.com/journals/laninf/article/PIIS1473-3099(12)70121-4/fulltext.

8. Kate E. Jones et al., "Global Trends in Emerging Infectious Diseases," *Nature* 451, no. 7181 (2008): 990–93, https://doi.org/10.1038/nature06536.

9. Fikre Germa, "Pandemics, Ebola, and the Family Doctor," *Canadian Family Physician* 62, no. 3 (2016): 203–5.

10. Gigi Kwik Gronvall, "Prevention of the Development or Use of Biological Weapons," *Health Security* 15, no. 1 (2017): 36–37, https://doi.org/10.1089/hs.2016.0096.

11. World Health Organization, "Report of the Ebola Interim Assessment Panel, July 2015," http://www.who.int/csr/resources/publications/ebola/ebola-panel-report/en/; Nuclear Threat Initiative, "A Spreading Plague: Lessons and Recommendations for Responding to a Deliberate Biological Event: Analysis," https://www.nti.org/analysis/reports/spreading-plague-lessons-and-recommendations-responding-deliberate-biological-event/.

12. World Health Organization, "Strategic Partnership for IHR and Health Security: Building Stronger Health Systems for Sustainable Health Security," https://extranet.who.int/sph/jee-dashboard.

13. Suerie Moon et al., "Will Ebola Change the Game? Ten Essential Reforms before the next Pandemic—The Report of the Harvard-LSHTM Independent Panel on the Global Response to Ebola," *The Lancet* 386, no. 10009 (November 2015): 2204–21, https://doi.org/10.1016/S0140-6736(15)00946-0; Lucia Mullen et al., "An Analysis of International Health Regulations Emergency Committees and Public Health Emergency of International Concern Designations," *BMJ Global Health* 5, no. 6 (2020): e002502, https://doi.org/10.1136/bmjgh-2020-002502.

14. Thomas J. Bollyky and Chad P. Bown, "The Tragedy of Vaccine Nationalism," *Foreign Affairs*, December 9, 2020, https://www.foreignaffairs.com/articles/united-states/2020-07-27/vaccine-nationalism-pandemic.

15. WHO Pandemic Influenza A(H1N1) Vaccine Deployment Initiative and World Health Organization, eds., *Report of the WHO Pandemic Influenza A(H1N1) Vaccine Deployment Initiative* (Geneva: World Health Organization, 2012).

16. Kavita Berger et al., "Policy and Science for Global Health Security: Shaping the Course of International Health," *Tropical Medicine and Infectious Disease* 4, no. 2 (2019): 60, https://doi.org/10.3390/tropicalmed4020060.

17. Coalition for Epidemic Preparedness Innovations, "Who We Are," https://cepi.net/about/whoweare/.

18. Board on Global Health, Institute of Medicine, and National Academies of Sciences, Engineering, and Medicine, *Global Health Risk Framework: Pandemic Financing: Workshop Summary*, edited by Gillian J. Buckley and Rachel E. Pittluck (Washington: National Academies Press, 2016), https://doi.org/10.17226/21855.

19. JHCHS website designer, "Public-Private Cooperation for Pandemic Preparedness and Response," Johns Hopkins Center for Health Security, https://www.centerforhealthsecurity.org/event201/recommendations.html.

20. Global Preparedness Monitoring Board, "A World at Risk," September 2019, https://apps.who.int/gpmb/assets/annual_report/GPMB_Annual_Report_English.pdf.

21. "WHO Director-General's Opening Remarks at the Media Briefing on COVID-19," March 11, 2020, https://www.who.int/director-general/speeches/detail/who-director-general-s-opening-remarks-at-the-media-briefing-on-covid-19---11-march-2020.

22. "Tracking Coronavirus in Countries With and Without Travel Bans: Think Global Health," Council on Foreign Relations, https://www.thinkglobalhealth.org/article/tracking-coronavirus-countries-and-without-travel-bansp; "Travel Restrictions on China Due to COVID-19: Think Global Health," Council on Foreign Relations, https://www.thinkglobalhealth.org/article/travel-restrictions-china-due-covid-19.

23. "The Global Health Security Index," https://www.ghsindex.org/.

24. Sanjana J Ravi et al., "The Value Proposition of the Global Health Security Index," *BMJ Global Health* 5, no. 10 (2020): e003648, https://doi.org/10.1136/bmjgh-2020-003648.

25. Ensheng Dong, Hongru Du, and Lauren Gardner, "An Interactive Web-Based Dashboard to Track COVID-19 in Real Time," *Lancet Infectious Diseases* 20, no. 5 (2020): 533–34, https://doi.org/10.1016/S1473-3099(20)30120-1.

26. Lauren Gardner et al., "A Need for Open Public Data Standards and Sharing in Light of COVID-19," *Lancet Infectious Diseases*, August 2020, S1473309920306356, https://doi.org/10.1016/S1473-3099(20)30635-6.

27. Thomas J. Bollyky and Jennifer B. Nuzzo, "Trump's 'Early' Travel 'Bans' Weren't Early, Weren't Bans and Didn't Work," *Washington Post*, October 1, 2020, https://www.washingtonpost.com/outlook/2020/10/01/debate-early-travel-bans-china/.

28. "The US Must Learn from COVID-19 to Prevent the Next Disaster," Council on Foreign Relations, 2020, https://www.cfr.org/report/pandemic-preparedness-lessons-COVID-19/.

29. WHO Solidarity Trial Consortium, "Repurposed Antiviral Drugs for COVID-19: Interim WHO Solidarity Trial Results," *New England Journal of Medicine*, December 2, 2020, https://doi.org/10.1056/NEJMoa2023184; John H. Beigel et al., "Remdesivir for the Treatment of COVID-19: Final Report," *New England Journal of Medicine* 383, no. 19 (2020): 1813–26, https://doi.org/10.1056/NEJMoa2007764.

30. "From Panic and Neglect to Investing in Health Security: Financing Pandemic Preparedness at a National Level," World Bank, https://documents.worldbank.org/en/publication/documents-reports/documentdetail.

31. "Preventing the Next Pandemic: A Challenge Fund to Build Health Security—NTI News, Preventing the Next Pandemic: A Challenge Fund to Build Health Security," Nuclear Threat Initiative, https://www.nti.org/newsroom/news/preventing-next-pandemic-challenge-fund-build-health-security/.

32. Nuclear Threat Initiative, "Spreading Plague."

Ten

Global Development Cooperation in the COVID World

H OMI K HARAS, *C ENTER FOR S USTAINABLE D EVELOPMENT,*
G LOBAL E CONOMY AND D EVELOPMENT AT B ROOKINGS

The Contours of the COVID World

COVID-19 and the economic response has amplified and changed the nature of development challenges in fundamental ways. Global development cooperation should adapt accordingly.

The most immediate challenge is to provide a level of liquidity support to countries ravaged by the global economic downturn. This is the broadest and deepest downturn in the global economy that has ever been seen. The International Monetary Fund projected a fall of 4.9 percent in global gross domestic product (GDP) in 2020, and a fall of a similar magnitude in emerging market and developing countries, excluding China.[1] The World Bank projected that 93 percent of all countries in the world would go into recession in 2020.[2] Many developing countries will see double-digit declines in GDP, with some recording downturns not seen in peacetime.

Alongside the short term challenge of recovery, COVID-19 has laid bare longer-term trends that have pointed for some time to the lack of sustainability in the way economic development was occurring in many places, including in advanced economies. The sharp reduction in productivity growth, the growing degree of inequality, the collapse of biodiversity, land degradation, ocean overfishing, and, of course, climate change all indicate the need for a reset of plans and priorities. This was already foretold in the negotiations leading to the adoption of the Sustainable Development Goals (SDGs) in 2015, but what was agreed to then as a theoretical concept of an improved development pathway has now given way to a recognition that decisive change is needed if countries are to avoid destabilizing forces.

This new landscape has significant implications for development cooperation in terms of scale, development/climate cobenefits, and transparency and accountability. First, our understanding of the scale of resources that could be made available has changed. There had already been a discourse about the increased needs to meet the SDGs (the "billions to trillions" discussion), but those were taken as aspirational rather than foundational, and often dismissed as impractical. COVID-19 has changed this. The IMF suggested that at least $2.5 trillion would be needed for emerging market and developing countries.[3] The African Union has called for $100 billion per year for that continent for the next three years.[4] Much higher levels of resource transfers to developing countries are now being discussed in global policy circles than was the case before COVID-19.

Perhaps the most telling statistic lies in the distinct fiscal response to the crisis.[5] Advanced economies had plans to raise fiscal deficits by 9 percentage points of GDP in 2020, and to add a further 11 percentage points of GDP to their gross public debt through loans and guarantees to keep their businesses afloat. In emerging markets, the equivalent numbers are 3 and 2 percentage points of GDP, while in low-income countries, they are 1 percentage point and negligible support. These differences are not due to differential health or economic impacts of COVID-19 but are purely the consequence of access to financing. Advanced economy governments have the exorbitant privilege of borrowing in their own currencies, while developing countries cannot; they are dependent on access to official development cooperation and to global capital markets. Scaling up finance for development has therefore moved to center stage in the COVID world. Advanced economies are being pressured, including by their own civil societies in some cases, to use their exorbitant privilege to help others. Whether they will resist, as in the past, or try to accommodate to a certain degree, is key to the COVID-19 discussion on development finance.

Second, the big effort to link climate change with development cooperation, which was agreed to in the SDGs, also has significant implications for development cooperation. At the risk of a vast oversimplification, climate change mitigation—with its focus on new investments in sustainable power, transportation, and buildings to transition to a low-carbon economy—requires a front-loaded agenda, in much the same way as IFFIm provided front-loaded resources for vaccinations after its introduction in 2003–4. Demographic and urbanization pressures require new infrastructure to be built now in the developing world. If done in a sustainable fashion, there is a chance to reduce carbon emissions thanks to the lock-in effects of sustainable infrastructure assets. But sustainable investments sometimes cost more up front, biasing liquidity-constrained countries to adopt least-cash solutions rather than least-cost solutions in their infrastructure choices. This must change.

In an additional complication, most infrastructure finance is debt finance, requiring long maturities and affordable rates. The COVID world has already reduced the creditworthiness of many developing countries, and every expectation was that the worst was still to come in 2021.

Third, if the focus does shift to a sustained expansion in sustainable infrastructure, where developing countries' needs could amount to 5 percent of GDP, then governments and state-owned utilities in developing countries will have a much larger role. Most sustainable infrastructure, with the exception of power generation and the information and communications technology backbone infrastructure, is implemented by the public sector or public agencies. But there is no shared understanding of the definition of sustainable development investment. Already there is a concern that the large volume of funds being mobilized to support recovery effort cannot be adequately tracked. With weakening parliamentary and civil society oversight in some places, there is a need for more radical transparency and monitoring of development spending that would give comfort to people in recipient and donor countries alike that money is being wisely spent. This is not "conditionality," something for which donors have rightly been criticized in their dealings with developing countries. It is a call for transparency; for finance to be sustainable and enjoy wide popular support, the links with expenditures and the development benefits that it brings about must be strengthened.

The remainder of this chapter looks at development cooperation through these three lenses of scale, links to climate change, and transparency and governance. The next section briefly discusses recent trends in development cooperation, and this is followed by a discussion of emerging gaps. The last section offers thoughts for opportunities to fill these gaps.

Recent Shifts in Development Cooperation Strategy

The United States, the European Union, and the United Kingdom have all recently embarked on major shifts in their development cooperation practices. This section briefly reviews these changes.

The United States

For many years, there has been a bipartisan consensus on development cooperation in the United States, resulting in several bipartisan initiatives—even in the divisive political atmosphere of the Trump administration. The United States passed the BUILD Act in 2018, transforming the Overseas Private Investment Corporation into the US Development Finance Corporation, and more recently passed the Global Fragility Act of 2019 to reestablish US leadership in the fight against extremism and violent conflicts. Both pieces of legislation enjoyed support among development stakeholders in the United States.

However, there have been efforts to roll back support for development cooperation. The Trump administration launched the Foreign Aid Review, which controversially would have placed more power over development cooperation in the hands of the State Department. Its core basis was to "realign foreign assistance for a new era of great power competition." The review was never been finalized, but some of its principles indicate the direction of change: a focus on friends and allies; a move toward self-reliance; links with bilateral trade; the voting record in the United Nations; and so forth. An example of this injection of foreign policy into development cooperation was the decision to cut off aid to the Northern Triangle countries—Guatemala, Honduras, and El Salvador—which did not cooperate with the administration's immigration agenda.

One major thrust of US development cooperation is to reduce the level of assistance. At 0.16 percent of gross national income, US assistance is among the lowest of any country that is on the Development Assistance Committee, but in absolute terms it remains the world's largest donor. Under the administration of President Trump, there was an annual dance on aid budgets; the administration routinely presented a budget with sharp aid cutbacks, often amounting to one-third reductions, while Congress equally routinely restored funding to previous levels. This dance appeared to give each party the political cover needed, but what is clear is that there is no appetite for large increases in aid in the Trump administration. What is more a cause for concern is that the United States has also used its influence to halt other global initiatives to expand financial assistance to developing countries. The most notable example was the opposition to a new issuance of Special Drawing Rights (SDRs) by the IMF, a move that would not have cost the US Treasury anything and which could have been accomplished without recourse to a congressional vote. The new US administration, under President Joe Biden, has reversed the US position on this, allowing the IMF's Board to approve a new issuance of $650 billion in SDRs. It has also submitted budgets with increased levels of US foreign assistance. These are welcome decisions, but budget politics may curb further expansion in US aid.

During the Trump administration, the politicization of foreign assistance by the United States spilled over into multilateral institutions. Those in good standing—such as the World Bank, the Global Fund, GAVI, the World Food Program, and

UNICEF—continued to receive US financial support. Those that were not perceived as advancing administration priorities—like the World Health Organization, the Green Climate Fund, and the Global Agriculture and Food Security program—had US support reduced to zero. Along with the decision to exit the Paris Agreement, and continued opposition to use of the terminology of the SDGs, the United States remained at odds with much of the rest of the development community. As in the case of SDRs, the Biden administration moved to undo some of these decisions and brought the United States more in line with other donors, but there is still little attention being given to make the major multilateral institutions fit for purpose in today's world.

Because US development cooperation is largely in the form of grants, its ability to front-load is quite limited. In theory, the US Development Finance Corporation could expand its operations, but it shows no signs of emerging as a large-scale player. Its capital is limited to $60 billion, and stringent accounting rules have been adopted. For example, each $1 in equity carries a $1 capital charge. There is no "expected loss" accounting.

US agencies are quite transparent in their activities—Publish What You Fund classifies the Millennium Challenge Corporation and the US Agency for International Development (USAID) as very good and good respectively on transparency—and the United States is an active supporter of the Open Government Partnership, which promotes tools for monitoring and accountability of SDG progress. But the lack of standardized definitions—a global problem—still hampers assessment of the US contribution to the SDGs. Without a very clear message on benefits achieved, the narrative for expanding US assistance becomes a muddy mixture of national security, promotion of democratic values, and humanitarian assistance.

Polling data suggest that the American public believes the United States should be spending more on aid and would be prepared to pay higher taxes to finance this. A University of Maryland poll, conducted in October 2019, found majority support among Republicans and Democrats to increase US aid for the purpose of eliminating hunger, providing universal vaccines, and water and sanitation coverage, as long as other countries also did their share. The polling reveals two points: a clear and strong link between spending and program objectives is needed to generate support for a scaled-up program; and collective action is preferred to national action.[6]

The European Union

The European Union's development cooperation footprint has been laid out in its Multiannual Financial Framework for 2021–27. This suggests a small increase in development cooperation compared with the current 2004–20 period. The "Neighborhood and the World" heading will receive €118.2 billion over the seven years, slightly more than 10 percent of the total EU budget. Given that the United Kingdom will no longer contribute, the EU framework represents a step increase in aid from all other member states, although most European countries remain behind the 0.7 percent target they endorse in principle.[7] The EU is second only to America as the largest aid provider in the world and is perhaps the least volatile among large aid donors.

In addition to its own financing, the EU has also taken the lead as a global convener for the Coronavirus Global Response. The Access to COVID-19 Tools Accelerator was sponsored by the EU and UN agencies and seeks to raise $35 billion to ensure equitable access to vaccines, diagnostics, and therapeutics.

Notwithstanding the planned increase in aid, the Multiannual Financial Framework has smaller amounts for development cooperation than the original proposal from European Commission technocrats. It allocates much higher amounts for humanitarian assistance, but very modest amounts for migration and for peace and fragility. Developing countries will not be able to access the large Next Generation Europe recovery fund. Aid to Africa, already on the decline, will not rise.

If the EU is to markedly increase its development cooperation, it will most likely be through the operations of the European Investment Bank (EIB). Already the largest development financial institution in the world, the EIB has long experience lending to small and medium-sized enterprises and has made a commitment to support €1 trillion in investments for climate action over the next decade. Most of this will of necessity be within Europe, but the EIB already has made loans to 162 countries; about 10 percent of its portfolio is outside the EU. There is active consideration of forming an affiliated European Development Bank to strengthen Europe's capacity to respond to global and regional economic challenges beyond its limited fiscal firepower.[8]

Europe has ambitions to become the first major climate-neutral continent, and it has allocated €400 billion to support EU member states' efforts to implement the European Green Deal. From this perspective, the EU is fully aligned with the idea of the post-COVID build-back-better, environmentally sustainable and socially inclusive agenda. For Central and Eastern European economies, the Just Transition Fund is available to support the transition away from coal and fossil fuels.

The EU is developing norms and standards for its sustainability transition. Its focus is on energy (renewables and buildings efficiency), transportation, and land use (carbon sinks and natural capital). By specifying targets in each area, and linking achievement of these to its spending instruments, the EU is modeling the kind of transparency and governance that will be needed globally.

The United Kingdom

The United Kingdom has the third-biggest aid budget and diplomatic network in the world. It made two of the most significant changes in decades to its development cooperation in 2020. The main headline was the decision to merge the UK Department for International Development (DFID) with the Foreign and Commonwealth Office into the new Foreign, Commonwealth, and Development Office (FCDO). While this was a major step for the UK, depriving the development community of its prized Cabinet-level seat, it represents a return by the UK to an institutional design that is common across the world and is favored by Conservative Party politicians. It codifies a movement among many aid donors to underline the links between aid and foreign policy to promote British interests and values overseas, a move in the direction taken by Canada and Australia in 2013. In this, the FCDO may depart from the more technocratic positions taken by DFID; indeed, in announcing the merger, Prime Minister Johnson explicitly spelled out the likely implications; should, he asked, the UK give the same amount of aid to Zambia (for poverty reduction) than to a strategically important European neighbor like Ukraine?

The experience of other countries in merging development and diplomacy suggests that it can take considerable time to align the different cultures and experiences of the two. The most recent merger of a similar nature was the absorption of Australia's AusAid into the Department for Foreign Affairs and Trade in 2014. According to an independent review undertaken five years later, the merger precipitated a considerable turnover of staff and loss of talent—1,000 staff years of experience left the department in the immediate aftermath of the merger, and an additional 1,000 staff years have since left.[9] Development professionals have specialized skills in planning and implementation that foreign office generalists often do not possess. Against this negative, the review also noted greater alignment with government priorities of shifting resources to the Pacific and toward infrastructure and humanitarian assistance.

A historical side note: When President Kennedy created USAID in 1961, one of his first actions was to take control of aid away from the US ambassador in Seoul and give it to a resident USAID official. With this move, US development cooperation shifted from a largely humanitarian operation to take on a more developmental orientation. The Korea Development Institute was established a decade later in 1971 to provide stronger domestic input into research and planning of South Korea's development path, something the State Department would never have contemplated. The tug-of-war for control over development cooperation, between diplomats and technocrats, continues today, as it has for seventy years.

The lesson for the United Kingdom is clear. It may be hard to scale up assistance even if desired. Scaling up is about both money, staff capacity to develop sound programs in partnership with local government officials with whom they have trusted relationships, and systems to expedite implementation. Each of these will face pressure in the merged office.

In terms of money, it is by no means assured that the UK government is committed to more aid. The second headline news event of 2020 was a government announcement of cuts of up to £2.9 billion, an 18 percent cut on 2019 aid levels, and an amount that is not consistent with the forecast fall of UK gross national income and the corresponding reduction in aid that would be consistent with the legally binding UK aid floor of 0.7 percent.[10] The uncertainty over aid levels and intentions is magnified by the recent UK history of efforts to count as aid more of the peacekeeping, demining and civil-military humanitarian expenditures carried out by the government.

In its efforts to align aid with the national interest, the United Kingdom has clearly signaled an intention to help developing countries transition to a green economy. At the UN General Assembly in 2019, Prime Minister Johnson announced a doubling of the United Kingdom's international climate finance commitments for the next five years.[11] As host of the COP26 climate meeting in Glasgow next year, the promotion of climate finance will be a priority for the UK's Global Britain campaign.

The United Kingdom is one of the most forward-looking countries in tracking attitudes toward aid and basing messaging (and perhaps policy) on the most effective messages. The Aid Attitudes Tracker, and its successor the Development Engagement Lab, show that the public's willingness to give aid depends critically on the topic and the way it is presented. For example, in the United Kingdom, three times as many people argue that aid should be given to those who need it most and because it is morally right than to those who think it will benefit UK businesses, jobs, or better trade deals.[12] These respondents would not respond well to Prime Minister Johnson's point about reducing aid to Zambia in favor of aid to Ukraine because the United Kingdom has a greater national interest in Ukraine.

As a pointer to why the prime minister may have taken this view, prior surveys had also shown that two-thirds or more of Britons felt that corruption made it pointless to give money to help reduce global poverty. From this perspective, Zambia would be less appealing than the Ukraine. The example reinforces the need for a better linkage between spending and "build-back-better" if the scaling up of development cooperation is to happen. Transparency, messaging, and good governance will be key.

Gaps in and Issues for Global Development

Some significant gaps remain in global development, all centering on financing issues: (1) sharing the burden of nurturing and safeguarding the global commons; (2) financing the building of sustainable infrastructure; and (3) plugging the leaks in the international financial system by fighting corruption and tax evasion. Although the principle of common but differentiated responsibilities provides a good starting point for discussing these issues, the divergence of interests among different countries has made it difficult to make breakthroughs.

The Global Commons

Perhaps the most obvious of the gaps in global development is the absence of any specific mechanism for discussing burden sharing and responsibilities for the global commons. This is a long-standing issue, covering peacekeeping, health research, biodiversity, oceans, and climate change. Part of the problem lies in accounting for official development assistance. According to the members of the Development Assistance Committee (DAC) of the Organization for Economic Cooperation and Development (OECD), who are the standard setters for what counts as aid, the principal purpose of any type of aid must be for the economic development and welfare of developing countries. But this definition is awkward when applied to spending on the global commons, where benefits accrue to everyone. In practice, it has meant that France counts research done by the Institut Pasteur on infectious tropical diseases (affecting developing countries), while the United States does not count research on HIV/AIDS conducted by the National Institutes of Health (affecting citizens of all countries, developed and developing). Yet both types of research save lives in developing countries and are important factors in development cooperation.

The absence of a consistent approach to funding the global commons has led to underinvestment, as the theory of public goods would suggest. Take the example of biodiversity conservation. The OECD estimates global biodiversity finance at $78 billion to $91 billion per year (2015–17 average), from all sources, public and private. Of this, $3.9 billion to 9.3 billion is international, with the higher figure including financing for projects where biodiversity is a secondary objective. However, an OECD report also notes that $500 billion a year is spent by the public sector around the world in ways that are potentially damaging to biodiversity.[13] This kind of conduct happens under the radar because metrics are not routinely collected on the management of the global commons, so there is no transparency or governance of the cumulative effort. The importance of new standards, definitions, and monitoring is such that four out of five key recommendations of the OECD report are for improvements in data definitions and monitoring, while the fifth recommendation is to analyze the effectiveness of spending.

The experience of other forms of delivery of public goods or management of the global commons is similar. Warnings about underinvestment in pandemic-related health monitoring have been made for some time. The Global Preparedness Monitoring Board issued just such a warning in September 2019, but little notice was taken. In its second report, issued in September 2020, it largely reiterated the same messages. Not enough financing for preparedness is available. The board estimates costs of better preparedness to be an increment of $5 per person per year, while benefits, as COVID-19 makes clear, could potentially be in the tens of trillions of dollars of losses averted.[14]

In a similar vein, even in the midst of the COVID-19 pandemic, the emergency appeal for $35 billion to ensure equitable access to vaccines, diagnostics, and treatments to speed up an end to the pandemic has not been quickly filled—despite Group of Twenty (G20) countries having committed more than $11 trillion to combating the effects of COVID-19 in their own countries.

On climate change, arguably the greatest challenge of all, there is confusion as to whether the original climate finance target of $100 billion by 2020 has actually been met, and no guidance for finance targets beyond. Partly, this is a reflection of the understanding that emissions reduction commitments must be improved upon and the financial targets would need to be correspondingly larger.

Regardless of the sector—health, oceans, climate, biodiversity—the message on the global commons is the same. Each area warns of a sense of urgency, of scientific tipping points that could lead to irreversible damage if action is not take now. Delay is viewed as unacceptable.

A second theme of reports on managing the global commons is that costs are modest compared with benefits—both positive, as in the creation of green economy jobs or recovery of fishing stocks; or in avoided losses, as in the case of pandemics and biodiversity. Prevention is called for. This is a challenge for development cooperation, which is at its best when reacting to a crisis, rather than in acting to prevent a crisis. The many cries for prevention, whether for conflict or preparedness for natural disasters, to be funded through development cooperation have largely gone unheeded.[15]

The third theme is the absence of any serious global collective effort for implementation: a secretariat body that can generate and analyze appropriate data, evaluate efforts and the impact of spending programs, and inform political leaders of the world for them to take action. The G20 provides a forum for political discussion, but for all the talk about expanding the G20's remit to "strong, sustainable, balanced, and inclusive growth," none of the reports by the IMF, World Bank, or OECD to the G20 have mentioned biodiversity or oceans.

The lack of a structure for delivering on global public goods is not new. The International Task Force on Global Public Goods laid out the challenges in 2006, but to no avail.[16]

Sustainable Infrastructure and the Debt Overhang

A second major gap that has been revealed is in the ability to scale up finance for sustainable infrastructure. There is an urgency to address infrastructure spending as a means of avoiding carbon lock-in. The evidence is overwhelming that getting infrastructure right is a far more efficient and effective solution than the grow-now-and-clean-up-later approach that has been followed by today's advanced economies. There is a narrow window to get infrastructure right in developing countries, while the dynamics of demographic change and urbanization are still in flux. But after a decade or so, this window will close, and any changes to infrastructure will involve a retrofit, a far more cumbersome and costly endeavor.

Rough estimates are that developing countries will need at least $1 trillion (5 percent of their aggregate GDP, excluding China) per year in additional infrastructure investment to be able to transition to sustainable trajectories.[17] This amount is mostly for power, transportation, and buildings. It will be concentrated in cities. Yet there are no mechanisms to allow cities to take advantage of global channels for development finance. In most countries, cities have to get approval to borrow from national authorities and have no independent revenue sources or credit rating. This asymmetry between city access and national access can also play into domestic politics.

The recognition that sustainable infrastructure will form a large part of the strategy for recovery from the COVID-19-induced economic downturn puts into sharp focus the debt problems of developing countries. Most infrastructure will be built by the public sector. A few sectors, like power generation and the information and communications technology backbone infrastructure, enjoy significant private provision, but well over 70 percent of infrastructure investment will be undertaken by government ministries or state-owned utilities in developing countries. Regardless of the sector, 70 percent or more of infrastructure financing is in the form of debt. Indeed, this has to be the case because it is essential for infrastructure to be kept affordable, and that requires cheap financing. The debt, in turn, comes from three main sources in roughly equal magnitude: official financing from multilateral institutions and OECD/DAC bilateral agencies; semiofficial financing by state-supported banks, like China Ex-Im Bank and the China Development Bank, which have financed Belt and Road Initiative projects, but also IndiaEximBank and other financial institutions in major emerging economies; and sovereign borrowing from global capital markets.

The problem is that many developing countries are faced with debt problems. Forty-three countries have already availed themselves of the Debt Service Standstill Initiative put forward by the G20 in April 2020. The initiative was widely expected to be extended to the end of 2021 and could potentially also be expanded in scope. These countries will have difficulty in raising funds on global capital markets. Other countries, too, face more expensive financing because of the downgrades of their credit ratings that have happened in the aftermath of COVID-19.

Official institutions make much of the potential to raise domestic tax revenues in developing countries as a way of paying for infrastructure. They have been doing this. But a rising tax effort is typically linked to economic growth and the broadening of the tax base. It happens slowly over time, not at the speed needed for front-loaded sustainable infrastructure investment. This is not to underplay the importance of domestic revenue mobilization—which is ultimately the foundation for improved creditworthiness—but it suggests that access to debt will continue to be important for the coming decade of action.

Plugging the Leaks

When the idea of official development cooperation took hold, after World War II, based on the success of the Marshall Plan and the establishment of new development agencies under the UN (IMF, World Bank, Food and Agriculture Organization, and UNICEF), the major purpose was to transfer resources and technical assistance to developing countries. On a gross basis, trillions of dollars have indeed been transferred; but on a net basis, the transfer has been far smaller. According to the IMF, capital has been flowing uphill from developing to developed countries. Since 2000, the net flow of resources to developed countries has been $4.4 trillion. Most of this uphill flow has taken the form of a build-up of foreign exchange reserves in Asia. Africa has enjoyed a net inflow of funds, but the volume has been small—less than $400 billion since 2000, or an average of less than $20 billion per year, equivalent to 5 cents per African per day.

The structures of the international financial system have not helped incentivize resource flows to developing countries. Developing countries have lost between $620 billion and $970 billion a year through questionable tax practices, customs fraud, corruption, and other illegal or illicit activities.[18] While accurate numbers are hard to verify, they are surely substantial, and of a roughly equivalent size to gross inflows for development.

The point is simple: development cooperation cannot succeed in its major objective of resource transfer unless leaks in the system are plugged. The OECD is working on new rules for the fairer taxation of multinational enterprises, including minimum tax provisions, and it provides technical assistance through its Tax Inspectors Without Borders program. Enablers in advanced economies who hide behind "ignorance" defenses, and secrecy laws protecting against disclosure of beneficial ownership of assets, are examples of mechanisms used to facilitate illicit flows.

Development cooperation agencies should work with counterparts in tax departments, and with prosecutors of fraud, embezzlement, and other financial crimes in justice departments in a whole-of-government approach to ensure that public channels for resource transfers to developing countries are not offset by the exploitation of private channels to reverse the flow of funds.

New Institutional Arrangements and Cooperation Strategies

At the end of World War II, the Bretton Woods Conference provided the setting for countries to devise institutional structures to meet the most pressing challenge at hand. At that time, the challenge was reconstructing European economies, which had been destroyed by war and were suffering from a severe shortage of hard currency liquidity. The United States provided this liquidity through the Marshall Plan, a program that disbursed $13.3 billion to sixteen European countries over four years, representing just over 1.1 percent of the US economy, and about 3 percent of the recipients' combined national income.[19]

The lesson from this history is that in the throes of the postwar crisis, a sense of international collective action and an understanding of the nature and scale of the problem led to new solutions. The diagnosis was one of a shortage of capital undermining trade and economic growth, which could make European countries vulnerable to the spread of communism. Times are different today, but there is a need for a similar sense of collective action to resolve issues of responsibilities for management of the global commons. A new Bretton Woods 2.0 conference could provide the basis for developing and implementing this agenda.

The Bretton Woods 2.0 conference should have a central focus on strengthening the global development finance system. Multilateral development banks (MDBs) and funds sit at the apex of this system. They have a long history of playing both the countercyclical role that is called for today in the recovery from COVID-19, as well as an investment financing role, particularly in infrastructure, that is called for by the need to transform economies. They have championed the transition to a green economy and have made strong commitments to help bring this about.

MDBs are unique institutions for these times. Their preferred creditor treatment helps them overcome the debt overhang problem. Their AAA credit rating helps them provide long-term financing at affordable rates to developing countries. They have a strong track record on promoting policy reform and good governance. Their financial business model permits high leverage of shareholder capital. They have significant size and volume of operations. And they have a range of instruments that can be deployed—grants, concessional credits, nonconcessional credits, guarantees, and technical assistance.

MDBs are, however, constrained by their shareholders. They have leaned forward to front-load their activities. They could do more, but they then risk a sharp curtailment in the future if funds and equity capital are not topped up, or if other risk management policies are not relaxed.

A number of fixes to raise the scale of MDBs' activities are possible. From a technical perspective, these are not difficult to identify. For example, while maintaining a AAA rating, MDBs could expand their loan books by at least $750 billion simply by using better accounting practices on how callable capital is measured.[20] They could move toward industry standards on risk management variables like the equity-loans ratio. They could mobilize more private capital and local counterpart funds, potentially using national banks as key local counterparts. They could sell selected loan assets, if these were properly priced initially. As a last resort, they could ask shareholders to provide them with additional equity. Each of these measures, however, requires shareholder support to take on greater ambition and potentially more risk. Shareholders have been reluctant to agree. Some have taken the view that markets could better play the role of resource transfers, a view best expressed in the Meltzer Commission's 2000 report on the future of the IMF and the World Bank.[21] That report famously called for getting the World Bank out of lending and turning it into a grant-making institution to the poorest countries. At that time, and still today, views on the appropriate role of the MDBs, especially in middle-income countries, were sharply divided.

If shareholders were to agree to allow MDBs to pursue far greater ambition, the technical fixes illustrated above would give them more financial firepower. However, to truly reach scale, they would also need to upgrade their effectiveness and move from a project approach to a program approach, something that is increasingly being done for middle-income countries receiving the World Bank's nonconcessional loans, but not for other countries. And program loans suffer from the absence of a strong link between funding and expenditures. It is hard to specify exactly what the money is used for, because it becomes mixed with general treasury resources.

To complement program loans and introduce greater specificity into the spending/finance nexus, a promising idea is the use of country platforms. These are being piloted by the World Bank, but so far they have been organized as coordination mechanisms across donors, in disparate sectors, with limited, if any, private participation. Alternative structures, including some with private sector governance, may be attractive.

Thinking on country platforms for sustainable infrastructure finance is fast evolving. The FAST-infra working group is developing a proposal for a technology-enabled securitization platform to simplify analysis and structuring, improve risk management and monitoring, and bring consistency to financial and regulatory reporting. The idea would be to develop a platform with enough transparency, standardization, and reporting to allow any bank to offer loans to a pool with modest transaction costs. If the pool initially contains projects in OECD countries, and gradually adds emerging market-based projects, risk can also be mitigated. This would broaden the scope of potential investors. For example, Solvency 2 rules would force a European insurer to charge about 40 percent of a loan for Latin American or African infrastructure against its capital; a pooled approach could reduce this substantially. The transparency and governance offered by a solid platform is part of its attraction to development cooperation providers as well as to commercial financial institutions.

Platform approaches could offer specialized portfolios. They would work best if there is a solid pipeline of projects to be financed. Here, national development banks could play a role. There are now 539 development finance institutions worldwide, defined as legally independent, financially sustainable, government-supported financial institutions (banks and insurance companies) in pursuit of public policy objectives[22] These are spread across the world, in Africa, Asia, Europe, and the Americas. With their public policy focus, national development banks are ideal partners to participate in platform approaches and provide origination, guarantee, and work-out services.

Managing Geopolitics

Overshadowing both of the suggestions offered above, for Bretton Woods 2.0 and for the establishment of expanded multilateral activities based on a platform approach, is the geopolitical contest between the United States and China. Much of the perceived shift in the use of aid to serve national interests can be understood in terms of the effort to align countries with one or the other side of this contest. This, too, has historical antecedents. Aid was used by both sides as a tool of foreign policy during the Cold War. From a development perspective, the results were not good. There was no focus on aid effectiveness until after the Cold War was over, when development cooperation could focus on results rather than relationships.

The irony of today's post-COVID-19 world is that it may have lessened the willingness of major powers to work together for the good of the planet or of national development. If development cooperation at both global and national levels turns into a struggle between competing geopolitical systems, there could be a race to the bottom, with dire consequences for all.

A better vision for development cooperation is for a significantly expanded scale that, like the Marshall Plan, could be a few percentage points (4–6 points in most countries) of recipient countries' economies. These need not be purely concessional resources, although those will have a role to play, especially for the management of the global commons. Given the low real interest rates prevailing in global capital markets, and the ability to expand intermediaries like MDBs, nonconcessional loans will be a major instrument for most countries. These need to be linked to climate change by prioritizing sustainable infrastructure. And this in turn requires platforms for transparency and good governance that are compatible with private financial institutional regulations.

Notes

1. International Monetary Fund, "World Economic Outlook Update, June 2020," https://www.imf.org/en/Publications/WEO/Issues/2020/06/24/WEOUpdateJune2020.

2. World Bank, "Global Economic Prospects, June 2020," https://openknowledge.worldbank.org/handle/10986/33748.

3. International Monetary Fund, "Transcript of Press Briefing by Kristalina Georgieva following a Conference Call of the International Monetary and Financial Committee," March 27, 2020, https://www.imf.org/en/News/Articles/2020/03/27/tr032720-transcript-press-briefing-kristalina-georgieva-following-imfc-conference-call.

4. UN Economic Commission for Africa, "Communiqué: African Finance Ministers' Meeting," https://www.uneca.org/sites/default/files/COVID-19/african_finance_ministers_meeting-_eca_-_covid_-01042020communiquefinaldvs1.pdf.

5. International Monetary Fund, "Fiscal Monitor Database of Country Fiscal Measures in Response to the COVID-19 Pandemic," October 2021, https://www.imf.org/en/Topics/imf-and-covid19/Fiscal-Policies-Database-in-Response-to-COVID-19.

6. University of Maryland, Program for Public Consultation, "Americans on US Contribution to Five Sustainable Development Goals," http://www.publicconsultation.org/wp-content/uploads/2020/07/SDG_Report_0720.pdf.

7. Center for Global Development, "The EU's Recovery Budget: How Prominent Is International Development?" June 20, 2020, https://www.cgdev.org/blog/eus-recovery-budget-how-prominent-international-development.

8. Erik Berglöf, "Commentary: Europe Needs Its Own Development Bank," Brookings, November 25, 2019, https://www.brookings.edu/opinions/europe-needs-its-own-development-bank/.

9. Richard Moore, "Strategic Choice: A Future-Focused Review of the DFAT-AusAID Integration," Susan McKinnon Foundation, February 17, 2019, https://apo.org.au/node/223736.

10. UK Government, "Prime Minister's Statement to the House of Commons: 16 June 2020," https://www.gov.uk/government/speeches/prime-ministers-statement-to-the-house-of-commons-16-june-2020; BBC, "Coronavirus: UK Foreign Aid Spending Cut by £2.9 Billion Amid Economic Downturn," https://www.bbc.com/news/uk-politics-53508933.

11. UK Government, "UK Aid to Double Efforts to Tackle Climate Change," September 23, 2019, https://www.gov.uk/government/news/uk-aid-to-double-efforts-to-tackle-climate-change.

12. University of Birmingham, "Changing How the World Works," no date, https://www.birmingham.ac.uk/research/quest/towards-a-better-society/Attitudes-towards-aid.aspx.

13. Organization for Economic Cooperation and Development, "A Comprehensive Overview of Global Biodiversity Finance," April 2020, https://www.oecd.org/environment/resources/biodiversity/report-a-comprehensive-overview-of-global-biodiversity-finance.pdf.

14. "Global Preparedness Monitoring Board," no date, https://apps.who.int/gpmb/assets/annual_report/GPMB_AR_2020_EN.pdf.

15. See, e.g., "Natural Hazards, Unnatural Disasters," World Bank and United Nations, 2010, https://issuu.com/world.bank.publications/docs/9780821380505.

16. International Task Force on Global Public Goods, "Summary: Meeting Global Challenges—International Cooperation in the National Interest," 2006, https://www.keionline.org/misc-docs/socialgoods/International-Task-Force-on-Global-Public-Goods_2006.pdf.

17. A. Bhattacharya et al., "Using Climate Models to Learn About Global Climate Change," *Science Teacher*, October 2020, https://www.researchgate.net/publication/376303347_Using_Climate_Models_to_Learn_About_Global_Climate_Change.

18. Fatima Kanji and Richard Messick, "Recommendations for Accelerating and Streamlining the Return of Assets Stolen by Corrupt Public Officials," Facti

Panel Background Paper 7, July 17, 2020, https://assets-global.website-files.com/
5e0bd9edab846816e263d633/5f15c02cd2766c40ce963878_FACTI%20BP7_return%20of
%20assets.pdf.

19. Curt Tarnoff, "The Marshall Plan: Design, Accomplishments, and Significance," Congressional Research Service, January 18, 2018, https://fas.org/sgp/crs/row/
R45079.pdf.

20. Chris Humphrey, "All Hands on Deck: How to Scale Up Multilateral Financing to Face the COVID-19 Crisis," Overseas Development Institute, April 2020, https://
media.odi.org/documents/200408_mbds_coronavirus_final.pdf.

21. Meltzer Commission on the Future of the IMF and World Bank, "Hearing
Before the Committee on Foreign Relations, United States Senate, One Hundred Sixth
Congress, Second Session, May 23, 2000," https://www.govinfo.gov/content/pkg/
CHRG-106shrg66721/html/CHRG-106shrg66721.htm.

22. Jiajun Xu, Xiaomeng Ren, and Xinyue Wu, "Mapping Development Finance
Institutions Worldwide: Definitions, Rationales, and Varieties." Peking University, May
2019, https://www.idfc.org/wp-content/uploads/2019/07/nse_development_financing_
research_report_no-1-2.pdf.

Eleven

Global Climate Politics in the Age of COVID-19

JONAS NAHM, JOHNS HOPKINS UNIVERSITY, SCHOOL OF ADVANCED
INTERNATIONAL STUDIES

The economic recession caused by efforts to contain the global COVID-19 pandemic has, at least in the short term, led to a considerable drop in global greenhouse gas emissions. Immediately after the first economic lockdown in China, observers began speculating about the potential impact of the COVID-19 crisis on global efforts to reduce carbon emissions. As other Asian economies, then Europe, and the United States followed China's attempts to curb the spread of the virus by restricting travel and imposing economic restrictions, headlines about climate change were dominated by reports of rapid reductions in air pollution, drops in carbon emissions, and widespread reductions in energy use, and, ultimately, the possibility that the COVID-19 crisis offered an opportunity to shift the global economy to a more sustainable path.

In this chapter, I examine the prospects for global climate politics in the age of the COVID-19 pandemic. I make three central points that caution against optimism that the economic recession resulting from the pandemic could trigger substantial shifts in global climate action toward long-term decarbonization. First, I show that the emissions reductions during the recession were small and were unlikely to have a lasting impact on efforts to reduce greenhouse gas emissions. Not only are such short-term emissions reductions tied to unstainable economic shutdowns, past recessions have also been followed by rapid increases in carbon emissions that have offset much of the reductions of the downturn. Such an emissions rebound may be offset by lasting changes in commuting patterns, but it is unclear whether such changes could prevail and whether their impact is significant, as public transit use also declined. Second, while economic stimulus spending expected in the post-COVID 19 recession recovery offers an opportunity to invest in long-term emissions reductions policies, I show that the majority of Group of Twenty economies have favored spending on fossil fuel industries over climate action in their recovery packages. Third, and perhaps most important, I argue that the United States–China relationship deteriorated at an unprecedented pace during the COVID-19 crisis and show that this was detrimental to all efforts to address the global climate crisis.

Economic Recessions and Climate Change

The economic recession caused by efforts to contain the global COVID-19 pandemic led, at least in the short term, to a considerable drop in global greenhouse gas emissions. In China, greenhouse gas emissions fell by more than 25 percent in early January 2020, as satellite data show reduced activity in coal power plants, manufacturing operations, and the transportation sector. Similar short-term effects of the pandemic response were documented in Italy, South Korea, and the United Kingdom.[1] Yet not only are such short-term emissions reductions tied to unstainable economic shutdowns; past recessions werre followed by rapid increases in carbon emissions that offset much of the reductions of the downturn. After the 2008–9 global financial crisis, for instance, greenhouse gas emissions from fossil fuel combustion and the global cement industry increased by nearly 6 percent to record levels in 2010. Similar rebounds in emissions occurred after the 1970s oil crises, the US savings and loan crisis in the late 1980s, the collapse of the Soviet Union in the 1980s, and after the Asian Financial Crisis in the late 1990s. In each case, emissions reductions caused by the economic recession were offset by rapidly increasing emissions in the immediate aftermath, further accelerating the accumulation of greenhouse gases in the atmosphere. The 2020 recession showed little indication of long-term structural changes in emissions patterns.

Two facts in particular are causes for concern. First, overall emissions reductions as a result of economic lockdowns have been negligible, even if substantial in the short term. The economic lockdowns enacted during the pandemic will likely yield the largest ever annual fall in greenhouse gas emissions. In the United States, for instance, demand for jet fuel and gasoline temporarily dropped by about 50 percent and 30 percent, respectively.[2] While the economic lockdowns enacted during the pandemic will likely yield the largest ever annual fall in greenhouse gas emissions, overall emissions for 2020 were estimated to only yield a 4 to 5 percent emissions reductions year over year.[3] Since climate change is driven by cumulative concentrations of greenhouse gases in the atmosphere, short-term emissions reductions have little impact on long-term climate patterns unless they are followed by structural changes in the economy. A 5 percent reduction in global emissions in 2020 would put the world on track to reach greenhouse gas concentrations of 414.1 parts per million in the atmosphere at the end of that year, compared with projected concentrations of 414.2 parts per million in the absence of the crisis.[4] It is not hard to discern from these numbers that for all the economic suffering caused by the pandemic, the recession has not relieved pressure to urgently forge decarbonization if the worst consequences of climate change are to be avoided.

Second, confirming the precedents of past economic crises, emissions have quickly begun to rebound wherever economies have indeed reopened. Globally, the transportation sector was the fastest to rebound, with some studies expecting post-COVID emissions to exceed prior levels as people prefer individual transportation to public transit in the postpandemic environment. At least in the United States, transportation is already the largest exacerbating factor in greenhouse gas emissions, a situation likely made worse as a result of the pandemic. As oil prices fell concurrently with the pandemic, consumers had less reason to switch to electric vehicles, particularly in the absence of regulatory incentives to facilitate such shifts. In China, greenhouse gas emissions surpassed 2019 levels by May 2020 as restrictions on the economy were lifted.[5] In June, global emissions were a mere 5 percent below 2019 levels. The transportation sector saw the fastest rate of emissions increases between April and June, but industrial activity and growing power demand also approached prepandemic levels.[6] Moreover, governments may be reluctant to pass stringent climate regulations in the aftermath of the recessions, out of concerns that environmental policy could harm the economic recovery. In short, the economic crisis itself at best caused short-term emissions reductions, making stringent climate policy and global collaboration on reaching climate goals more important than ever. The recession did not relieve pressure to urgently decarbonize the global economy if the worst consequences of climate change are to be avoided.

Possibilities for a Green Recovery

Existing research in the social sciences has frequently pitted environmental and climate policy against concerns about economic growth, particularly in the presence of externalities and market failures.[7] It has also demonstrated that individual attitudes and government policies prioritize growth over climate during economic downturns.[8]

If the 2008–9 financial crisis is any guide, governments rarely live up to the promise of using stimulus funds to produce long-term emissions improvements. Government stimulus spending offers an opportunity for decarbonization through long-term investments in infrastructure, transportation electrification, building efficiency, and clean energy technologies that can reduce emissions and help sustainably shift the global economy away from fossil fuels.[9] During the 2009 recession, governments in the Group of Twenty (G20) economies responded by including climate objectives in their stimulus packages. Fifteen percent of G20 stimulus spending focused on reducing emissions reductions while supporting economic recovery. In the United States, about 12 percent of stimulus funds pursued such objectives.[10] It is important to note that these figures only include large stimulus packages. As a percentage of overall recovery spending in 2009, the numbers were likely significantly smaller.

Continued cross-national divergence in decarbonization efforts during the economic recovery was highly likely, and my ongoing research on G20 stimulus efforts confirms wide variation in patterns of stimulus spending. Ongoing research conducted at Johns Hopkins University with support from the Johns Hopkins Alliance for a Healthier World and the Initiative for Sustainable Energy Policy suggests that green recovery efforts in G20 economies fell short of 2009.[11] Focusing on fiscal stimulus policies starting with the beginning of the COVID-19 pandemic (excluding loans, loan guarantees, and monetary policy), our preliminary data suggest that 7 percent of stimulus spending through August 2020 targeted a green recovery. According to our analysis, about the same amount of global stimulus funds aim to support fossil fuel sectors, suggesting that G20 economies did not yet use the recession to shift the global economy on a more sustainable path. Research conducted by other organizations supports our preliminary findings.[12]

While our findings are preliminary, they suggest that the majority of green recovery efforts were taking place in Europe. The European Union planned to spend 30 percent of its stimulus efforts on green objectives, with the dual goal of meeting stringent climate targets and increasing competitiveness in critical industries of the future. France, Germany, and the United Kingdom also accelerated efforts to combine economic and environmental objectives in the recovery through support for renewable energy, hydrogen, and electric vehicles, among others. In Asia, South Korea included a Green New Deal in its recovery plans, which both set more ambitious targets for decarbonization and increased funding for clean energy sectors and vehicle electrification. China, meanwhile, accelerated the long-planned New Infrastructure Initiative, with the goal of spending $2.5 trillion on seven major industries, most notably 5G, electric vehicles, and ultra-high-voltage transmission. Stimulus bills in South Korea contained 30 percent green stimulus spending, followed by China and the European Union, with 18 percent. Efforts to fund a green recovery in Germany and the United Kingdom amounted to 9 and 8 percent of stimulus spending, respectively. At the same time, we estimate that Russia and India were on track to spend more than 80 percent of their stimulus funds on fossil fuel sectors. China's support for activities likely to increase carbon emissions exceeded 40 percent of its stimulus spending.

Green recovery efforts fell into three distinct categories. First, governments used stimulus packages to accelerate investments in infrastructure, support clean energy industries, fund research and development, and set up green financing institutions. Priorities under such direct spending initiatives varied. For instance, the European Union, Germany, France, and South Korea announced plans to invest in the research and development of hydrogen technologies. Producing hydrogen from renewable sources was part of long-term plans to reduce emissions in heavy industrial sectors. In the short term, governments focused on the expansion of electric vehicle charging networks, support for the establishment of a European battery industry, and upgrades to electric grids to accommodate the growing share of renewable energy. Common to such efforts was the goal to improve national competitiveness in key clean energy industries and improve national capabilities in the development, production, and deployment of clean energy technologies.

Second, green recovery plans funded incentives to accelerate the clean energy transition. Such incentives include subsidies for electric vehicles as well as rebates and tax credits for building retrofits and energy efficiency. Many such programs were similar to measures adopted in the United States in the American Recovery and Reinvestment Act in 2009. Germany, for instance, raised its incentives for electric vehicle purchases to €9,000 ($10,000), while also reforming vehicle taxes to reward energy-efficient cars. In the United Kingdom, homeowners were reimbursed two-thirds of energy-efficient building retrofits, and low-income households will be fully reimbursed.

Third, governments made financial support for private sector firms conditional on emissions reductions. In return for a €7 billion ($8.3 billion) bailout, Air France reduced domestic flights by 40 percent to encourage the use of France's high-speed rail system. The Dutch government attached similar conditions—including a requirement to reduce per-passenger emissions by 30 percent—to support KLM, half of the Air France–KLM group. While details about the enforcement of such conditions remain to be resolved, they suggest experimentation with new types of climate conditionalities that could more generally make state support for the private sector dependent on environmental goals.[13]

Although there is the possibility that stimulus packages primarily focused on economic rescues during the lockdown period and focused on a green recovery in subsequent rounds, two trends in our data are causes of concern. First, the vast majority of spending was on climate-neutral activities unconcerned with forging structural change in national economies toward a more sustainable path. Second, many economies that invested substantial sums in climate-related recovery packages also compensated fossil fuel sectors, again offering little indication that the recession yielded a global shift to decarbonization. According to our analysis, China in particular did not play a strong role in using the economic recession to invest in emissions reductions efforts, and instead used its stimulus packages to bail out suffering fossil fuel industries. Efforts to combine climate and economic objectives during the recovery fell short of the 2008–9 financial crisis, even though global emissions substantially increased.[14]

COVID-19, United States–China Relations, and Climate Change

The United States and China jointly account for 40 percent of global greenhouse gas emissions, putting these two nations at the center of any successful attempt to curb emissions to the levels required to prevent catastrophic climate change. Yet long before the onset of the COVID-19 pandemic, voices across the political spectrum in Washington began advocating for economic decoupling from China. Although opinions differed on what exactly such measures should entail, a bipartisan consensus emerged that China was unwilling to accept global rules of engagement, requiring the United States to shift strategy. At its core, such views originated in the realization that the core assumptions underlying United States–China relations in recent decades were unsound: economic integration did not in fact lead China to align with Western political norms and economic practices. China was increasingly unwilling to "play our game."[15] On the left, the Center for American Progress called for the need to "limit, leverage, and compete" with China, essentially advocating a strategy of putting US interests first and using economic interdependence as a political gain.[16] On the right, the Trump administration discovered tariffs as its preferred instrument for leveraging economic interdependence in a renegotiation of the United States–China economic relationship. The COVID-19 pandemic significantly accelerated such tendencies, highlighting not only the vulnerability of the world's economic supply chains to external shocks but also strengthening mercantilist calls for national self-sufficiency in China, the United States, and elsewhere.[17]

Yet few industries have more at stake in these battles than those producing low-carbon energy technologies, including wind turbines, solar panels, electric vehicles, and the lithium-ion batteries that are increasingly needed for electric cars and on-grid storage. Since joining the World Trade Organization in 2001, China has increased its share of global solar photovoltaic production from less than 1 percent to over 60 percent of the world's solar panels. China now makes more than one-third of global wind turbines, is the world's largest producer of (and market for) electric cars, and commands more than two-thirds of global production capacity for lithium-ion batteries.[18] In large part because of China's unprecedented investment in manufacturing capacity in these sectors, costs of clean energy technologies have fallen sharply. Since 2009, prices for wind turbines and solar panels have decreased by 69 percent and 88 percent, respectively, making these technologies competitive with conventional sources of energy in many parts of the world. This is particularly the case when they are deployed in conjunction with battery storage, where China's massive investments in new manufacturing capacity have also led to rapid cost declines.[19]

The development of these capabilities in manufacturing innovation relied on two unique institutional features of China's domestic economy that supported investments in both innovation and manufacturing: central government incentives for research and development (R&D) and local government support for manufacturing. To date, no other economy has been willing and able to devote a similar level of resources in the expansion of manufacturing capacity and manufacturing R&D in clean energy sectors. Since the beginning of the reform period in the 1980s, the central government in Beijing has used state incentives to encourage the development of domestic R&D, including applied research in manufacturing. Such government R&D support expanded in 2006, when the central government began encouraging "indigenous innovation" to reduce dependence on foreign technologies through increased domestic R&D efforts. Efforts further accelerated under President Xi's "Made in China 2025" initiative, which has also designated the development of domestic clean energy sectors as a strategic national priority. Provincial and municipal governments, dependent on tax revenue from the local manufacturing economy, augmented central government R&D support with incentives for mass production. China's provincial and municipal governments repurposed the central government's resources to broker bank loans and provide land, facilities, and tax incentives to manufacturers, including those in clean energy sectors that were unable to attract large-scale financing in other parts of the world. Such loans for manufacturing facilities were provided even as the central government's policies encouraged industry consolidation. It is estimated that between 2010 and 2012 alone, wind and solar firms received credit lines of $47 billion from Chinese banks. The China Development Bank, one of three state-owned policy banks, reportedly extended $29 billion in credit to the fifteen largest wind and solar firms.[20] Other reports suggest that state-owned banks provided $18 billion in loans to large wind and solar firms for the expansion of manufacturing facilities. These loans were backed by municipal and provincial governments, allowing firms to expand manufacturing capacity even after the global financial crisis of 2008–9, when the collapse of European markets led to global overcapacity and few lenders were willing to fund further expansion of manufacturing plants.[21]

While national policies designated strategic technologies and provided funding for R&D, local policies diverted those resources into mass manufacturing clusters. In this environment, Chinese manufacturers continued to center their R&D efforts on production improvements rather than R&D for new products.[22] To ensure that firms would rapidly contribute to the local economy, local administrations frequently made subsidies conditional on meeting production targets and revenue requirements. In many instances, firms were contractually obliged to build facilities with a predetermined manufacturing capacity by a particular date or risk losing government grants, tax reductions, and discounts on land prices. In other cases, local governments informally exerted pressure on firms to rapidly scale up production.[23] As Chinese manufacturers in clean energy sectors focused on commercialization, scaling up, and cost reduction, their innovative manufacturing capabilities (rather than basic factor cost advantages) emerged as a key source of competitive advantage.[24] Yet even with China's highly supportive domestic institutions and rapid developmental pace, it took nearly four decades for Chinese firms to establish the capabilities in commercialization and scaling up that the world now needs to bring new energy technologies to market. It is highly unlikely that any other economy will be able to replicate China's skills in scaling up and mass production in the time frame required to avoid the worst consequences of climate change.

Climate change is a global problem of unparalleled dimensions that requires a global response, including in the invention, commercialization, and production of technologies that can forge deep decarbonization. In the United States, some attribute China's rapid rise in clean energy sectors to unfair industrial policies, such as forced technology transfers, subsidies, and outright intellectual property theft, aimed at strategically dominating the next generation of energy technologies. This common narrative is based on the mistaken assumption that the Chinese state is a monolithic actor, when in fact different levels of government and administrative agencies have pursued different (and often conflicting) interests in the clean energy industries. This misunderstanding has led to a series of misguided policy responses, including the ongoing tariff battles between the United States and China. Missing from this conversation is an understanding of Chinese manufacturers' critical contributions of knowledge and innovation to the global ecosystem of clean energy development and commercialization.

We already have many of the technologies needed to begin making significant progress toward decarbonization, and recent cost reductions of solar and wind in particular mean that such progress is becoming ever more affordable. The unique geography of clean energy supply chains—some of the first industries to emerge after globalization led to a wholesale reorganization of the global economy in the 1990s—make US collaboration with China fundamental in any effort to avoid the worst consequences of climate change and, indeed, be beneficial to the United States. Meeting the goals of the Paris Agreement will require net-zero emissions by 2050 and substantial reductions before then. Already by 2030, emissions must have peaked and begun declining among major industrialized economies, given the limited remaining carbon budget.[25] In this time frame, it is unrealistic to expect that any other economy will be able to replicate or surpass China's infrastructure for the production of clean energy technologies required to meet these goals.

Collaboration was central to the development of contemporary renewable energy sectors, including collaboration between US innovators and Chinese producers with skills in rapid scaling up and cost reduction, and manufacturers of production machinery in Germany that supplied China's growing number of factories. Trade battles and widespread talk of decoupling have begun to undermine the relationships needed to quickly and efficiently bring new technologies to market and deploy them at the scale required. If successful, such decoupling would thwart progress on decarbonization, making it highly unlikely that global warming can be contained to acceptable levels. Collaboration will continue to be central to rapid decarbonization in the deployment of clean energy technologies, and the US and Chinese governments in particular should work to foster such collaboration. Initiatives like the US–China Clean Energy Research Center are one promising path to achieving this goal.

Zero-sum approaches to the United States–China economic relationship also obfuscate what the United States has to gain from such a collaboration.

This is certainly true for US renewable energy industries, which have suffered losses as a result of trade barriers to Chinese technologies that were first put in place under the Obama administration and were extended under Trump. It is important to note that such trade barriers have not brought manufacturing "back" to the United States. In clean energy sectors, the removal of barriers and the restoration of open trade relationships is imperative for meeting global climate goals. Addressing grand challenges like climate change will require fundamental advances in technology, where the United States is uniquely equipped to be at the global frontier. In United States, this means continuing to support the core strengths of US firms and universities—the invention of new technologies—through investments in basic and applied research. China was on course to overtake the United States in R&D spending in 2020, unless domestic efforts were ramped up. Particularly on climate-related technologies, the United States should accelerate its research and development investments to defend its technological lead.[26] Yet the technologies that emerge from these efforts must eventually be scaled up and deployed, and, for now, working with Chinese manufacturers can accelerate this process. Instead of competing with Chinese firms that have access to an institutional infrastructure supportive of mass production, US renewable energy start-ups might benefit from working with Chinese partners instead of trying to be self-sufficient in an economy devoid of similarly supportive manufacturing institutions.

The division of labor between US inventors (and the global economy more generally) and Chinese manufacturers is not fixed or inevitable. Collaboration with China entails working with and learning from Chinese partners on development and deployment in clean energy sectors, but it also comprises efforts to improve domestic competitiveness, including in segments of clean energy supply chains that are currently not well supported in the US economy. The United States should continue to address attempts by China to discriminate against foreign firms and provide institutional support for domestic clean energy firms trying to work with Chinese partners. It should also continue investing in domestic manufacturing capabilities as part of a national strategy for technological innovation. The creation of a domestic infrastructure bank that could finance domestic manufacturing projects, renewed investments in vocational training and technical colleges, and a stable regulatory framework to support domestic markets for clean energy technologies would improve national competitiveness in clean energy sectors. This is especially important since China, too, continues to engage in technonationalism and to pursue national self-sufficiency in key technology areas.

Yet only long-term investments in domestic clean energy industries will allow the world to change the terms of its relationship with China in clean energy industries without jeopardizing global climate goals. Even then, it is unlikely that entire value chains for complex energy technologies will lie entirely within national boundaries. As trade conflicts between and China and the United States threaten to undercut efforts to strengthen global ties in local carbon energy industries, the United States should not lose sight of the climate challenge or risk missing the narrow remaining window to sufficiently reduce global carbon emissions. Building on the advanced capabilities of Chinese firms in mass manufacturing is currently the most promising path to rapid global decarbonization, but it does not preclude smart investments in domestic alternatives. For now, the United States cannot solve the climate crisis without collaborating with China, but the politics surrounding the COVID-19 pandemic have made such collaboration less likely.

Conclusion

If the economic recession in the aftermath of the COVID-19 pandemic in principle offered an opportunity to "build back better" by shifting the global economy to a more sustainable path, there is little evidence that governments did so. In the long term, the recession offered an opportunity to improve conditions for segments of clean energy supply chains that were not well supported in countries around the world domestically. This means investing in domestic manufacturing capabilities as part of a national strategy for technological innovation. European recovery strategies offer instructive lessons on how stimulus spending can improve national competitiveness in clean energy industries, while maintaining open trade relationships with China. In the short term, the world should not lose sight of the substantial economic benefits from investments in clean energy industries, even if a share of these technologies is, for now, manufactured abroad. Investments in clean energy infrastructure, upgrades to the grid, sustainable transit solutions, renewable energy installations—including offshore wind—and energy-efficient building retrofits create local jobs in construction, installation and maintenance, and related service industries, regardless of where these products are manufactured. Green recovery spending would support the creation of such jobs in the near term and rapidly deploy capital in the economy.[27]

Even aggressive investments in clean energy sectors through economic stimulus packages will need to be complemented by stable regulatory measures to create domestic markets for clean technologies and reduce greenhouse gas emissions to levels required to avoid the worst consequences of climate change.[28]

Within recovery legislation, attaching climate conditions to corporate bailouts is one way to shift corporate behavior without incurring additional costs, such as France and the Netherlands attempted in the aviation sector. Combining financial incentives with changes in the tax code, as Germany did in the auto sector to accelerate the deployment of electric vehicles, is another way to combine regulatory policies with stimulus spending. Nonetheless, long-term regulatory measures will need to follow green recovery investments to reach global climate goals.

If the economic recession in the aftermath of the COVID-19 pandemic in principle offered an opportunity to shift the global economy to a more sustainable path, there is little evidence that governments did so sufficiently. At best, the recession caused short-term emissions reductions and led to some investment in clean energy industries to stimulate economic recovery. But governments also bailed out fossil fuel companies and invested in polluting technologies—including coal power—that threaten to lock in greenhouse gas emissions for generations. At worst, the pandemic fueled a pushback against globalization that is likely to complicate efforts to decarbonize, challenging both diplomatic relations and those global supply chains that are most needed to collectively shift away from fossil fuels.[29] The vast majority of stimulus funds were spent on climate-neutral activities. And spending on decarbonization was offset by compensation for fossil fuel industries. Given the limited time remaining to reduce greenhouse gas emissions and avoid the worst consequences of climate change, these patterns signal a missed opportunity to shift the global economy to a more sustainable path.

Notes

1. J. Watts and N. Kommenda, "Coronavirus Pandemic Leading to Huge Drop in Air Pollution," *Guardian*, March 23, 2020, www.theguardian.com/environment/2020/mar/23/coronavirus-pandemic-leading-to-huge-drop-in-air-pollution.

2. K. T. Gillingham, C. R. Knittel, J. Li, M. Ovaere, and M. Reguant, "The Short-Run and Long-Run Effects of COVID-19 on Energy and the Environment," *Joule* 4, no. 7 (2020): 1337–41.

3. Breakthrough Institute, "COVID-19 Could Result in Much Larger CO2 Drop in 2020," 2020, https://thebreakthrough.org/issues/energy/covid-co2-drop.

4. Breakthrough Institute.

5. L. Myllyvirta, "China's CO_2 Emissions Surged Past Pre-Coronavirus Levels in May," 2020, https://www.carbonbrief.org/analysis-chinas-co2-emissions-surged-past-pre-coronavirus-levels-in-may.

6. C. Le Quéré, R. B. Jackson, M. W. Jones, A. J. P. Smith, S. Abernethy, R. M. Andrew, A. J. De-Gol, D. R. Willis, Y. Shan, J. G. Canadell, P. Friedlingstein, F. Creutzig,

and G. P. Peters, "Temporary Reduction in Daily Global CO_2 Emissions during the COVID-19 Forced Confinement," *Nature Climate Change* 10, no. 7 (2020): 647–53.

7. K. Palmer, W. E. Oates, and P. R. Portney, "Tightening Environmental Standards: The Benefit-Cost or the No-Cost Paradigm?" *Journal of Economic Perspectives* 9, no. 4 (1995): 119–32; M. E. Porter and C. Van der Linde, "Toward a New Conception of the Environment–Competitiveness Relationship," *Journal of Economic Perspectives* 9, no. 4 (1995): 97–118; T. P. Conca and Ken Michael Maniates, *Confronting Consumption* (MIT Press, 2002); W. Pizer, M. Adler, J. Aldy, D. Anthoff, M. Cropper, K. Gillingham, M. Greenstone, B. Murray, R. Newell, R. Richels, A. Rowell, S. Waldhoff, and J. Wiener, "Using and Improving the Social Cost of Carbon," *Science* 346, no. 6214 (2014): 118–90; G. Kostka and J. Nahm, "Central–Local Relations: Recentralization and Environmental Governance in China," *China Quarterly* 231 (2017): 567–82; S. Tiba and A. Omri, "Literature Survey on the Relationships Between Energy, Environment and Economic Growth," *Renewable and Sustainable Energy Reviews* 69 (2017): 1129–46; T. Jackson, "The Post-Growth Challenge: Secular Stagnation, Inequality and the Limits to Growth," *Ecological Economics* 156 (2019): 236–46.

8. C. Burns and P. Tobin, "The Impact of the Economic Crisis on European Union Environmental Policy," *Journal of Common Market Studies* 54, no. 6 (2016): 1485–94; A. P. J. Mol, "The Environmental Nation-State in Decline," *Environmental Politics* 25, no. 1 (2016): 48–68.

9. K. Tienhaara, "Varieties of Green Capitalism: Economy and Environment in the Wake of the Global Financial Crisis," *Environmental Politics* 23, no. 2 (2014): 187–204; J. Meckling and B. B. Allan, "The Evolution of Ideas in Global Climate Policy," *Nature Climate Change* 10, no. 5 (2020): 434–38; P. Tobin, "Economics from Zero-Sum to Win-Win," *Nature Climate Change* 10, no. 5 (2020): 386–87.

10. N. Robins, R. Clover, and C. Singh, *A Climate for Recovery: The Colour of Stimulus Goes Green* (London: HSBC Global Research, 2009).

11. G. P. Peters, G. Marland, C. Le Quéré, T. Boden, J. G. Canadell, and M. R. Raupach, "Rapid Growth in CO_2 Emissions after the 2008–2009 Global Financial Crisis," *Nature Climate Change* 2, no. 1 (2012): 2–4. For this ongoing research, I collaborate with Johannes Urpelainen at the Johns Hopkins School of Advanced International Studies and Scot Miller at the Johns Hopkins Whiting School of Engineering. We are supported by an excellent research team: Jacob Brunell, Santiago Cunial, Alex Haag, Daniel Mathew, Zubeyde Osul, and Will Zhao.

12. See the analysis of International Monetary Fund data conducted by the Rhodium Group: https://rhg.com/wp-content/uploads/2020/09/Its-Not-Easy-Being-Green-Stimulus-Spending-in-the-Worlds-Major-Economies.pdf. The International Institute for Sustainable Development is collecting energy sector recovery policies: https://www.energypolicytracker.org.

13. J. Strecker and J. Meckling, *Green Bargains: From Crisis Response to Sectoral Transformation* (University of California Press, forthcoming).

14. P. Friedlingstein, M. W. Jones, M. O"ullivan, R. M. Andrew, J. Hauck, G. P. Peters, W. Peters, J. Pongratz, S. Sitch, C. Le Quéré, D. C. E. Bakker, J. G. Canadell, P. Ciais, R. B. Jackson, P. Anthoni, L. Barbero, A. Bastos, V. Bastrikov, M. Becker, L. Bopp,

E. Buitenhuis, N. Chandra, F. Chevallier, L. P. Chini, K. I. Currie, R. A. Feely, M. Gehlen, D. Gilfillan, T. Gkritzalis, D. S. Goll, N. Gruber, S. Gutekunst, I. Harris, V. Haverd, R. A. Houghton, G. Hurtt, T. Ilyina, A. K. Jain, E. Joetzjer, J. O. Kaplan, E. Kato, K. Klein Goldewijk, J. I. Korsbakken, P. Landschützer, S. K. Lauvset, N. Lefèvre, A. Lenton, S. Lienert, D. Lombardozzi, G. Marland, P. C. McGuire, J. R. Melton, N. Metzl, D. R. Munro, J. E. M. S. Nabel, S. I. Nakaoka, C. Neill, A. M. Omar, T. Ono, A. Peregon, D. Pierrot, B. Poulter, G. Rehder, L. Resplandy, E. Robertson, C. Rödenbeck, R. Séférian, J. Schwinger, N. Smith, P. P. Tans, H. Tian, B. Tilbrook, F. N. Tubiello, G. R. van der Werf, A. J. Wiltshire, and S. Zaehle, "Global Carbon Budget 2019," *Earth Syst. Sci. Data* 11, no. 4 (2019): 1783–1838.

15. E. S. Steinfeld, *Playing Our Game: Why China's Rise Doesn't Threaten the West* (Oxford University Press, 2010).

16. M. Hart and K. Magsamen, "Limit, Leverage, and Compete: A New Strategy on China," 2019, https://www.americanprogress.org/issues/security/reports/2019/04/03/468136/limit-leverage-compete-new-strategy-china/.

17. H. Farrell and A. Newman, "Will the Coronavirus End Globalization as We Know It?" *Foreign Affairs*, May–June 2020.

18. J. Helveston and J. Nahm, "China's Key Role in Scaling Low-Carbon Energy Technologies," *Science* 366, no. 6467 (2019): 794.

19. Lazard, "Lazard's Levelized Cost of Energy Analysis," 2018, https://www.lazard.com/media/450784/lazards-levelized-cost-of-energy-version-120-vfinal.pdf.

20. S. Bakewell, "Chinese Renewable Companies Slow to Tap $47 Billion Credit," Bloomberg, 2011.

21. K. Bradsher, "Glut of Solar Panels Poses a New Threat to China," 2012, http://www.nytimes.com/2012/10/05/business/global/glut-of-solar-panels-is-a-new-test-for-china.html?_r=0.

22. J. Nahm and E. S. Steinfeld, "Scale-Up Nation: China's Specialization in Innovative Manufacturing," *World Development* 54 (2014): 288–300.

23. J. Nahm, "Exploiting the Implementation Gap: Policy Divergence and Industrial Upgrading in China's Wind and Solar Sectors," *China Quarterly* 231 (2017): 705–27.

24. E. S. Steinfeld and J. Deutch, *A Duel in the Sun: The Solar Photovoltaics Technology Conflict between China and the United States—A Report for the MIT Future of Solar Energy Study* (Massachusetts Institute of Technology, 2013).

25. Intergovernmental Panel on Climate Change, "Global Warming of 1.5°C," Geneva, 2018.

26. K. S. Gallagher and Z. Myslikova, "The Important Outcomes of Mission Innovation: First Evidence," 2020, https://www.climatepolicylab.org/climatesmart/2020/9/8/the-important-outcomes-of-mission-innovation-first-evidence.

27. R. Hanna, Y. Xu, and D. G. Victor, "After COVID-19, Green Investment Must Deliver Jobs to Get Political Traction," *Nature* 582 (2020): 178–80.

28. N. Kaufman, "The Greenest Stimulus Is the One That Delivers Rapid Economic Recovery," 2020, https://energypolicy.columbia.edu/sites/default/files/file-uploads/Green%20stimulus%20commentary,%20final%20design,%206.09.20.pdf.

29. A. Goldthau and L. Hughes, "Protect Global Supply Chains for Low-Carbon Technologies," *Nature* 585 (2020): 28–30.

Index

www.ingramcontent.com/pod-product-compliance
Lightning Source LLC
Chambersburg PA
CBHW020857270326
41928CB00006B/743